The Poetry of Limitation

The Poetry of Limitation:

A Study of Edmund Waller

by Warren L. Chernaik

New Haven and London, Yale University Press, 1968

Ezra Pound, "Envoi (1919)," from *Personae.*
Copyright 1926, 1954 by Ezra Pound. Reprinted by
permission of New Directions Publishing Corporation,
New York, and Faber and Faber, London.

Library of Congress catalog card number: 68–27749

Designed by Helen V. Buzyna,
set in Baskerville type,
and printed in the United States of America by
The Carl Purington Rollins Printing-Office of
the Yale University Press, New Haven, Conn.
Distributed in Great Britain, Europe, Asia, and
Africa by Yale University Press Ltd., London; in
Canada by McGill University Press, Montreal; and
in Latin America by Centro Interamericano de Libros
Académicos, Mexico City.

Published with assistance from
the Kingsley Trust Association Publication Fund
established by the Scroll and Key Society of Yale College.

For Judith

Acknowledgments

This study is loosely based on my Yale dissertation, "The Poetry of Edmund Waller." Over the course of the years I have incurred a large number of debts to scholars who patiently read one or another version of portions of the book or the whole. My first long-standing debt is to Maynard Mack, whose careful criticism of my original disordered thoughts enabled me to find out what I was trying to say. Five years later, David Vieth's detailed, perceptive commentary provided an invaluable fresh perspective and enabled me to give the manuscript its final form. I am grateful to Cleanth Brooks, George deF. Lord, and the late Alexander Witherspoon, who read and criticized the earliest version; to Anne Barbeau, who read and criticized the final version; and to the many friends and colleagues who read intermediate versions: Samuel Mintz, Rose Zimbardo, Albert J. Kuhn, Robert C. Elliott, John Harold Wilson, Wallace Maurer, Steward LaCasce, and Elizabeth Dalton. Portions of this book appeared, in slightly different form, in *Studies in English Literature, 4* (1964), and in *Modern Language Quarterly, 26* (1965); I am grateful to the editors of these journals for permission to reprint. The editors of New Directions have graciously permitted me to quote from *Personae: The Collected Poems of Ezra Pound* (New York, 1926; copyright by Ezra Pound). I am grateful for the editorial advice and assistance of Ann MacLean and to the clerical assistance of Barbara Miranda and Holly Hagedorn. I am particularly indebted to the courtesy and helpfulness of Wayland W. Schmitt of Yale University Press, and to the

ACKNOWLEDGMENTS

Graduate School of Boston University, for financial assistance extended me during the period of final revision and preparation of the manuscript. The last and greatest of my debts is to my wife Judith, who knows the green isles in the sea through which the weary mariner travels, and knows how it feels when he finally reaches the shore.

W. L. C.

Boston, Mass.
March 19, 1968

Contents

When our two dusts with Waller's shall be laid,
Siftings on siftings in oblivion,
Till change hath broken down
All things save Beauty alone.

Ezra Pound, "Envoi," *Hugh Selwyn Mauberley*

All, all, of a piece throughout;
Thy Chase had a Beast in View;
Thy Wars brought nothing about;
Thy Lovers were all untrue.
'Tis well an Old Age is out,
And time to begin a New.

John Dryden, *The Secular Masque*

Introduction

The rise and fall of the reputation of Edmund Waller is spectacular. "No poetical reputation of the seventeenth century," Douglas Bush tells us, "has been so completely and irreparably eclipsed."[1] It was not always so. The preface to *The Second Part of Mr. Waller's Poems* (1690), a volume of previously uncollected poems, begins, "The Reader needs be told no more in commendation of these Poems, than that they are Mr. Waller's: a Name that carries every thing in it, that's either Great or Graceful in Poetry."[2] In Gerard Langbaine's *An Account of the English Dramatick Poets* (1691), Waller is described as "a Gentleman not many Years deceas'd; whose Name will ever be dear to all Lovers of the *Muses*. His compositions are universally applauded, and they are thought fit to serve as a Standard, for all succeeding Poems."[3] As late as 1766, the *Biographia Britannica* can call Waller "the most celebrated Lyric Poet that ever England produced."[4]

The high point of Waller's reputation is probably to be found in the fervent, evangelistic praise bestowed upon him by Thomas Rymer. Rymer writes in *A Short View of*

[1]. *English Literature in the Earlier Seventeenth Century, 1600–1660* (Oxford, Clarendon Press, 1945), p. 166.

[2]. (London, 1690). The preface, generally attributed to Francis Atterbury, is reprinted in G. Thorn-Drury, ed., *The Poems of Edmund Waller* (2 vols. London, [1905]), *1*, xviii–xxvii. Page numbers of Thorn-Drury's introduction, which precedes the table of contents, are italicized; prefatory material following the table of contents is numbered in roman type.

[3]. (Oxford, 1691), p. 507.

[4]. (London, 1747–66), *6*, pt. 2, 4099.

Tragedy (1692), "And one may observe by his Poem on the Navy . . . that Not the language only, but His Poetry then distinguish'd him from all his contemporaries, both in *England* and in other Nations; and from all before him upwards to *Horace* and *Virgil*."[5] Waller remained highly regarded through most of the eighteenth century; at the end of the century, however, we begin to hear a new tone. "The whole editions of his works may be thrown in the fire, without any diminution of English poetry."[6] Perhaps the shrillness of the late eighteenth-century antiquary, aesthete, and hack, John Pinkerton, is less damning than the casual certainty of a number of Victorian pronouncements. "He is feeble poetically, quite as surely as morally and politically."[7] "Edmund Waller, in my estimation, hardly deserves a place among the best names in English literature, either as a poet or as a man."[8] "A few flowing lines are not bribe sufficient to pervert the judgment of posterity."[9]

The decline of Waller's reputation in the nineteenth century is comprehensible. In some ways, Waller is a valley between hills. He challenges comparison with poetry before and after him, sharing certain qualities with each, and he comes out badly. Moreover, neither his personal nor his poetic character shows the expected vatic dignity. He is too much the timeserver, too much the politician. "What true poet, who felt as a poet, would have said this?"[10] "Waller's poetry is exactly what might have been anticipated from

---

5. In *Critical Works of Thomas Rymer*, ed. Curt A. Zimansky (New Haven, 1956), p. 127.

6. Robert Heron [John Pinkerton], *Letters of Literature* (London 1785), p. 131.

7. Elizabeth Barrett Browning, "The Book of the Poets," in *The Greek Christian Poets and the English Poets* (London, 1863), p. 168.

8. Charles Dexter Cleveland, *A Compendium of English Literature* (Philadelphia, 1847), p. 268.

9. Thomas Babington Macaulay, "Lord Bacon," *Critical, Historical, and Miscellaneous Essays* (6 vols. New York, 1877), *3*, 387.

10. [Anna B. Jameson] *The Loves of the Poets* (2 vols. London, 1829), *2*, 32.

the character of the writer,—always polished and sparkling, —never commanding or sublime. . . . His poetry is that of a cool, calculating and ingenious man."[11] "With all his brilliant poetic gifts and social accomplishments, Waller's seems to have been a mean and poor nature—selfish and pleasure-loving in prosperity, and abject and servile in adversity. Society pardoned his public baseness for his private pleasantries."[12]

The last editor of Waller, George Thorn-Drury, devotes only three of the seventy-four pages of his informative, chatty introduction to the poetry, and those pages are embarrassed and deprecatory. Douglas Bush in the *Oxford History of English Literature* treats Waller with a cheerful summary contempt. The best Mr. Bush can find in Waller is an occasional "attenuated cavalier grace." His account is full of such words as "dwindle"; he speaks of "the loss involved in the whole poetical mode that Waller stood for." "There is little attraction in Waller. . . . For us he remains a fluent trifler, the rhymer of a court gazette. . . . Since there is so little to put to Waller's credit, perhaps we should remember that he greatly enjoyed Chapman's Homer."[13]

The most elaborate treatment of Waller in modern times is Edmund Gosse's *From Shakespeare to Pope*.[14] Gosse finds Waller's influence on English poetry deplorable and in accordance with the critical clichés of the nineteenth century, treats the rise of neoclassicism as a disaster. His book has been deservedly attacked as vague and full of inaccura-

---

11. George Godfrey Cunningham, *Lives of Eminent and Illustrious Englishmen* (8 vols. Glasgow, 1836–40), *3*, 348.

12. John Tulloch, *Rational Theology and Christian Philosophy in England in the Seventeenth Century* (2 vols. Edinburgh and London, 1872), *1*, 110–11. There is a full account of the fluctuations of Waller's reputation in Netty Roeckerath, *Der Nachruhm Herricks und Wallers* (Leipzig, 1931). See also Charles Wells Moulton, ed., *The Library of Literary Criticism* (Buffalo, N. Y., 1901–05), 2, 378–84.

13. *English Literature in the Earlier Seventeenth Century*, p. 167.

14. Cambridge, 1885.

cies.[15] But at least Gosse recognizes that Waller *had* an influence on English poetry, although he does not define that influence satisfactorily. The modern reappraisal of the Augustans has reawakened interest in the poets they took as their forerunners; thus some recent critics have begun to analyze Waller's contribution with something like sympathy. My own study, similarly, takes Waller's historical position as a point of departure and seeks as well to look with a fresh eye on his poetry.

In writing this book, I am indebted to several recent studies which have sought to place Waller in historical perspective. I would particularly single out H. M. Richmond's *The School of Love,* an examination of the traditions and development of Cavalier love poetry; Ruth Nevo's *The Dial of Virtue,* a study of seventeenth-century political poetry; George Williamson's *The Proper Wit of Poetry,* which traces the changing conceptions of wit in the course of the seventeenth century; and Alexander Ward Allison's *Toward an Augustan Poetic: Edmund Waller's "Reform" of English Poetry,* a careful study of Waller's language and versification.[16] Each of these works is illumi-

---

15. See J. Churton Collins, "English Literature at the Universities," *Quarterly Review, 63,* (1886), 289–329, a slashing attack on Gosse's book as an example of "dilettantism" in the study of literature.

16. *The School of Love: The Evolution of the Stuart Love Lyric* (Princeton, Princeton University Press, 1964); *The Dial of Virtue: A Study of Poems on Affairs of State in the Seventeenth Century* (Princeton, Princeton University Press, 1963); *The Proper Wit of Poetry* (Chicago, University of Chicago Press, 1961); *Toward an Augustan Poetic: Edmund Waller's "Reform" of English Poetry* (Lexington, University of Kentucky Press, 1962). Briefer but suggestive treatments of Waller's early poems include Robin Skelton, *Cavalier Poets,* Writers and their Work Series, No. 117 (London, 1960); and Josephine Miles, *The Primary Language of Poetry in the 1640's,* University of California Publications in English, Vol. 19, No. 1 (Berkeley and Los Angeles, 1948). The detailed analyses of the versification and rhetoric of Waller's couplets in Ruth Wallerstein, "The Development of the Rhetoric and Metre of the Heroic Couplet, Especially in 1625–1645," *PMLA, 50,* (1935), 166–209; and George Williamson, "The Rhetorical Pattern of Neoclassical Wit," *Modern Philology, 33* (1935), 55–81, illuminate

nating for the student of Waller and of seventeenth-century poetry, but each treats Waller from a single perspective only. My aim in this study is to provide a comprehensive treatment of the man and his work, tracing the relationships of Waller's poetry to the events of his life and the age he lived in. Waller's poems are interesting in their own right, and even more interesting from the standpoint of literary history. As I will attempt to show by detailed examination of his early lyric poetry and his later poems on affairs of state, Waller is a key figure in the seventeenth-century "line of wit" and its eventual reconciliation with neoclassical standards of clarity and harmony.

Though Waller is not one of the great English poets, in English poetry written between 1630 and 1740 his figure looms large. He lived more than half of those years, and his poetry was widely read during the entire period;[17] his effect on the poetry written during that time was profound. "I am desirous of laying hold on his memory, on all occasions," Dryden wrote of Waller in 1691, "and thereby acknowledging to the world, that unless he had written, none of us could write."[18] I think it can be assumed that when Dryden speaks of Waller in this manner, or when Rymer, Pope, and Steele treat him in a roughly similar way, they do so with good reason.

For a very long time after he began writing, Waller remained, in effect, not a poet of the former age, but a contemporary. His position was always special: his great longevity and the affinities of his poetry with later poetry

Waller's role in the development of neoclassicism. The latter essay is reprinted in George Williamson, *Seventeenth Century Contexts* (London, Faber and Faber, 1960).

17. Collected editions of his works were published in 1645 (4x), 1664, 1668, 1682, 1686, 1690 (2x), 1693, 1694 (2x), 1698, 1705, 1711, 1712, 1722, 1729, 1730, and 1744.

18. Preface to William Walsh's *Dialogue Concerning Women* (1691), in Sir Walter Scott and George Saintsbury, eds. *The Works of John Dryden* (18 vols. London, 1882–93), *18*, 6.

forced him, as it were, into a later time, distant from that in which he wrote at least half his poems. It is true that Dryden and Pope tend to make Waller over in their own image. Still, their testimonies can be valuable in giving us a knowledge of Waller. They are close, as we are not, to Waller and Waller's age. Even as they turn him to their own uses, they are aware of his roots in his own time: both the age of Charles I, in which he found a style and subject matter that he maintained, with a minimum of changes, for sixty years, and the age of Charles II, through which he lived, wrote, and was read.

1 The Poet as Politician

Edmund Waller was born on March 3, 1606, in Coleshill in Hertfordshire, the eldest son of a wealthy father. Waller's father had studied law, but he devoted most of his life to the care of his extensive estates in Hertford and Buckinghamshire. When he died in 1616, Waller was left heir to an estate worth £3500 a year. After brief residence in Eton and in King's College, Cambridge, Waller was elected to Parliament at an unusually early age (sixteen or eighteen, according to various accounts).[1] He remained a member throughout most of his life.

In 1631, Waller increased his already large fortune by marrying the heiress of a wealthy London merchant. After her death in 1634, he paid court to Lady Dorothy Sidney, daughter of the Earl of Leicester, under the name of Sacharissa. Most of his love poems date from the period in which Parliament was in suspension; once Parliament met again in 1640, politics became his main interest.

1. See Thorn-Drury, *1, xvi–xvii.* His introduction is indispensable for any future biographer of Waller, as is Samuel Johnson's "Life of Waller" in *Lives of the English Poets,* ed. George Birkbeck Hill (3 vols. Oxford, 1905). An anonymous "Account of the Life and Writings of Edmond Waller, esq.," prefixed to *Poems, &c. Written upon several Occasions, and to several Persons. By Edmond Waller, Esq.* (10th ed. London, 1722), supplies a good deal of biographical information, some of doubtful validity. The "Life" originally appeared in the 1711 edition of the *Poems;* all my references are to the 1722 edition. The fine edition of Waller prepared by Elijah Fenton in 1729, *The Works of Edmund Waller, Esq., in Verse and Prose* (2d ed. London, 1730), includes "Observations on some of Mr. Waller's Poems" (over 150 pages in the 1730 edition), which includes much incidental biographical information.

The two major intellectual influences upon the early Waller were his friends George Morley and Lucius Cary, Lord Falkland. Both men were witty and erudite. Morley, who later became a bishop and a conservative pillar of the Anglican establishment, was in his early days a minor poet and "son of Ben," noted for his irreverent wit (when asked by "a grave Country Gentleman . . . what the Arminians held," Morley answered, "the best Bishopricks and Deaneries in England"). Waller paid Morley's extensive debts, and Morley, an excellent Latin scholar, in return "assisted and instructed him" over a period of years, beginning in the late 1620s, "in the reading of many good Books . . . especially the Poets."[2] Nearly all of Waller's poetry was written after he met Morley, and most of it after Morley had introduced him to the Falkland circle in the 1630s. Falkland's ideals of reason and detachment, of humane learning and urbane conversation, exercised a lasting influence over Waller. The poet was a regular member of the *convivium philosophicum* meeting at Falkland's estate at Tew, and he continued to hold ideas characteristic of the Falkland group many years after Falkland's death.[3]

When Parliament assembled in 1640, Waller (like Falkland) was a leader of the party of Constitutional

2. *The Life of Edward Earl of Clarendon . . . Written by Himself* (3 vols. Oxford, 1761), *1*, 47–50. Another account of the relationship between Morley and Waller may be found in the "Life" in Waller's *Poems* (1722), viii. A good brief discussion of Morley's career is F. Bussby, "George Morley: Caroline Divine," *Church Quarterly Review, 165* (1964), 186–97.

3. For a discussion of the religious and intellectual ideas of the Falkland group, see Wilbur K. Jordan, *The Development of Religious Toleration in England* (4 vols. Cambridge, Mass., 1932–40), 2, 371–412; and William Haller, *The Rise of Puritanism* (New York, Harper Torchbooks, 1957), pp. 236–48. Ruth Wallerstein, in "The Development of the Rhetoric and Metre of the Heroic Couplet," *PMLA, 50* (1935), 187, speaks of Falkland's influence upon the form of Waller's verse; but Falkland was only incidentally a poet, and his primary influence on Waller lies in the ideas the poet habitually expressed in his verse and acted upon in his life.

Royalists, who began by attacking the abuses of arbitrary rule but ended up defending the crown against the demands of the Puritan majority. His efforts to serve as broker between the two sides and as a voice of moderation collapsed utterly with the debacle of "Waller's plot," an attempt to bring the war to an end by a coup d'etat, and with the cowardice of his behavior after the discovery of the plot. He escaped with no greater punishment than a fine and banishment.

After living comfortably in France for several years, Waller received in 1651 a pardon from his kinsman Cromwell. Though he lay under suspicion in some quarters for his Royalist sympathies, he was soon on terms of familiarity with Cromwell. In 1655 he published *A Panegyric to my Lord Protector,* perhaps his best poem, urging support of Cromwell's regime. But when the King came back, Waller was among the first to greet him with a poem *(To the King, upon His Majesty's Happy Return)*. The poet again became a favorite at court and a leading member of the House of Commons, and this time he did nothing to bring disgrace on his name.

Waller was associated with the court throughout his career; his poems are by-products of a courtier's and politician's life. Poetry to him was not a divine calling, a fire burning within, but the avocation of a gentleman. He was at all times the celebrated wit, the good companion. While yet young, he was "known at Court, and caress'd by all the People of Quality, who had a Relish of Learning and Wit." Clarendon, who knew him well at this time, speaks of him as familiar in "that Company, which was most celebrated for good Conversation; where he was received, and esteemed, with great Applause, and Respect. He was a very pleasant Discourser, in Earnest, and in Jest, and therefore very grateful to all Kind of Company, where He was not the less esteemed for being very rich."[4]

4. "Life," in *Poems* (1722), vii; Clarendon, *Life, 1,* 48.

After the Restoration, his reputation as a wit was even greater. "In a time," says Johnson, "when fancy and gaiety were the most powerful recommendation to regard it is not likely that Waller was forgotten. He passed his time in the company that was highest, both in rank and wit."[5] Like his friend St. Evremond, whose letters comment upon his "delicious Conversation," Waller was a great frequenter of salons, a connoisseur of pleasures, and an expert in the gallant and courtly phrase.

> King *Charles*, in his Diversions at the Duke of *Buckingham's*, and other Places, always made Mr. *Waller* one of the Party, excusing to the Company his not being able to drink; upon which Mr. *Saville* us'd to say, *No Man in England should keep him Company without drinking, but Ned Waller.*[6]

The younger generation occasionally scoffed at the stodginess of "old Waller," but in general he was respected, almost exaggeratedly so, as an elder statesman of wit.[7]

Waller exercised his wit inside Parliament as well as out. He was known for the brilliance of his speeches; one of

---

5. *Lives of the Poets, 1*, 272. According to Aubrey, "When King Charles II returned, he received Mr. Waller very kindly, and no man's conversation is more esteemed at Court now then his. The Dutches of Yorke . . . very much delights in his company" (John Aubrey, *Brief Lives*, ed. Oliver Lawson Dick [Ann Arbor, 1957], p. 309).

6. John Hayward, ed., *The Letters of Saint Evremond*, tr. Pierre Des Maizeaux, 1728 (London, 1930), pp. 75, 127, 194; "Life" in *Poems* (1722), xxxiii. Several letters written by and to Waller, illustrative of his life as an aging courtier and gallant, may be found in Thorn-Drury, *1, lxv–lxviii.*

7. In 1664, Waller collaborated with the Earl of Dorset, Sir Charles Sedley, and others in a translation of Corneille's *Pompée;* in *The Session of the Poets* (1668), his presence "among these young fellows that spoil the French plays" is remarked on as odd. See George deF. Lord, ed., *Poems on Affairs of State: Augustan Satirical Verse, 1660–1714, 1* (New Haven and London, 1963), p. 334. For an example of the irreverence with which the younger wits could treat Waller, see two letters from Henry Savile to the Earl of Rochester, in John Harold Wilson, ed., *The Rochester-Savile Letters 1671–1680* (Columbus, Ohio, 1941), pp. 48–49, 51.

them is said to have sold twenty thousand copies in a single day.[8] A number of the speeches have been preserved: they are, for the most part, witty, sententious, and erudite, epigrammatical almost to excess, and stuffed with historical and literary allusions.[9]

To be a courtier, a wit, a polished orator, are dangerous skills. A remarkable number of people, from the time of the English Civil War to the present day, have written attacks on Waller. The attacks find their origin not only in Waller's particular character and deeds, but in a general suspicion of the kind of activities he preferred to engage in. To many people a court is necessarily frivolous, wit and rhetoric necessarily methods of perverting truth, panegyric necessarily venal. Nineteenth-century critics heap scorn on Waller's poetry and his character; for them the two are inseparable. But the adverse criticism does not rest on prejudice alone: the critics find ample material in the events of the poet's life.

The most damning thing ever written about Waller— and, directly or indirectly, the most influential—is the brilliant portrait of the poet in the Earl of Clarendon's autobiography. Clarendon was strong-willed, stern, and unforgiving, a man of unshakable moral rectitude; Waller, who shared none of these qualities, had been a companion of the statesman's youth and later became his political enemy. Clarendon thus has sufficient cause for drawing up a powerful indictment, and he accuses Waller of such shortcomings as "a Narrowness in his Nature to the lowest Degree; an Abjectness, and Want of Courage to support him in any virtuous Undertaking; an Insinuation, and servile Flattery to the Height, the vainest, and most Imperious Nature could be contented with." Waller's good qualities

8. "Life," in *Poems* (1722), xv.

9. Fenton prints three of Waller's speeches before the Short and Long Parliaments. Excerpts from the poet's speeches after the Restoration may be found in Anchitell Grey, ed., *Debates of the House of Commons, From the Year 1667 to the Year 1694* (10 vols. London, 1763).

were no less suspect to Clarendon than his bad: his abilities and parts, "the Excellence and Power of his Wit, and Pleasantness of his Conversation . . . preserved and won his Life from those, who were most resolved to take it; and in an Occasion in which He ought to have been ambitious to have lost it; and then preserved him again, from the Reproach and Contempt that was due to him, for so preserving it, and for vindicating it at such a Price." Thus, throughout his long life, "his Company was acceptable, where his Spirit was odious, and He was at least pitied, where He was most detested."[10]

Clarendon condemns Waller especially for his behavior during the Civil War and the years immediately subsequent to it. Instead of going to a noble death after his plot was discovered, Waller bargained for his life and then, a few years later, came out in support of the government Clarendon detested. As Clarendon saw him, Waller was ruled not by principle but by expediency and self-interest.

Later writers have shared Clarendon's general view. Bishop Richard Hurd, in an imaginary dialogue between Waller and Henry More, presents the poet as the consummate timeserver, who holds that "fine stoical lessons must all give way to a little common sense, I mean, to a prudent accommodation of ourselves to time and circumstances; which, whether you will dignify it with the name of philosophy, or no, is the only method of living with credit in the world, and even with safety."[11] In a somewhat similar work of the same period, John Langhorne's *Letters Supposed to have Passed between M. de St. Evremond and Mr. Waller,* the poet is presented as the perfect flowering of Restoration cynicism, a man who believes in nothing except change. "The end of all philosophy is to set the heart

---

10. *Life, 1,* 48–49. Clarendon's character sketch of Waller is conveniently reprinted in Johnson's "Life of Waller," *Lives of the Poets, 1,* 278–79.

11. "Dialogue, On Sincerity in the Commerce of the World, between Dr. Henry More, and Edmund Waller, Esq.," *Works* (London, 1811), *3,* 53.

at ease. . . . I comply with fortune upon the same principles as I would with any other mistress, to keep her in good-humour. . . . Enjoy the chace while it lasts—If you are thrown out, smile at the disappointment, and start some other game."[12] How else but by an absolute and shameless lack of principle, critics ask, could a man have written poems in praise, successively, of Charles I, Cromwell, Charles II, and James II? (Waller died before he could write in praise of William, though he managed to praise him as Prince of Orange.) Dr. Johnson writes, with measured severity,

> Neither Cromwell nor Charles could value his testimony as the effect of conviction, or receive his praises as effusions of reverence; they could consider them but as the labour of invention and the tribute of dependence. Poets, indeed, profess fiction, but the legitimate end of fiction is the conveyance of truth; and he that has flattery ready for all whom the vicissitudes of the world happen to exalt must be scorned as a prostituted mind that may retain the glitter of wit, but has lost the dignity of virtue.[13]

The same stern and censorious tone, the same tendency to use Waller as a moral exemplum, may be found in most treatments of the poet in the nineteenth and early twentieth centuries—most notably in the great Civil War historian, Samuel Gardiner. Any study of Waller must rely heavily on Gardiner's work, which so thoroughly illuminates the context in which Waller acted. Yet his remarks on Waller are consistently moralistic, even indignant. The poet is denigrated again and again as "dishonourable," a man "whose own life was so dissolute as to cast off all moral restraints," "a precursor of Restoration morals and of Restoration politics," representing "pure Royalism . . . in all its native offensiveness." His political beliefs are dis-

12. (2d ed. London, 1770), Letter XI, pp. 41–42. See also Letter VIII, pp. 29–31.

13. *Lives of the Poets, 1,* 270–71.

missed as "patriotic sentiments" uttered "for fashion's sake."[14]

The images of Waller in Clarendon, Hurd, Langhorne, Johnson, and Gardiner are all drawn in illustration of a point. It is possible, of course, to see Waller as the quintessential Restoration man, or the quintessential courtier, or cynic, or literary hack with his pen for hire. But surely there is more to be said. Surely it should be possible to examine his character and actions in a manner relatively free from bias, analytic rather than intent on proving a thesis.

This study is heavily indebted to the reinterpretations of seventeenth-century history by Christopher Hill, Irene Coltman, C. V. Wedgwood, and others (and even more heavily indebted to Gardiner, who made all revisionist history possible).[15] But each of these works treats Waller only insofar as he supports a particular thesis or approach: economic determinism in Hill, neo-royalism in Miss Wedgwood, persistent analogies with twentieth-century liberalism in Miss Coltman. Other historical studies are more damagingly thesis-ridden, while literary critics, when they mention Waller at all, generally treat him as ammunition, while they belabor the sins of neoclassicism, extol the virtues of high seriousness, or ride some more currently fashionable hobbyhorse. This study, then, is an attempt not to rehabilitate Waller but to do him simple justice—to seek to understand the man, his actions, his writings, and his

14. Samuel R. Gardiner, *History of the Great Civil War* (4 vols. London, 1886), *1*, 8–10. See also Gardiner's *History of England, 1603–1642* (10 vols. London, 1883–84), *8–10*.

15. Christopher Hill, *The Century of Revolution 1603–1714* (Edinburgh, Thomas Nelson and Sons, 1961); Irene Coltman, *Private Men and Public Causes: Philosophy and Politics in the English Civil War* (London, Faber and Faber, 1962); C. V. Wedgwood, *The King's Peace* (London, Collins, 1955), and *The King's War* (London, Collins, 1959). Though none of these works treats Waller at any length, I have found their incidental remarks on Waller and their general treatment of Constitutional Royalism in seventeenth-century politics very helpful.

beliefs by examining them in their own right and seeing them in their appropriate contexts.

Through all the twistings and turnings of Waller's career, there is a certain consistency. Like Dryden, he changed his allegiances without changing his basic beliefs —and indeed, the attacks on Waller in the later eighteenth and in the nineteenth centuries, like the similar attacks on Dryden, err by neglecting the mainspring of his actions. The charges that Waller acted purely from expediency have approximately the same validity as the charges that Dryden turned Catholic to get a pension. In Parliament, Waller always chose the role of peacemaker, broker between opposing factions. When he alternately supported and opposed the government in the Parliaments of Charles I and Charles II, he was not being blown by every wind; he held consistently to a middle-of-the-road position, opposing what he considered the excessive demands of each of the claimants to power. His support of Cromwell in 1655 did not mean he abandoned his Royalist principles. Instead, he adapted them, presenting Cromwell in his *Panegyric to my Lord Protector* as an ideal king, a leader under whom the nation could achieve new greatness. The *Panegyric,* an immensely skillful piece of political argumentation, is a plea for peace, unity, and harmony; from unity, the poet argues, comes strength.

> Your drooping country, torn with civil hate,
> Restored by you, is made a glorious state.[16]

Waller's characteristic position throughout the century was that of a trimmer. The term in its original application was pejorative: to trim one's sails to the prevailing wind. But the greatest of trimmers, George Savile, Marquess of Halifax, changed the metaphor.

---

16. *A Panegyric to my Lord Protector*, 13–14. In quoting Waller, I follow the text in Thorn-Drury's edition, unless otherwise noted.

> This innocent word *Trimmer* signifieth no more
> than this, That if Men are together in a Boat, and one
> part of the Company would weigh it down on one side,
> another would make it lean as much to the contrary;
> it happeneth there is a third Opinion of those, who
> conceive it would do as well, if the Boat went even,
> without endangering the Passengers.

> Our *Trimmer* . . . thinketh fit to conclude with these
> Assertions, That our Climate is a *Trimmer,* between
> that part of the World where Men are Roasted, and the
> other where they are Frozen; That our Church is a
> *Trimmer* between the Phrenzy of Platonick Visions,
> and the Lethargick Ignorance of Popish Dreams; That
> our Laws are *Trimmers,* between the Excess of
> unbounded Power and the Extravagance of Liberty not
> enough restrained; That true Virtue hath ever been
> thought a *Trimmer,* and to have its dwelling in the
> middle between the two Extreams.[17]

Like Halifax, Waller believed in a mixed form of
government, a balance of power within the state. While he
jealously guarded Parliament's privileges, the poet repeatedly cautioned the House of Commons against the dangers
of meddling where they had no right and of attempting to
eat into the King's prerogative.[18] He attacked the House of

17. George Savile, Marquess of Halifax, *Complete Works,* ed. Walter
Raleigh (Oxford, 1912), pp. 48, 103.

18. The British constitution was frequently cited as an example of a mixed
and balanced polity, even before the settlement of 1688. Most seventeenth-
century English political theorists agreed that "the monarch has certain
prerogatives, the subjects certain rights—particularly rights of property—
and neither could be infringed without a dangerous imbalance resulting";
see J. P. Kenyon, *The Stuart Constitution 1603–1688* (Cambridge, Eng.,
Cambridge University Press, 1966), p. 9. Dryden's formulation in "To my
Honour'd Kinsman, John Driden," 171–74, is typical: "A Patriot, both the
King and Country serves; / Prerogative, and Privilege preserves: / Of Each,
our Laws the certain Limit show; / One must not err, nor t'other overflow"
(James Kinsley, ed., *The Poems of John Dryden* [4 vols. Oxford, 1958]). Cf.
also Halifax, *Complete Works,* p. 62; or Swift's "Discourse of the Contests

Lords when it claimed a position of superiority but opposed attempts to circumscribe the powers of this House: "The two Houses are the two hands; the right will want the left. . . . They may err; so may we; sometimes we can never have enough; at other times any thing contents us."[19] The poet's ideal of government finds expression in a speech which attacks Charles II and his ministers for mismanagement of finances: "We believed, when the King was called back, that the law was come again. . . . No Government can be more advantageous to him than this. 'Tis a monarchy. The King governs by Law."[20]

Again like Halifax, Waller advocated a strong navy and a strong foreign policy.[21] As an island power, he felt, England depended on the sea, and she was able to hold the balance of power in Europe while not becoming embroiled in Europe's petty rivalries. The rule of law within the state

---

and Dissentions between the Nobles and Commons in Athens and Rome," in *A Tale of a Tub, with Other Early Works,* ed. Herbert Davis (Oxford, 1957), p. 197: "It will be an eternal Rule in Politicks, among every free People, that there is a Ballance of Power to be carefully held by every State within it self, as well as among several States with each other."

19. Grey, *Debates, 1,* 191. According to J. P. Kenyon, "some of the fiercest parliamentary battles" of 1660–88 "were fought not between king and Parliament but between the two Houses" *(The Stuart Constitution,* p. 413). Waller's speeches, both before and after the Restoration, are full of allusions to the rights and duties of Parliament and the limitations upon the power of either house. For the earlier period, see Fenton, pp. 258, 261, 268–70, 275–77; for the later, see (e.g.) Grey, *Debates, 1,* 12, 128; *2,* 25, 266; *3,* 121, 244–45, 302–03.

20. Ibid., *3,* 302. For a discussion of the significance of *concordia discors*—harmony, the mixed state, the balance and reconciliation of opposites—in seventeenth-century political theory, especially as reflected in poetry, see Earl Wasserman, *The Subtler Language* (Baltimore, 1959), pp. 53–61.

21. For Waller's views on the navy and foreign policy, see the poems "To the King, on his Navy," and *A Panegyric to my Lord Protector,* 17–24, 41–48; see also speeches printed in Fenton, pp. 270–71, and Grey, *Debates, 1,* 28; *3,* 175, 452–53. Halifax expresses ideas very close to Waller's in "A Rough Draught of a New Model at Sea," *Complete Works,* p. 168; cf. also Dryden's "To my Honour'd Kinsman, John Driden," 146–49.

should guarantee internal peace, enabling England to extend the rule of law to all Europe. On the other hand, arbitrary and lawless practices divide and weaken the state and prevent it from accomplishing "any great matter abroad."[22]

Throughout his career, Waller was concerned with the growth of trade and with colonization, arguing the importance of trade for the health of the nation and the folly of narrow restrictive measures, such as the prohibition of exports, which protected a particular group at the expense of the national interest.[23] He was appointed a commissioner of trade by Cromwell in 1655 and after the Restoration served on the Councils of Trade and Foreign Plantations, which were at first separate bodies but later combined into one. The position was no sinecure; he worked hard at his job, attending meetings regularly and helping draft reports and instructions as part of the Council's day to day business.[24]

The poet's several years' residence in Europe and his cos-

---

22. Fenton, p. 236. Cf. the remark of Louis XIV's foreign minister Arnauld de Pomponne, quoted in G. N. Clark, *The Later Stuarts* (Oxford, 1934), p. 105: "This perpetually divided state of England is that which suits us best. So long as she is divided within herself she will be little equal to making herself considerable abroad and to holding that balance which seems to lie naturally in her hands among the contentions of Europe."

23. See *Memoirs of Sir John Reresby*, ed. James J. Cartwright (London, 1875), p. 97, an account of a debate in Parliament in 1675: "Mr. Waller, the poet, an old Parliament man, said this was the most necessary thing that could be, for the riches and strength of all nations are proportionate to their trade, and therefore trade must both enrich the country and maintain itself." See also Grey, *Debates*, *1*, 443, and *5*, 157; and *The Diary of John Milward*, ed. Caroline Robbins (Cambridge, 1938), p. 270, reporting a speech by Waller in 1668.

24. After 1670, working members (including Waller) were paid £500 annually. There is a full account of the Trade and Plantations Councils and of Waller's role in them in Charles M. Andrews, *British Committees, Commissions, and Councils of Trade and Plantations, 1622–1675*, Johns Hopkins University Studies in Historical and Political Science, Series 26, Nos. 1–3 (Baltimore, 1908), esp. pp. 40, 68, 76–77, 97–98, 106.

mopolitanism, together with his interest in colonization and
in trade, led him to see domestic events in broad, international perspective. Again and again on the floor of Parliament he urged the examples of other nations and of history
to argue against the narrow, tightfisted provincialism of
many of his colleagues. "At *Paris* there are many bridges—
At *Venice* hundreds—We are still obstructing public
things."[25] Men are imperfect, but the idea of the nation
stands above anything individual men can do. Waller's ideal
commonwealth, the empire of peace, finds its clearest
expression in *A Panegyric to my Lord Protector,* but the
idea lies behind much of his work. When he celebrates
British power, he is praising not force, but law; the best
conquests are bloodless. The dream of empire shades off
into the dream of a golden age, a world where (to quote a
line Pope adapts from Waller) "Seas but join the Regions
they divide."[26] In the *Panegyric* and again in *Instructions
to a Painter,* Waller speaks of England as a second Rome.
This is no casual metaphor but embodies his central vision,
the universal rule of peace, civility, and law.

It is not easy, however, to pursue a trimming policy under
the pressure of events and emotions. Those who, like
Waller, consistently urged moderation, constitutionalism,
and compromise during the Civil War period met with
continual failure and frustration; as C. V. Wedgwood puts
it, they were "cheated . . . and repudiated" by the two parties
they sought to reconcile. Waller's career as a whole, and
particularly that part of it which is most fully documented,

25. Grey, *Debates, 1,* 415; see also *1,* 227; *3,* 176, 452–53.
26. *Windsor-Forest,* 400, in John Butt, ed., *The Poems of Alexander Pope*
(New Haven, 1963). Cf. *Panegyric,* 99–100: "While by your valour, and your
bounteous mind, / Nations, divided by the sea, are joined." The vision of
the triumph of peace (and of British empire) at the end of *Windsor-Forest*
owes a good deal to Waller's poetry, especially the *Panegyric.* A similar
prophecy concludes Dryden's *Astraea Redux,* 293–322; all three poets draw
on the classical and biblical prophetic tradition (Virgil, Isaiah) in presenting
their vision of a *pax Britannica,* a paradise restored.

his political activities during the years 1640–43, provides a particularly interesting case history illustrating the strengths and weaknesses of moderation.[27]

When Parliament was reconvened in 1640 after an intermission of eleven years, Waller's sympathies were divided between the two sides. His family connections linked him to Puritanism: John Hampden was the poet's first cousin and neighbor in Buckinghamshire, while Cromwell, Sir William Waller, the parliamentary general, and Sir Hardress Waller, later a regicide, were more distant cousins. On the other hand, Waller's own inclinations, his friends at court, and his great respect for the idea of monarchy would lead him to favor the Royalists. There is indirect corroboration of Waller's middle position and its uncertainties in the fact that he sat for the Puritan borough of Agmondesham, Buckinghamshire, in the Short Parliament, while in the Long Parliament he sat for St. Ives, in the Royalist stronghold of Cornwall.[28]

Waller's position in the Parliaments of 1640 was that of

27. *The King's War*, p. 27. There are good brief accounts of Waller's political career, with particular emphasis on these years, in Thorn-Drury's introduction, *1, xxxi–xxxvii* and *lxiii–lxiv;* and in Jordan, *The Development of Religious Toleration 4,* 40–44. I am indebted throughout this section to Samuel Gardiner's monumental *History of England, 7–10,* and to Willson H. Coates' edition of *The Journal of Sir Simonds D'Ewes,* Oct. 1641–Jan. 1642 (New Haven, 1942).

28. Waller's native county was one of the bastions of Independency, and he held a seat in the Long Parliament only through the influence of friends. Lord Lisle (brother of Lady Dorothy Sidney, Waller's Sacharissa) had been elected to two separate seats and chose to sit for the other; the seat thus vacated, for which Waller was chosen in a second election, was a preserve of the Godolphin family, with whom Waller (through his good friend Sidney Godolphin) was also closely associated. See Mary Frear Keeler, *The Long Parliament, 1640–1641, A Biographical Study of its Members* (Philadelphia, 1954), p. 376. Divided allegiances were of course common in the Civil War period. Waller's mother, according to the poet's biographers, remained on good terms with Cromwell in spite of her Royalist sympathies, until, "finding in time that she acted for the king as well as talked, he made her a prisoner to her own daughter, in her own house" (Johnson, *Lives of the Poets, 1,* 269).

his good friend Lord Falkland and his old acquaintance Edward Hyde: constitutionalist, Anglican, and ultimately royalist. Like Falkland, he was eager in the Short Parliament and the early days of the Long Parliament for the redress of grievances, political and economic. The autocratic methods of Charles I had offended both the sense of right and wrong and the pocketbooks of the gentry who composed the Short Parliament. To Waller, as to Locke half a century later, the right to property was the keystone of all rights:

> The propriety of goods is the mother of courage, and the nurse of industry; makes us valiant in war, and good husbands in peace. . . . 'Tis not the fear of imprisonment, or, if need be, of death it self, that can keep a true-hearted *English*-man from the care to leave this part of his inheritance as entire to posterity, as he received it from his ancestors.[29]

As soon as Parliament had assembled, the King presented it with an immediate, peremptory demand for funds. Waller's speech of April 22, 1640, in which he argued that guarantees of "the fundamental, and vital liberties, the propriety of our goods, and freedom of our persons" must precede any consideration of finances, expressed the nearly unanimous feeling of the House. What was particularly characteristic of Waller and his closest associates was an optimistic, conciliatory tone, together with a conservative dislike of innovations in government. The King's advisers, Waller said, had urged a foolish absolutist course upon him, ignoring the long-established, sensible, balanced English form of government, in which the King ruled with the advice of Parliament. But with fair dealing on every side, he maintained, the problems would be worked out, the liberties of the people restored, and all things would run smoothly again:

> By new ways they think to accomplish wonders; but, in truth, they grasp the wind: and are at the same time

29. Fenton, pp. 258–59.

> cruel to us, and to the King too. For if the Common-
> wealth flourish, then he that hath the Sovereignty can
> never want, nor do amiss; so as he govern not according
> to the interest of others; but go the shortest, and the
> safest, ways, to his own, and the common Good.[30]

There are many similarities between the position argued in this speech and the views later expressed by Locke. Both men were primarily concerned with refuting the claims of absolutism (Locke arguing against the doctrines of Filmer and Hobbes, Waller against the claims of divine right and *ad libitum* prerogative represented by Strafford, the ship-money judges, and the Laudian divines), both saw the right to personal property as fundamental and inalienable, and both presented an ideal of limited, responsible government, a king ruling in harmony with his people.[31] The primary difference between them is that, for all his love of compromise, Locke faced up to the problem of royal power where Waller did not. Waller relied on the hope that kings and men will be ruled by reason, Locke on a right of revolution when reason failed.

When it became evident that the King did not share in Waller's conception of the common good and intended to dissolve Parliament for not complying with his financial demands, Waller unsuccessfully tried to convince court officials to ask for less. He laid the blame for Parliament's dissolution not on the King, but on the King's intermediaries.[32] Here as elsewhere the poet managed to combine severe criticism of royal policies with exaggerated respect

30. Ibid., p. 261.

31. It has several times been pointed out that the political beliefs of the Constitutional Royalists of 1640 received a belated confirmation in the constitutional settlement of 1688–89; see e.g. B. H. G. Wormald, *Clarendon: Politics, History and Religion, 1640–1660* (Cambridge, Cambridge University Press, 1951), p. 153; and Jordan, *Development of Religious Toleration*, 2, 318.

32. "Life" in *Poems* (1722), xv.

for the King's person by the fiction that the King himself was not responsible for the arbitrary rule of the past few years but had been the victim of evil counsellors. The accompaniment of this view was the complementary fiction that Parliament was united in its pursuit of the common good and that temporary disunities within it could be resolved by an appeal to reason. Neither fiction was able to hold up under the pressures of civil war.

When the Long Parliament met, a split immediately became evident between moderates and revolutionaries—those who desired minor changes in the existing system, ecclesiastical and political, and those who considered the system the work of the devil. Parliament was able to act with some unanimity in rectifying the legal and financial abuses of ship money and royal courts; Waller conducted the impeachment of Sir Francis Crawley, one of the ship-money judges, as Hyde and Falkland had managed the prosecution of Lord Keeper Sir John Finch, the chief legal spokesman for absolutism. But the temporary unity of the House was split asunder when the Long Parliament came to consider fundamental religious and constitutional questions. In the debates on church government in February and June 1641, as in the debates on parliamentary approval of officials and on the proposed Grand Remonstrance in October and November, Waller and his allies used the same arguments against innovations and extremes that they had used earlier in the session, but these arguments were powerless against those who, not content with half measures, were determined to wrest sovereign power from the King and frame the government of the church to their own liking.

In the prosecution of Justice Crawley, Waller was working with the Puritan majority, while in his speech defending episcopacy, he stood in opposition to that majority. Yet on both occasions he argued the importance of law, the dangers of arbitrary government and of unchecked selfish ambition, and the evils of "mutation." In both speeches, a sharp attack on abuses is coupled with an appeal for resolution of differences by compromise. The philippic against Crawley is an eloquent and lengthy indictment of the attempt by Charles' kept judges to destroy the law on which the health of the state depends, claiming "necessity" to justify arbitrary encroachments on liberty. It is clear from the speech that Waller believed such abuses were no longer possible now that Parliament was in session: "the chief troublers of our State" were few in number, and "the foundation of our laws" and the strength of the nation could be restored. By implication, Waller was appealing to Parliament to preserve its unity and not split into factions.[33]

In Waller's view (and Falkland's), Archbishop Laud and his adherents were directly responsible for the political divisions that racked the nation.[34] Yet the main point of Waller's speech on church government in June, and the position argued by the Constitutional Royalists in all the debates on church government, was that the evils brought about by the political divines were correctable. Men were at fault, not the system. Parliament had "disarmed" the bishops of their power and "cut and pared" their "Hornes and Clawes." "Episcopacy, and the evils thereof," Waller argued, "are mingled like water and oyle," but "our Lawes and the present Government of the Church are mingled

---

33. Fenton, pp. 267–74.

34. Waller devoted a good part of his speech on supply to an attack on "those Divines, who would persuade us, that a Monarch must be absolute, and that he may do all things *ad libitum*" (Fenton, pp. 261–63). Cf. Falkland's speech on church government, Feb. 8, 1641, in John Rushworth, *Historical Collections, 3, i* (London, 1692), 184–85:

> This kingdom hath long laboured under many and great oppressions, both in *Religion* and *Liberty;* and . . . a principal cause of both these have been some *Bishops* and their adherents. . . . Some have evidently laboured to bring in an *English,* though not a *Roman Popery;* I mean not only the *outside,* and *dress* of it, but equally absolute, a blind dependence of the People upon the Clergy, and of the Clergy upon themselves.

like Wine and Water . . . inseparable."[35] Waller was a
member of the Anglican communion all his life, but
religious feeling entered only slightly into his support of
the episcopate. As W. K. Jordan puts it, "the truth or
falsity underlying episcopacy" was "far less important" to
him "than the fact that it enjoy[ed] institutional validity in
the life and traditions of England. . . . Religion was to him
a matter of constitutional rather than of personal significance." The defense of episcopal church government was
the defense of law and order: "*Nolumus mutare Leges
Angliae.*"[36]

It is difficult to disentangle political, religious, and economic motivations during the Civil War period; any
position, any decision, may be seen as partly the product
of economic interest or the automatic loyalties of social
class, partly the result of deeply held religious or political
convictions, and partly reasoned, partly instinctive. Historical accounts of the Constitutional Royalists and of
Civil War politics tend to fall into two camps: the moderates
either become embattled Abdiels, blessed with the gift of
prophecy and serene, self-effacing courage, or they become
mere pawns of economic determinism. The truth lies
somewhere between these two points of view. The actions

---

35. *A Speech Made by Master Waller Esquire, in the Honorable House
of Commons, Concerning Episcopacie* (London, 1641), pp. 3–4. The speech
is reprinted in Johnson, *Lives of the Poets.* Cf. Falkland: "Let us give but
good men good Rules, we shall have both good Governors, and good Times"
(Rushworth, *3, i,* 185).

36. *A Speech Concerning Episcopacie,* p. 4; Jordan, *4,* 42–43. In his support of episcopacy for prudential, political reasons, Waller resembled John
Selden; see Jordan's discussion of Selden, *2,* 479–88. Selden, a thorough
erastian who believed "the State still makes the Religion, and receives into
it what will best agree with it," supported bishops as "useful to the King or
State." See John Selden, *Table Talk* (London, 1898), pp. 14, 129. Hyde, a
more conventional defender of the church with none of Selden's (or Waller's)
religious skepticism, also saw the institution of episcopacy primarily in
political terms, "as it was a part of the Government of England"; see
Wormald, *Clarendon,* p. 301.

of these men (who like any group differed widely among themselves) were neither wholly noble nor wholly base, but shared in the complex and problematical nature of all human behavior.

The transformation of Waller and his friends into Royalists was in large part caused by events over which they had no control. For all their efforts to retain a middle position, critical both of the demands of the parliamentary radicals and the demands of the King, ultimately they were forced to take sides. It was their allegiance to the principle of order and their fear (practical rather than philosophical) of what uncontrolled change might bring that determined their choice.

The ultimate position of the Falkland group in the debates on church government was that expressed in James I's famous dictum: "No Bishop, no King." Their conservatism was in part the product of class solidarity. "If we make a parity in the Church," Sir John Strangways protested, "we must come to a parity in the Commonwealth."[37] The fear of "the multitude," of "irregular and tumultuous assemblies of people," who first petitioned and then besieged Parliament, played a large part in turning the moderates into Royalists. In his speech on episcopacy, Waller cautioned the House against allowing "the people" too much power:

> I see some are moved with a number of hands against the Bishops, which I confesse, rather inclines Me to their defence, for I look upon Episcopacy, as a counterscarp or outwork, which if it be taken by this assault of the people, and withall this Mysterie once revealed, that we must deny them nothing when they ask it thus in troopes, we may in the next place, have as hard a taske to defend our propriety, as we have lately had to recover it from the prerogative. If by multiplying hands, and petitions, they prevail for an equality in

37. Gardiner, *History of England, 9,* 285.

things Ecclesiasticall, the next demand perhaps may be
Lex Agraria, the like equality in things temporall.[38]

Waller proved a good prophet. But the accuracy of his
analysis does not make it any less a piece of special pleading,
a defense of one class against another. The metaphors of
war and battle, with the underlying assumption that man in
his natural state is ruled by boundless selfish ambition, are
revealing; here Waller sees political institutions and human
nature in a manner far more akin to Hobbes than Locke.

In the debates of October, November, and December
1641, political theory and religious beliefs played a far
smaller role than fear, hatred, distrust, and the exigencies of
power. John Pym, the leader of the parliamentary majority,
was regularly using mob pressures to bring wavering members in line and build up party solidarity; the presence of the
mob had the concomitant effect of strengthening the
instinctive conservatism and royalism of the minority. In
December, troops under the Earl of Dorset fired on a crowd
assembled outside Parliament. "Mr. Waller . . . much
inveighed against the Londoners in comming down after soe
tumultuous a manner, and crying openlie *No Bishopp Noe
Bishopp.* And he iustified the Earle of Dorset in what hee
had done; saying that hee had done nothing but what hee
was necessitated unto."[39] The Constitutionalists had clearly
become Royalists; Sir Edward Nicholas' letter to the King
on October 29 recognizes them as allies and suggests that the
King give them concrete encouragement.

Yo[r] Ma[ties] long absence encourages some to talke in
Parliamt of highe matters. . . . Howsoever I may not

38. *A Speech Concerning Episcopacie,* pp. 4–5 (I have corrected several
obvious misprints). In his speech two years later, after the discovery of his
"plot," he issued a similar warning, and his prediction was equally accurate.
"The people" in the first speech, the army in the other, would soon find
they desired power by themselves, until "they never suffered the Senate to
have a voyce any more" (ibid., p. 5; cf. Fenton, pp. 275–77).

39. Coates, p. 225. In his introduction (xxxii–iii) the editor discusses the
role of mob pressure during these months.

> forbeare to let yor Matie know, that the Lo: ffalkland, Sr Jo. Strangwishe, Mr. Waller, Mr. Ed. Hide, & Mr. Holborne, & diverse others stood as Champions in maynten'nce of yor Prerogative, and shewed for it unaunswerable reason and undenyable p^esedents, whereof yor Matie shall doe well to take some notice (as yor Matie shall thinke best) for their encouragm't.[40]

The bitterness between the two parties increased as the session wore on. When Pym used reports of a rebellion in Ireland to push through measures for parliamentary control over appointment of ministers and over the army, Waller angrily accused him of dictatorial tactics and was forced to ask pardon of Pym and the House.

> Mr. Waller . . . saied that as the Earle of Strafford had advized the King that because wee did not releive him he was absolved from all rules of government; soe by this addition on the contrarie, wee should pretend that if the King did not remove his ill Counsellors wee weere absolved from our duties in assisting him in the Recoverie of Ireland.[41]

Intent on a struggle for power, the parliamentary majority scorned any policy of compromise, and the minority fought bitterly to keep from being overwhelmed. In the lengthy debate on the Grand Remonstrance, an appeal to the nation listing the abuses of Charles' rule, Waller and his allies pleaded legality and custom in a desperate rearguard action. Sir John Culpeper attacked the Remonstrance as "daingerous for the publique peace," and Waller attacked it as "a remonstrance against the lawes." "Lawes are the children of the parliment," he objected, "and wee must not destroy

---

40. *Diary and Correspondence of John Evelyn, F.R.S., to which is subjoined the Private Correspondence between King Charles I and Sir Edward Nicholas*, ed. William Bray (4 vols. London, 1902), *4*, 100–01.

41. Ibid., p. 95.

them with orders and declarations.''[42] Waller's words in defense of his fellow member Geoffrey Palmer have a noble ring: "Let not the successe make any man a delinquent. . . . Let noe man be punished for temperance, least wee seeme to punish vertue." Yet Palmer's actions had hardly represented temperance. At one in the morning of November 23, when after long debate the Remonstrance had finally passed by a close vote of 158–149, Palmer

> stood upp and desired that a protestation might be entered in the name of himselfe and all the rest upon which divers cried *All, All,* and some waved their hatts over their heads, and others tooke their swords in their scabberds out of their beltes and held them by the pumells in their hands setting the lower part on the ground, soe as if God had not prevented it there was very great danger that mischief might have been done.[43]

During the next two weeks, members were repeatedly threatened with expulsion or censure for remarks made in debate. On December 16, Pym demanded that Waller and Orlando Bridgeman "give a reason why they saied *No*" on a bill; it was finally agreed, after discussion, that "noe reason should be given of anie man's vote which ought to be free."[44]

Clearly, it was an atmosphere in which moderation and compromise were impossible. The moderates were equally frustrated when, admitted into the King's councils, they tried to influence the King. Two days after Falkland and Sir John Culpeper were appointed Secretary of State and Chancellor of the Exchequer, respectively, Charles, without their knowledge, brought armed troops into the House of

---

42. *Verney Papers: Notes of Proceedings in the Long Parliament, by Sir Ralph Verney, Knight,* ed. John Bruce (London, Camden Society, 1845), pp. 122–24.

43. Ibid., p. 128; Coates, p. 186.

44. Coates, pp. 233, 298; cf. also pp. 228, 245–47. One of the members threatened with censure was Waller's friend Sidney Godolphin.

Commons in an attempt to arrest five members. Though Hyde and Falkland succeeded in providing constitutional rationalizations for events as they occurred, they and their associates had little effect on policy during the next few years. "My Lord Falkland," Charles complained, "commonly brought me my instructions in so fine a dress, that I did not always own them." The royalist Oxford Parliament, a parliament-in-exile established at the advice of Hyde and his friends to give an aura of constitutionality to the royal cause, was to Charles "the place of base and mutinous motions (that is to say, our Mungrel Parliament here)."[45] In the words of Gilbert Burnet, the King "hated all that offered prudent and moderate counsels: he thought it flowed from a meanness of spirit, and a care to preserve themselves by sacrificing his authority, or from republican principles: and even when he saw it was necessary to follow such advices, yet he hated those that gave them."[46] At no point did the constitutional moderates have the slightest hope of changing Charles I into either a constitutionalist or a moderate—and the remnant of the party who survived the Civil War and interregnum had no greater success with Charles II.

Waller's trimming policy shows itself at its absolute worst in the unhappy affair of "Waller's plot." On the other hand, if we look at Waller's behavior in Parliament after the Restoration, we see him at his best. The King and Parliament did not follow his advice in the 1660s and 1670s any more than in the 1640s. But where in the earlier period he was swamped by the pressure of events and the need for action, in the later period he could rest comfortably above the battle, the elder statesman benignly offering advice.

45. Coltman, *Private Men and Public Causes*, pp. 104, 110. For a similar view of the impotence of the moderates, see Wedgwood, *The King's War*, p. 27.

46. Gilbert Burnet, *History of my Own Time*, ed. Osmund Airy (2 vols. Oxford, 1897–1900), *1*, 47.

Under different circumstances, his principles could lead him to act nobly or abominably. His actions could take on the glamour of a lost cause or a mellow, Lockean wisdom; his vision of unity could serve as a splendid affirmative creed; or the desire for moderation, peace, and unity could be shot through with weakness.

After the outbreak of the Civil War, Waller remained in Parliament, speaking "with great sharpness and freedom . . . as the boldest champion the Crown had in both Houses."[47] He was thus in a position to capitalize on the strong sentiment for peace that had grown up in the city of London and among the parliamentary moderates (mostly Presbyterians like D'Ewes, Whitelocke, Maynard, and Holles) who had chosen Parliament over the King but still longed for a reconciliation. Such sentiment was economic as well as idealistic in its motivation. London merchants chafed under the high taxes imposed by Parliament to carry on the war, while the leaders of the parliamentary peace party were for the most part wealthy men whose estates had suffered particular diminution by the war.[48] In its original form, "Waller's plot" seems to have entailed some form of passive resistance by citizens of London, backed by members of both houses, to urge a negotiated settlement upon Parliament. One of the plotters, Richard Chaloner, a wealthy linen draper, described its inception as follows:

> It came from Mr. Waller under this Notion, That if we could make a moderate Party here in London, to stand betwixt, and in the Gap, to unite the King and the Parliament, it would be a very acceptable Work; for now the Three Kingdoms lay a Bleeding, and unless that were done, there was no hopes to unite them.[49]

47. Edward Hyde, Earl of Clarendon, *History of the Rebellion and Civil Wars in England*, ed. W. Dunn Macray (6 vols. Oxford, 1888), *3*, 38–39.

48. See Hill, *The Century of Revolution*, pp. 126–27; Wedgwood, *The King's War*, p. 161; and John Langton Sanford, *Studies and Illustrations of the Great Rebellion* (London, 1858), pp. 528–43.

49. Rushworth, *3, ii*, 327.

But the peace plan quickly turned to war: in its final form, the plot called for an armed rising and seizure of the key points of the city in order to let the King's army in. The pragmatic soldier's mind of the Viscount Conway had elaborated the plans in a way quite distant from Waller's rather vaguely formed original intentions, demanding concrete information from his fellow plotters on "In what places the Magazines were laid . . . Where the Rendezvous should be . . . Where was the Place of retreat, if there should be occasion . . . By what marks and tokens they should be distinguished from others, and know their friends from their enemies . . . What strength there was within the walls, and what strength without?" When Pym revealed the plot to the House of Commons, he placed particular emphasis on the contrast between the "pretences" of peace and the actuality of "blood and violence":

> The City should have been put into such a combustion, as to have your swords imbrued in one anothers bloud: The Parliament should have been corrupted, and betrayed by their own Members. . . . Under pretence of securing themselves by force against the Ordinances of Parliament, and under pretence of procuring peace, they would have made themselves Masters of the City, yea of the whole kingdom, and they would have ruined and destroyed all those that should have interrupted them in their mischievous intentions.[50]

Perhaps Waller cannot be held fully responsible for the plot's final form;[51] yet the readiness with which the plot and

50. *A Discovery of the great Plot For the utter Ruine of the City of London, and the Parliament. As it was at large made known By John Pym, Esq; On Thursday being the Eighth of June, 1643. At a Common Hall: And afterwards corrected by his own hand for the Presse* (London, 1643).

51. Clarendon attempts to separate Waller's design from a military uprising organized by Sir Nicholas Crispe (whose name appears on the Commission of Array used as evidence in the trial of Waller's co-conspirators). Waller seems to have opposed the transformation of his plot from peace

its chief actor were diverted from their course is an index to their fundamental weakness.

Pym and the other leaders of the Puritan party used the plot as a pretext to annihilate the moderates, destroying any possibility of peace. Members of the House of Commons who had spoken up strongly for a negotiated settlement in the previous months were hard pressed to clear themselves of charges of complicity in the plot.[52] The peace party, which had held a majority in the House of Lords and a large minority in the House of Commons, was in a moment reduced to impotence. Moreover, a covenant was imposed upon the Parliament, the city, and the army, by which all signatories declared their innocence of the plot and vowed support of "the Forces raised by the Two Houses of Parliament . . . for the Defence of the true Protestant Religion and Liberty of the Subject, against the Forces raised by the King."[53]

When Waller was questioned in prison by a parliamentary committee, he confessed his own guilt and implicated others freely. He was, as Clarendon put it, "so confounded with fear and apprehension that he confessed whatsoever he had said, heard, thought, or seen, all that he knew of himself, and all that he suspected of others, without

---

to war: he told the House he "had nothing to do with the other army; or any intention to begin the offer of violence to any body," and "ever disallowed, and utterly rejected" the "propositions of letting-in part of the King's army" (Fenton, p. 277). But Clarendon's charge that the details of the plot were largely fabricated by Pym *(History of the Rebellion, 3, 40, 47, 50–51)* is highly dubious. The Commission of Array for raising an army was smuggled from Oxford to Waller's co-conspirators Tomkins and Chaloner, and even if Waller served primarily as "the Mouth from the Lords" to the citizens (Rushworth, *3, ii,* 327), he was certainly aware of the final details of the plot.

52. Bulstrode Whitelocke, *Memorials of the English Affairs from the Beginning of the Reign of Charles the First to the Happy Restoration of King Charles the Second* (4 vols. Oxford, 1853), *1,* 203–04; see also Gardiner, *Civil War, 1,* 173–74; and Wedgwood, *The King's War,* p. 219.

53. Rushworth, *4, 325.*

concealing any person, of what degree or quality soever."[54] In accusing such figures as the Earls of Portland, Holland, and Northumberland of complicity in the plot, Waller hoped to save his own life by shifting the blame on others whom the House of Commons and the army would be unable or unwilling, because of their rank, to punish. Apparently he agreed to cooperate fully with his captors; in a petition to the House the following year, he speaks of "the free and ingenuous confessions and discoveries made upon promised favour." But the vagueness and desperation of his charges caused his reputation to sink still lower.[55]

The poet managed to have his trial put off until the furor had died down, and then, after distributing bribes copiously, was allowed to appear before the House. His air of "despairing dejectedness" did not prevent him from making a shrewd appeal to the self-interest of his hearers, and his plea to the House of Commons not to surrender one of its own members to the military "preserved," in Clarendon's phrase, "his dear-bought life."[56] After remaining a year in prison without trial, he was fined £10,000 and permitted to go into exile. Though he had saved his life, he had managed by his conduct to alienate all parties. The Puritan D'Ewes and the Royalist Clarendon could never speak of him afterwards without contempt.

54. *History of the Rebellion, 3,* 44.

55. Thorn-Drury, *1, xlviii–liii, lvii.* Waller's confrontation with the Earl of Portland before a committee of the House of Lords is reported fully in Historical Manuscripts Commission, *Fifth Report,* p. 94. Waller's letters to Portland and to Arthur Goodwyn, both pleading for his life, are printed in Fenton, pp. 280–81, and in George Grenville, Lord Nugent, *Some Memorials of John Hampden, His Party and His Times* (London, 1854), pp. 352–53.

56. *History of the Rebellion, 3,* 52. Waller's speech on the occasion is printed in Fenton, pp. 275–79. Aubrey, with characteristic brio, says the poet "bribed the whole House, which was the first time a house of Commons was ever bribed" *(Brief Lives,* p. 309); Clarendon and the author of the 1722 "Life" more reasonably make the bribes selective, directed to "some leading Members of the House" and influential Puritan clergymen. See *History of the Rebellion, 3,* 51–52; and "Life" in *Poems* (1722), xxiv.

The role Waller played in the parliaments of Charles II, on the other hand, showed him at his best. Though basically friendly to the court, he was found a good part of the time in the opposition; his central allegiance was not to the particular government, but to his idea of the nation. In the bitterness between the Parliament and King over such issues as the King's Declarations of Indulgence in 1662 and 1672, the Third Anglo-Dutch War, and the crown's management of finances, he endeavored to reconcile the opposing parties. A substantial country gentleman with ties to the court and the city, Waller was less likely to take a partial view than most of his associates; divided allegiances have their advantages as well as disadvantages. Dryden's account of his cousin as an M.P. in "To My Honour'd Kinsman, John Driden," fits Waller very well:

> Well-born, and Wealthy, wanting no Support,
> You steer betwixt the Country and the Court;
> Nor gratifie whate'er the Great desire,
> Nor grudging give, what Publick Needs require.
>
> (127–30)[57]

Personal factors helped determine Waller's allegiances at various times. When Clarendon, his enemy, was in power, Waller leaned toward the opposition, and when his friend Buckingham was in power, he favored the court. Party organization lists drawn up in the 1670s show him now a seeming ally of one side, now the other. It is possible that Danby purchased his support in early 1678 with a large bribe. His speeches in February 1677/8 are markedly more friendly to the court than they had been a year before; his increased trust in the court may have been due to the King's temporary abandonment of a pro-French policy for a Dutch alliance, but it may also have been due to £1000 paid him

57. In a speech delivered in February 1667/8, Waller speaks of himself as having "ever resisted both the extremes of giving and not giving" (Grey, *Debates, 1*, 93).

out of secret service funds in January.[58] At other times
he was far less sympathetic toward the court. Bishop Burnet
lists him among the leaders of the opposition party in Parliament, "the chief men that preserved the nation from a very
deceitful and practicing court, and from a corrupt house of
commons."[59] Yet through all the varying circumstances of
politics, Waller's essential position remained the same: a
distrust of extreme measures and violent emotions and an
ideal of government based on the sharing of power and
responsibility. Again and again in his speeches, he invoked
the memory of the Civil War to show that neither king nor
parliament should attempt to rule alone.

As the temper of the House swung from violent Tory to
violent Whig, from the Clarendon Code to the Popish Plot,
Waller pursued a steady course of moderation. He was a
steadfast proponent of religious toleration in a house bent
on persecution of Papists and Dissenters. In the years when
English prestige was at its lowest and Charles' foreign
policy was entirely supine, Waller generally voted with
the opposition, at the same time working to prevent open
breach between the factions. A letter to his friend Jane
Middleton in 1675 indicates the persistence and ill success
of his efforts at mediation:

> I went from you on fryday last immediately to the
> house. . . . But finding a better occasion than I expected,
> to persuade them to Union among themselves, agree-
> ment with the Lords & a better understanding with his

58. Andrew Browning, *Thomas Osborne, Earl of Danby and Duke of
Leeds* (3 vols. Glasgow, 1944–51), *3*, 55. See also *3*, 42, 80, 95; *Calendar of
Treasury Books, 1676–1679*, p. 1322; and Grey, *Debates*, *5*, 90–91, 164–65,
327–28, 375. The payment may not have been a bribe, but I can find no
other likely explanation for it; Andrew Marvell is celebrated as the only
member of that Parliament known to have refused a bribe.

59. *History of my Own Time*, *2*, 91, 93; the passage refers specifically to
the year 1675. Marvell also speaks of Waller as a leader of the opposition
in the late 1660s; see "Last Instructions to a Painter," 263–64, 267–68, in
H. M. Margoliouth, ed., *The Poems and Letters of Andrew Marvell* (2 vols.
Oxford, 1927).

Majty, I did it with as much success as one could expect
in that house, as now it is constituted, with approbation
from one Party. . . . I thinke both the Weather and the
House at this tyme too hot for me.[60]

Waller's position in the Popish Plot controversy was
similar to that of Halifax: initially sympathetic with the
Whigs, he opposed their attempts to exclude James from the
succession. In the early stages of the controversy, he held the
confidence of the Whig leaders sufficiently to be appointed
to committees to investigate the murder of Sir Edmund
Berry Godfrey and to translate and report on the intercepted
letters of Coleman, the Duke of York's former secretary. But
at this time, as earlier, he urged unity and caution upon the
House. Though he did not serve in the three Exclusion Bill
parliaments of 1679–81, his attitude at that time may be
discerned from his warnings against proposals in 1678 to
send James into exile:

There may be more danger in removing the Duke,
than in letting him alone. . . . *Absalom* asked his father
leave to go out of his Court, and you know what
followed. At Court the Duke will keep none but good
company, abroad Catholics. . . . From my experience
abroad, and what I have read at home, I have ever
observed, that Princes of the Duke's magnitude are like
fire out of the chimney, and put in the middle of the
room; it makes a great blaze, but sets all on fire. . . .
Foreign Princes will make use of the discontents.[61]

60. British Museum MS. Egerton 922, fol. 27. The letter in the MS., a
transcription in the hand of Mrs. Middleton's daughter, is dated May 12,
1670, but that date is obviously incorrect, since Parliament was not in
session at that date or any other May between 1668 and 1674. Its probable
date is May 12, 1675; see David Ogg, *England in the Reign of Charles II*
(2 vols. Oxford, 1956), 2, 532, for the letter's apparent occasion.

61. Grey, *Debates, 6,* 143, 246–47, Nov. 4 and 21, 1678. For Waller's further
speeches and committee assignments at this time, see *6,* 128, 196, 206–07, 232,
372, 382; and *Journals of the House of Commons, 9,* 518a, 532a. It has been
suggested that Waller's use of the story of David and Absalom in this speech

It may be that Waller prudently chose to withdraw from active politics at the height of the Exclusion Bill crisis. In a letter to Halifax dated July 8, 1680, and largely devoted to complaints about the unsettled nature of the times and the "cabals" of the Whigs ("The storm is grown very high this fortnight; God knows what does encourage them"), the Countess of Sunderland (Sacharissa) remarks, "Mrs. Middleton and I have lost old Waller; he is gone away frightened."[62]

When James II ascended the throne, Waller greeted him with two poems, both of which are thinly disguised pleas to the new King to pursue a policy of reconciliation and national unity. Like other moderate Anglicans, the poet soon became dissatisfied with James; he is said to have predicted that the King's intransigence would cause him to be left "like a Whale upon the Strand" and is reported to have been privy to negotiations with William before his death.[63]

---

gave Dryden a hint for *Absalom and Achitophel;* see Wallace Maurer, "Who Prompted Dryden to Write *Absalom and Achitophel?*" *Philological Quarterly,* 40 (1961), 130–38. But the parallel between Charles and David was a commonplace, and the identification of the Duke of York with Absalom is, if anything, closer to the Whig version of the story (as presented e.g. in Elkanah Settle's *Absalom Senior*).

62. *Some Account of the Life of Rachael Wriothesley Lady Russell . . . To which are added, eleven letters from Dorothy Sidney Countess of Sunderland, to George Saville Marquis of Hallifax,* ed. Mary Berry (London, 1819), pp. 129–30. In a letter to Jane Middleton at the time of the Oxford Parliament in 1681, Waller writes as an uncommitted moderate: "The King . . . never was seen in better humour nor more confident then now as may well appear by his Speech, wch lessens our hope of the wished accord with the same men whom he thinkes were unreasonable the last parliament" (British Museum MS. Egerton 922, fol. 28).

63. "Life," in *Poems* (1722), xxxvi. Characteristically, Waller "charg'd some about him not to meddle, 'till they saw the Prince of Orange actually landed." His two poems to James II, "A Presage of the Ruin of the Turkish Empire" and "To His Majesty, upon his motto, Beati Pacifici," both urge the King to unite warring Christendom by engaging in a crusade against the Turks. His funeral poem on Cromwell praises the Protector for following a similar policy: "From civil broils he did us disengage, / Found nobler

Whether defending or attacking the government, he stressed common sense, the importance of law, and the primacy of the national interest. To Waller, rights implied responsibilities; the House of Commons should serve as watchdog of the interests of the nation.

> Let us look back to the evils we had, in order to prevent more. There was loan, and ship-money, and extremes begat extremes. . . . We give public money, and must see that it goes to public use. . . . We cannot live at the expense of *Spain,* that has the Indies; or *France,* who has so many millions of revenue. Let us look to our Government, Fleet, and Trade. 'Tis the advice that the oldest Parliament-man among you can give you; and so, God bless you![64]

As one might expect, the same principles which animate Waller's speeches and actions in Parliament are central to his poetry. Images of order, reconciliation, and harmony recur again and again in his poems; the belief in the value of precedent, the dangers of innovation, and the desirability of peace find expression there as on the floor of Parliament. Waller's poems, like his speeches, oddly combine idealism and pragmatism: ideals are expressed for a highly pragmatic purpose. Waller wrote a large number of panegyrics—

---

objects for our martial rage; / And, with wise conduct, to his country showed / Their ancient way of conquering abroad" *(Upon the Late Storm and of the Death of His Highness Ensuing the Same,* 23–26).

64. Grey, *Debates, 3,* 302–03, speech of Oct. 19, 1675. Waller's conception of the relative powers of King and Parliament differed at various times. In general, he was willing to grant Parliament greater power in the 1660s and 1670s than in 1640–43—perhaps because Parliament in fact had little power in the later period and a great deal of power in the earlier. At all times, his ideal government was King-in-Parliament, a limited monarchy under law. But in the later period he supported close parliamentary supervision of finances, where in 1641–42 he had argued against Pym and his party for limitations on Parliament's power.

formal poems on affairs of state—and nearly all are political documents, written on a particular occasion for a particular purpose.

The poems are generally more royalist in tone than the speeches, partly because, as panegyrics, they are committed to praising something. In the speeches, historical allusions and comparisons are likely to be cautionary rather than ennobling. But poems and speeches reflect similar beliefs and advocate similar policies. When he defends the controversial ship-money tax in 1636 and attacks the policy with equal eloquence five years later, we may accuse him of lack of foresight, of selecting and arranging evidence for purposes of persuasion, or of confounding metaphor with reality, but we should not accuse him of inconsistency. "To the King, on his Navy" (1636), written at the time of the ship-money writs, represents the court position, extolling the royal navy as the glory of the nation and seeking by implication to counteract popular complaints of waste, extravagance, and illegal taxation. In 1641 he excoriates the court for failing to do what five years earlier he had praised the King for doing—maintaining a strong navy. The poem and the speech contain similar patriotic sentiments:

> Where'er thy navy spreads her canvas wings,
> Homage to thee, and peace to all she brings.   (1–2)

The poem goes on, through imagery of order and disorder, floods and protection, to express the limitlessness of British power.

> Should nature's self invade the world again,
> And o'er the centre spread the liquid main,
> Thy power were safe, and her destructive hand
> Would but enlarge the bounds of thy command;
> Thy dreadful fleet would style thee lord of all,
> And ride in triumph o'er the drowned ball.   (19–24)

In his speech five years later the ideal remains the same, but he is far less sanguine about the actuality; instead of erecting bulwarks against the flood, Charles' advisers have neglected their naval defenses and flooded the land:

> God, and Nature, has given us the sea as our best guard against our enemies; and our ships, as our greatest glory above other nations: and how barbarously would these men have let-in the sea upon us, at once to wash away our liberties, and to overwhelm, if not our land, all the propriety we have therein! . . . Alas! my Lords, the daily complaints of the decay of our navy tell us how ill Ship-Money has maintained the sovereignty of the sea.[65]

There is almost always a concrete political intention lying beneath the smooth and carefully elaborated surfaces of Waller's political poems; he is always either giving advice or arguing in support of a particular policy. Yet if Waller is a partisan, he is a remarkably gentle one. The repairs to St. Paul's Cathedral undertaken by Charles I and Archbishop Laud in the 1630s were bitterly attacked by Puritans.[66] "Upon His Majesty's Repairing of Paul's" (c. 1635) is thus a party piece, arguing the Anglican and Royalist position, justifying and glorifying the King's behavior (Laud is not mentioned in the poem). Yet the tone of the poem is not in the least combative; here as always, Waller seeks to reconcile, to persuade his audience toward his version of the common good. When one thinks of the devastation that lay a few years ahead, the poet's picture of the triumph of reason, order, and beauty over sectarianism seems particularly fragile and pathetic. The repairs, we are told, illustrate Charles' "grand design" for church and nation:

> To frame no new church, but the old refine;
> Which, spouse-like, may with comely grace command,
> More than by force of argument or hand.

65. Fenton, pp. 270–71.
66. E.g. "it was more agreeable to the rules of piety to demolish such old monuments of superstition and idolatry than to keep them standing" (Gardiner, *History of England*, 7, 246); see also p. 307.

For doubtful reason few can apprehend,
And war brings ruin where it should amend;
But beauty, with a bloodless conquest, finds
A welcome sovereignty in rudest minds.[67]

Yet the attractive idealism of lines like these suggests the fundamental inadequacy of Waller's position when we move from poetry to political action. The poet can create his own world, while the statesman is forced to deal with the world as it is. As the history of Waller and his fellow Constitutional Royalists in 1640–43 shows, the position of the moderate is always difficult, at times impossible—in part because the moderate is subject to incessant pressures from the two sides, and in part because it is an enormous strain to sustain a policy of negation and questioning, as against one of positive and angry conviction. "They who hated bishops," Falkland said, "hated them worse than the devil and they who loved them did not love them so well as their dinner."[68] Waller's motives were neither more nor less mixed than those of any other man involved in the politics of the seventeenth century. Even Falkland, whom Clarendon describes as living in *republica Platonis* rather than in the ordinary world, was capable of being led by self-interest, pride, or misdirected idealism (and indeed, Falkland was seriously involved in Waller's plot).[69] Waller's love of unity proved inadequate because too often it simply provided flimsy rationalizations for self-interest and because, for all its apparent flexibility, it was in reality inflexible, a ritual gesture.

Clarendon, for all his moral sternness, was a practical

67. "Upon His Majesty's Repairing of Paul's," 35–42. The particular brand of Anglicanism expressed in the passage, with its emphasis upon conciliation and its distrust of "doubtful reason," force, and argument (physical or theological), is characteristic of Falkland and his circle.

68. Clarendon, *History of the Rebellion, 1,* 363.

69. *History of the Rebellion, 3,* 184. On Falkland's role in Waller's plot, see Wedgwood, *The King's War,* p. 185; Wormald, *Clarendon,* pp. 127–32; and Pym, *A Discovery of the great Plot,* Sig. A3.

politician able to distinguish essential principles from expendable details; writing to Sir John Culpeper in 1647 about negotiations with the Scots, he cautions, "Let not the landmarks be removed, no pillars, upon which the fabric relies, be taken away, [but] let them have all circumstantial temporary concessions."[70] Compromise to Halifax, Locke, and Clarendon (for all the differences among the men and their beliefs) meant the application of principles to circumstances, holding on to "landmarks" while working out a position appropriate for a particular situation. Clarendon's decision to remain loyal to the exiled king is not morally superior to Waller's decision to support the de facto government of Cromwell. In supporting Cromwell, Waller made a conscious, reasoned choice, and his *Panegyric* on Cromwell is an admirable defense of a particular political philosophy and course of action. Clarendon's stand is the result of a consistent belief directly opposed to Waller's—that moral imperatives are more important than the maintenance of order, "private Duty" more important than "publick peace."[71] But more often, Waller avoided making a choice. Even though politics is one of his two abiding interests (the other is poetry as an art), he characteristically retreats from commitment, from ideology, from unpalatable, unmalleable fact. Perhaps the preeminence of the *Panegyric* among his political poems comes from the fact that he faces up to the problems inherent in the position he is arguing; the poem is far more forthright than most of his works in its treatment of political theory and practical politics. For all his sensitivity to particular circumstances, his usual approach was not to come to terms with them but to rationalize them out of existence. Circumstances are adapted to fit principles, not the other way around. In his poems and in Parliament, Waller was guided not by practical politics or by unshakable principle, but by metaphor.

70. Wormald, *Clarendon*, p. 218. In another letter he contrasts "landmarks" and "foundations" with distribution of "personal obligations."
71. Coltman, *Private Men and Public Causes*, p. 96.

Waller's politics and aesthetics are closely connected. His ideals of reason and moderation are consistently reflected in the smooth flow of balanced, controlled verse. Antithesis is his favorite poetic device, opposites played off against one another or held in balance, and certain key pairs of terms recur, in varying forms, throughout his works. The first set of terms is "the arts of peace" and "the martial rage," fury and destructiveness against harmony and creativity, peaceful order against warlike chaos. Standard royalist images presenting divine builders and harmonizers—Orpheus and Amphion, the sun benignly shining in its sphere—take on particular weight in Waller's verse by constant juxtaposition with their grim opposites. Thus, England in the interregnum is like "Blind Polypheme . . . in a wild rage," while with the return of Charles II she "has got her eye again." It is easier, Waller tells us several times, to destroy than to build. He writes of Cromwell, "Tigers have courage, and the wounded bear, / But man alone can, whom he conquers, spare."[72] Order and peace are so important to Waller that he is willing to support any government that is able to assume the protective functions (ignoring any questions of the legitimacy or justice of its rule). In this way he resembles Hobbes, and it is significant that he was an admirer of Hobbes' *De Cive*.

> I have heard him say that he so much admired Mr. Thomas Hobbes booke *De Cive*, when it came forth, that he was very desirous to have it donne into English, and Mr. Hobbes was most willing it should be done by Mr. Waller's hand, for that he was so great a Master of our English language. Mr. Waller freely promised him to doe it, but first he would desire Mr. Hobbes to make an Essaye; he (T. H.) did the first booke, and did it so

72. *Panegyric*, 109–16; *To the King, upon His Majesty's Happy Return*, 19–24; "Upon His Majesty's Repairing of Paul's," 64; *Upon Her Majesty's New Buildings at Somerset House*, 1–22; "Of Her Majesty, on New Year's Day, 1683," 17.

extremely well, that Mr. Waller would not meddle with it, for that nobody els could doe it so well.[73]

It requires an unusual feat of acrobatics to be at once a Hobbesian and a constitutionalist. The difficulties in Waller's politics come when the love of order and the love of moderation conflict, when peace and justice are not one. The second and more problematical kind of antithesis in Waller's works, then, occurs when the contrast is not black against white, but two terms which are both positive but to some degree opposed. He praises Cromwell for ruling "with a strong and yet a gentle hand," William of Orange for reconciling "empire and freedom" in the government of Holland.[74] But empire and freedom, order and individual rights, are not that easily reconcilable, and when forced to choose Waller characteristically chose the side of order.

One of his repeated antitheses is "power" and "piety" or "clemency" in a monarch: power is justified by inner restraint in using it. It is unlikely that the French, Spanish, or Dutch navy ever agreed that the British were the agent of divine justice, ordained to impose "nobler laws" on the sea.[75] As other nations were unwilling to grant England sovereignty of the seas, few Englishmen were willing to trust the unrestrained power of a King or Protector. Though Waller consistently opposed absolutism and in a traditional fashion stressed the limited nature of British monarchy,[76] his conception of the polity did not include constitutional

73. Aubrey, *Brief Lives*, p. 310. A letter from Hobbes to Waller about the proposed translation of *De Cive* is excerpted in Thorn-Drury, *1*, *lviii–lix*. A long, interesting letter from Waller to Hobbes (c. 1657) is printed in *Huntington Library Quarterly*, *11* (1948), 431–33.

74. *Panegyric*, 1; *Of the Lady Mary*, 21.

75. "To the King, on his Navy," 9; cf. ibid., 32, *Panegyric*, 124.

76. "'Tis a monarchy. The King governs by law" (Grey, *Debates*, *3*, 302). Hobbes and the defenders of Charles I's absolute rule had argued that the King was entirely above the law. Waller, in the British constitutional tradition, opposed to this belief the conviction that British rule was "dominium politicum et regale" (to cite the classic formulation of Sir Thomas Fortescue

guarantees against absolutism or any diminution of sovereign power. Instead, he relied on voluntary restraint, on an unspoken consensus and will to compromise, on mutual assumptions of good faith. These things were not enough in 1629, or in 1641, or in 1649, or in 1660, or in 1688: the constitutional crises of the seventeenth century all hinged on this very issue of power and trust. "Power unbounded, and a will confined"[77] is not a formula which, on reflection, could satisfy anyone other than the ruler himself—and, indeed, seventeenth-century rulers generally found even tacit restrictions too confining.

Waller was preeminently a man of his times, and it is only to be expected that his political beliefs should reflect his roots in the moneyed middle class. His love of peace and moderation was partly the product of his wealth and social position. The fiasco of Waller's plot had many causes: economic self-interest or disguised self-interest, a real longing for peace, and genuinely divided allegiances, both in political beliefs and (as a wealthy landowner with close ties among both the aristocracy and the London merchants) in social class. Gardiner and Thorn-Drury have a simple explanation for Waller's plot and for Waller's politics in general, claiming that he was primarily interested in protecting his own estate and ensuring the continuance of his own comfort.[78] But this is at best a half-truth. Throughout Waller's poems and speeches, the ideal of harmony is presented in positive terms as that which makes true glory possible. The poet's wealth gave him a feeling of noblesse oblige. He could think of his views as representing the public interest because his wealth (which allowed him the

---

in the fifteenth century), a limited monarchy under law. For a good discussion of the two traditions in the seventeenth century, see Francis D. Wormuth, *The Royal Prerogative 1603–1649* (Ithaca, 1939).

77. *To the King, upon His Majesty's Happy Return,* 104.

78. Thorn-Drury, *1, xxxviii–xxxix;* Gardiner, *Civil War, 1,* 8–10, 169.

leisure to write and to pursue a parliamentary career) enabled him much of the time to remain remote from private interests. His tendency to look on all sides of a question and his sanguine belief that any problem could be straightened out by the application of reason kept him at all times in the middle of the road, advocating compromise, distrusting all extremes. It is in character for Waller to advocate religious toleration, a more humane poor law, and an end to fratricidal war, appealing to reason and open-mindedness and basing his arguments on utilitarian grounds: these policies would be more to everyone's interest than restrictive measures or the pursuit of private ambitions. It is equally understandable that his arguments should have convinced very few of his fellow members of Parliament. The appeal of reason is stronger in theory than in practice.

Perhaps if Waller had been wholly a poet or wholly a practical politician, his career would have been very different. But he was both, and at all times oddly combined a penchant for idealizing with a strong sense of reality. Indirect evidence of Waller's practical side is apparent in a letter his mother addressed to him during his exile. The poet's daughter had reached marriageable age, and the letter concerns itself with her prospects. After coolly ana-lyzing the merits of two suitors, a knight and an alderman's son, Mrs. Waller gets down to the business of the dowry. The alderman's son, a good catch, would require £2000. "I am not in hast to mary hir, she is yong enough to stay, but the danger is if she should catch the small poxe or hir beauty should change, it would be a great lose to hir."[79] Her son's political beliefs reflect the same bourgeois common sense. He had the liberalism and the conservatism of the middle class, with his belief in the primacy of property rights and his conviction that enlightened self-interest and the public interest can be reconciled.

As a thoroughgoing rationalist and man of the world, Waller greatly preferred the practical to the speculative.

79. Thorn-Drury, *1, lx*.

Moreover, he had a deeply ingrained caution, a distaste for
controversy, and a belief in the relativity of truth. Though
he was a close friend of Hobbes and sympathized with
many of that author's beliefs, he declined a request to write
verses in praise of Hobbes because "he was afrayd of the
Churchmen." Similarly, when "a fellow upon a barrel in
Westminster-Hall" was haranguing a mob during the trial
of Strafford, Waller escaped possible danger by a decision
"at that instant to feign himself Sir Arthur Haslerigg."[80]
There is something Falstaffian about Waller. D'Ewes tells
an amusing story about his attitude toward the sanctity of
promises made. When the poet was ill "with a dangerous
feaver" his aunt Lady Scudamour "thought it seasonable to
deale plainly with him and therefore wisht him to consider
of that prophane and luxurious life which he lead and
especially of that great and most dangerous sinne of lust by
his use of strange women." "With many deepe sighs" the
sick man acknowledged his sin and swore solemnly that if
he recovered "hee would become a new man." On his
recovery, "forgetting or rather wilfully neglecting his
solemn vow . . . he returned to his old beloved and emascu-
lating sinne of lust"; when his aunt "admonished him of
what hee had done . . . hee in a slight and joculary way
replied that there was noe regard to bee had to such words
spoken by him when hee was distempered by sicknes." One
is reminded of Dorimant's cavalier reply to Loveit's angry
accusations of unfaithfulness in *The Man of Mode:* "I made
'em [Oaths, Vows, and Protestations] when I was in love.
. . . What we swear at such a time may be a certain proof of
a present passion, but to say truth, in Love there is no
security to be given for the future."[81]

80. Aubrey, *Brief Lives*, p. 156; Grey, *Debates, 1,* 13.

81. MS. journal of Sir Simonds D'Ewes, British Museum MS. Harleian 165,
fol. 144. The incident is discussed and the passage from D'Ewes' journal
summarized in Gosse, *From Shakespeare to Pope,* p. 90. Cf. *The Man of
Mode*, II.ii.211–18, in *The Dramatic Works of Sir George Etherege,* ed.
H.F.B. Brett-Smith (2 vols. Oxford, 1927).

His religious views were close to those of Falkland and his circle: a latitudinarian, noncombative Anglicanism, with a total lack of sympathy for religious "enthusiasm" or theological disputes, and a strong emphasis upon consensus theology, the unity of Christendom. But he went beyond them in the direction of skepticism and anti-clericalism. In his speech on church reform before the Long Parliament, he was coldly contemptuous of both Laudian bishops and Puritan reformers, and his support of episcopacy was purely political. He supported religious toleration after the Restoration for similarly secular reasons: "a sense of kindness for any persons that suffer," a skepticism about the importance of doctrinal distinctions, and, primarily, a conviction that persecution was futile and pointless, that uniformity of worship could never be compelled—that, indeed, persecution made a persecuted party stronger.[82]

In his old age, he underwent a religious reaction, wrote a series of *Divine Poems,* and was quoted as saying "that Poetrie was abused when 'twas turned to any other way, than hymnes."[83] His religious poetry is an extension of his political ideas to the religious sphere. Its main subject, a familiar one in seventeenth-century religious verse, is the superiority of the heavenly perspective over the earthly one. Yet the divine truths Waller finds in his old age all revolve around peace, harmony, and love, as set against ordinary human ambition, jealousy, and factionalism.

> Could we forbear dispute, and practise love,
> We should agree as angels do above
>
> . . .
>
> 'Tis with our minds as with a fertile ground,
> Wanting this love they must with weeds abound
>
> . . .

82. See e.g. Grey, *Debates, 1,* 2, 128, 146, 160, 220; 2, 33, 132.
83. Aubrey, *Brief Lives,* p. 310; cf. "Of Divine Poesy," I.21–32, 47–50; "On the Fear of God," II.47–54.

> This love, the centre of our union, can
> Alone bestow complete repose on man;
> Tame his wild appetite, make inward peace,
> And foreign strife among the nations cease.[84]

In general the important truths for Waller were those of political morality—prudence, common sense, the wisdom of the world. Though he writes movingly of the new knowledge gained in old age, of how "The soul's dark cottage, battered and decayed, / Lets in new light through chinks that time has made,"[85] yet in most of his work his perspective is entirely worldly. His idealism is always tempered with practicality. When he addressed Parliament in 1667 about an anonymous libel that was being circulated, his remarks were not based on a swordsman's ideal of honor or an inflexible morality, but on more practical considerations: "Liberty of accusing, and no liberty of calumniating, [are] the security of all rights. Rewards were in the *Romans* time given to accusers. If the dogs that guarded the Capitol should have set upon and bit all the worshippers that came, none would have come to worship."[86] History, in his view, provides man with a set of clear lessons to follow. He was enough of an idealist to hope that men would realize the limitations of mere self-interest and private ambition, but enough of a skeptic to believe that more often than not men ignore what history and reason should teach them.

To stay afloat on various tides as long as Waller did is an achievement in itself. With "a tender weake body . . . not at all robust,"[87] he lived to be eighty-two. He seldom drank

---

84. "Of Divine Love," III.25–26, 49–50; V.43–46. Cf. "On the Fear of God," II.1–6. "Earth praises conquerors for shedding blood, / Heaven those that love their foes, and do them good. / It is terrestrial honour to be crowned, / For strowing men, like rushes, on the ground. / True glory 'tis to rise above them all, / Without advantage taken by their fall."

85. "Of the Last Verses in the Book," 13–14.

86. Grey, *Debates, I,* 92.

87. Aubrey, *Brief Lives,* pp. 309–10.

anything but water because of his health, yet he was accepted as a drinking companion by the wits; he "had the dexterity to accommodate his discourse to the pitch of the others' as it sunk."[88] One feels the same husbanding of resources, the same careful choice of an advantageous position, in his poetry.

88. *Biographia Britannica* (London, 1747–66), *6*, pt. 2, 4100.

2 Beauty's Sovereignty: Waller's Cavalier Lyrics

Though we tend to think of Waller's work as all one, there are differences in subject matter, treatment, and emphasis between his early and his later poems. In the middle and late 1630s, when most of his lyric poetry was written, Waller was a wealthy young man, witty and handsome, attached to the court. His poems are those of a closed society—love poems of a highly conventional kind and occasional pieces dealing with events of importance in the court world; he is in many ways a typical Cavalier poet. The poems he wrote in the years following the Restoration, on the other hand, are those of a middle-aged, then an old, man. Almost none of them are love poems; he continues to enjoy the society of great ladies, but now as "old Waller," a regular visitor at their salons. Instead of love poems, he writes gallant inscriptions inside the books of various duchesses. As his shorter poems become slighter and more inconsequential, his longer poems become more elaborate and grand. In his later years, Waller is primarily an official poet, a writer of state panegyric. Old Waller differs from young Waller further in being a determined moralist; at one point he expresses his desire to "blot from his works any line that did not contain some motive to virtue."[1]

In this chapter I shall consider Waller's shorter poems— poems, largely written in the first half of his career, which may be loosely grouped together as lyrics. Some of them are in short lyric stanza, some in couplets; they have such

1. Johnson, *Lives of the Poets, 1,* 283.

titles as "Of Loving at First Sight," "To the Mutable Fair," and "On a Girdle." As he writes a panegyric on the King's repairs upon St. Paul's Cathedral or on the recovery of the Queen from an illness, he also writes of Sacharissa's experience in "passing through a crowd of people," or of her ability to "sleep when she pleases," addresses lines "to a friend, on the different success of their loves," draws several witty conclusions from the spectacle of a young couple tumbling down, and casts indirect light on the nature of love in an account of the marriage of two dwarfs at court. Many of Waller's verses are jeux d'esprit, entirely products of the moment: bits of gallantry on a tree cut in paper, on the return of a poem which had for some years been lost, on the gift of a silver pen, on a piece of embroidery woven in divers colors, on tea, on the Queen's tearing a card at ombre. In his consistent preference for the small occasional subject, the poem made out of the minutiae of daily court life, Waller shows his affinities with the epigrammatists of the *Greek Anthology* and with such contemporary poets as Marino—a deliberate limitation of scope and subject matter, a search for novelty within the confines of a well-worn tradition, a feeling that "in a small space the more Perfection's shown, / And what is exquisite, in Little's done."[2]

The twenty-odd poems that concern themselves with Waller's courtship of Sacharissa (Lady Dorothy Sidney) are almost entirely occasional and tend, particularly in poems addressed to Sacharissa herself, to be rather formal.[3]

2. The lines quoted come from a poem by Thomas Yalden, "The Insect. Against Bulk" (1693), quoted in Kitty Scoular, *Natural Magic* (Oxford, 1965), p. 93; Miss Scoular's remarks about the connection between "small poems," small subjects, and "the high value placed upon fine craftsmanship" (pp. 85–94) are quite illuminating. On the characteristic subjects of Marino's verse, see James V. Mirollo, *The Poet of the Marvelous: Giambattista Marino* (New York, 1963), pp. 121–25.

3. The characteristic tone of the Sacharissa poems is due in part to her social position as the daughter of an Earl. Though Waller actively courted

Sacharissa is portrayed as the typical mistress of the Petrarchan tradition: she is the sum of all virtues, a creature of more than human beauty, admired to idolatry by all who came in contact with her. Conforming to type, she is unmoved by her "servants' " protestations of love, remote, haughty, unapproachable.[4] In one poem, "At Penshurst," the last of the series, Waller bewails his fair one's cruelty, calls her an enemy of love, with a heart harder than stone; but in most of the poems, Sacharissa's unwillingness to love is proof of her perfection, a subject for praise (and occasion to prove the lover's constancy and sincerity).

The Sacharissa poems bear a strong resemblance to another group of his poems, the addresses to great ladies. Waller uses the language of love and gallantry to praise the Queen and other ladies of high position, but he is always conscious of court decorum and speaks as a distant admirer of clearly inferior rank. The sight of Henrietta Maria, he tells us in one poem, would kindle love in any heart; it is fortunate that, like the sun, she is "placed in so sublime a seat," where except for Charles "never love durst fly," or, again like the sun when Phaeton seized its reins, she might have made a bonfire of all the youth of England, burning with love for her. All who come in contact with the Countess of Carlisle, he tells us elsewhere, fall in love with her, while she "like Phoebus so divides her light, / And warms us, that she stoops not from her height."[5]

Lady Dorothy with a view toward marrying her and writes in some detail about the competition for her hand, yet when Lady Leicester writes to her husband in France about various suitors for their daughter, the only names she takes seriously are peers (see Thorn-Drury, *1, xxviii*). Lady Dorothy eventually married Lord Spencer, later Earl of Sunderland, who was killed in the early stages of the Civil War.

4. See e.g. "On My Lady Dorothy Sidney's Picture," 2–6; "To Vandyck," 37–44; "At Penshurst" ("Had Sacharissa lived"), 7–16; and "To my Lord of Leicester," 19–24.

5. "To the Queen, Occasioned by Sight of Her Majesty's Picture," 13–32; "Of her Chamber," 21–22.

The basic component of most of Waller's poems, lyrics as well as formal poems of state, is praise. As a result, there is a certain sameness of tone in all his verse; most seventeenth-century poetry is more varied in its tone and its central concerns. The sun is always shining over Waller's poetry, whose inhabitants are presented as "fair," "great," "good," "noble," "bright," "high," creatures of "power" and beauty, the "care" of "heaven," the cause of "love."[6] Where the poetry of Donne and Jonson is strongly masculine, Waller writes for an essentially feminine audience; he is the apostle of softness, the poet of salons. We do not find in him the colloquial tone, the calculated spontaneity of Suckling and several Restoration poets, any more than we find the tone of the human voice and byplay of the human mind so characteristic of Donne. One cannot imagine Waller's writing "Upon T. C. Having the Pox" any more than his writing "The Good-morrow."

In his own age and the next, he was the favorite of fops and ladies. A certain air of the beau monde attached itself to his name; both Etherege's Dorimant and Congreve's Mirabell come onstage quoting Waller. Yet, as several entertaining papers by Addison and Steele indicate, it was the Sir Fopling Flutters of the age who took Waller up. Addison prints a letter purportedly from a young fop in *Spectator*, No. 8:

> As soon as the Minuet was over, we ogled one another through our Masques; and as I am very well read in *Waller*, I repeated to her the four following Verses out of his Poem to *Vandike*.

> The heedless Lover does not know
> Whose Eyes they are that wound him so;
> But confounded with thy Art,
> Enquires her Name that has his Heart.

6. Statistically these are Waller's favorites terms, according to the tabulations of Miles, *The Primary Language of Poetry in the 1640's*, pp. 31–35, 79.

> I pronounced these Words with such a languishing Air,
> that I had some reason to conclude I had made a Con-
> quest.[7]

The fullest treatment of Waller's reputation among the
fops occurs in *Tatler,* No. 163, again by Addison.

> Ned Softly is a very pretty poet, and a great admirer of
> easy lines. Waller is his favourite: and as that admirable
> writer has the best and worst verses of any among our
> great English poets, Ned Softly has got all the bad ones
> without book, which he repeats upon occasion, to show
> his reading, and garnish his conversation.

To show Ned Softly's tastes more clearly, Addison presents
us with one of his poems:

> To Mira on her Incomparable Poems.
>
> I
>
> When dressed in laurel wreaths you shine,
>   And tune your soft melodious notes,
> You seem a sister of the Nine,
>   Or Phoebus' self in petticoats.
>
> II
>
> I fancy, when your song you sing
>   (Your song you sing with so much art),
> Your pen was plucked from Cupid's wing;
>   For ah! it wounds me like his dart.[8]

And yet, the ease and grace which make Waller a model
to the minor poets whose verses fill the miscellanies also
mark him as a product of the seventeenth-century tradition
of wit. His verse depends upon the techniques of witty

---

7. *The Spectator,* ed. Donald F. Bond (5 vols. Oxford, 1965). See also
Steele's *Spectator* papers on "Woman's Men," Nos. 156, 158.

8. *The Tatler,* ed. George A. Aitken (4 vols. London, 1898–99). Ned Softly
goes on to analyze the beauties of his poem in detail. " 'Phoebus,' says he,
'was the God of Poetry. These little instances, Mr. Bickerstaff, show a
gentleman's reading.' "

analogy, paradox, juxtaposition of like and unlike, and precise analysis, which are usually taken to characterize Cavalier and metaphysical poetry; it shows a similar "alliance of levity and seriousness."[9]

His allegiances to the tradition of wit are the source of a number of Augustan caveats on his poetry. Addison, in the paper on Ned Softly quoted above, as in his papers on true, false, and mixed wit, condemns Waller for falling prey to the allure of "the little Gothic ornaments of epigrammatical conceits, turns, points and quibbles," ignoring "simplicity in its natural beauty and perfection" *(Tatler, No.* 163). In *Spectator,* No. 62, Addison cites Waller along with Cowley as a chief practitioner of "mixt Wit" (consisting "partly in the Resemblance of Ideas, and partly in the Resemblance of Words"). Such wit to Addison is somewhat better than acrostics and anagrams, but still "its Foundations are laid partly in Falsehood and partly in Truth," it is contrary to "good Sense" and "the Nature of things." Johnson does not list Waller among the metaphysical poets, praising him for writing understandably, with imagery "free . . . from philosophical pedantry."[10] Still, the operations of his wit, his choice of images, Johnson feels, are not sufficiently guided by the requirements of literal truth.

> His thoughts are sometimes hyperbolical, and his images unnatural . . . Some applications may be thought

---

9. T. S. Eliot, "Andrew Marvell," *Selected Essays* (New York, Harcourt, Brace and Company, 1950), p. 255; see also F. R. Leavis, "The Line of Wit," *Revaluation: Tradition and Development in English Poetry* (London, Chatto and Windus, 1936). Recent discussions of Waller's lyric poems and their connection with the seventeenth-century "line of wit" include Williamson, *The Proper Wit of Poetry,* and Richmond, *The School of Love.* I have found both books very helpful in writing this chapter.

10. "He seldom indeed fetches an amorous sentiment from the depths of science; his thoughts are for the most part easily understood, and his images such as the superficies of nature readily supplies; he has a just claim to popularity, because he writes to common degrees of knowledge" *(Lives of the Poets, 1,* 284–85).

> too remote and unconsequential . . . His images are not
> always distinct, as in the following passage ["Of Loving
> at First Sight," 15–20], he confounds *Love* as a person
> with *love* as a passion . . . [In his] amorous verses . . .
> little things are made too important; and the Empire
> of Beauty is represented as exerting its influence further
> than can be allowed by the multiplicity of human
> passions, and the variety of human wants.[11]

To these writers, Waller is a step removed from the extravagance of the metaphysicals, but his "improvements"
over the earlier writers have not gone far enough. A passage
earlier than any of those I have quoted leaves no doubt that
its author considers Waller's kind of wit mere trickery and
affectation. Waller's celebrated ease is to Samuel Butler, in
his "Character of a Quibbler" (1667–69), simply a new
variant of an old con game.

> There are two Sorts of Quibbling, the one with Words,
> and the other with Sense, like the Rhetoricians *Figurae
> Dictionis* and *Figurae Sententiae*—The first is already
> cried down, and the other as yet prevails; and is the
> only Elegance of our modern Poets, which easy Judges
> call *Easiness;* but having nothing in it but *Easiness,* and
> being never used by any lasting Wit, will in wiser times
> fall to nothing of itself.

In his notebooks, Butler defines quibbling with sense as
"expressing of Sense by Contradiction, and Riddle"; "Mr.
Waller," he tells us, "was the first most copious Author" of
this new fad, and has "so infected our modern writers of
Heroiques [i.e. couplets] with it, that they can hardly write
any other way."[12] Though none goes as far as Butler, all the

11. Ibid., *1,* 285–87.

12. Samuel Butler, *Characters and Passages from Note-Books,* ed. A. R.
Waller (Cambridge, Eng., 1908), pp. 90, 414–15. Cf. the account of Butler in
Aubrey, *Brief Lives,* p. 46: "He has often sayd, that way (e.g. Mr. Edmund
Waller's) of Quibling with Sence will hereafter growe as much out of fashion
and be as ridicule as quibling with words."

critics I have cited object to Waller's wit as illegitimate. The easy elegance, the "beautiful turns" for which Waller was noted, Butler, Addison, and Johnson condemn to varying degrees as contrary to the exacting requirements of truth.[13]

A transitional figure between Caroline wit and Augustan clarity, straddling two worlds, Waller attempts to reconcile "dignity" with "spriteliness,"[14] grandeur with concision, large general truths with witty particularity. Even the events of his poetic career show him to be a Janus: the amateur who writes verses in his spare time "only to please himself, and such particular persons to whom they were directed"[15] devotes a good part of his career to the writing and publishing of formal poems upon public occasions, proclaiming his belief that verse should infuse "heroic thoughts and virtue" by praising and publicizing "great acts."[16] In very many ways, Waller owes a double allegiance.

13. Dryden's attitude toward these matters is somewhat more complex. In the "Discourse concerning Satire," he praises Waller's elegant "turns" at the expense of the "points of wit, and quirks of epigram" of Cowley, but in other essays he condemns both turn and conceit as "unnatural," "trifling . . . little ornaments." See W. P. Ker, ed., *Essays of John Dryden* (2 vols. Oxford, 1900), *2*, 108–10, 219, 256–57. Though he couples Waller with Ovid in their fondness for verbal ornamentation, he continues to treat Waller with respect, even while his successive mentions of Ovid, the conceit, and the turn grow increasingly hostile. For a fuller discussion of Dryden's attitude toward Waller and of Waller's devices of verbal ornamentation (including the "turn") see chaps. 4 and 5, below.

14. Johnson calls these "the characters, by which Waller intended to distinguish his writing" *(Lives of the Poets, 1, 283)*.

15. The statement comes from the publisher's preface to the 1664 edition of Waller's poems (Thorn-Drury, *1*, xiii). An earlier dedicatory epistle, written by Waller himself for a manuscript collection of his works and printed with the editions of 1645, carries the pose of gentlemanly indifference even farther. His poetry, he says, was the "diversion of [his] youth"; if the lady to whom the poems have been presented and her "fair friends" wish, they may "cast them into the fire" or "tear them to pieces, wherein you shall honour me with the fate of Orpheus." The letter is printed in Thorn-Drury, *1*, vii–x.

16. "Upon the Earl of Roscommon's Translation of Horace, 'De Arte Poetica'; and of the Use of Poetry," 23–36.

Though all seventeenth-century poets have a certain family resemblance, several broad distinctions can be made between the metaphysical and Cavalier lines. The Cavalier poets are more worldly in their concerns (poetic and extra-poetic) and in their choice of subjects, more classical in their models and their aesthetic assumptions. Poetry to the Cavaliers is a part-time occupation, one of the many concerns of a gentleman, and they are careful to preserve their amateur status—the ideal in behavior and in poetry is *sprezzatura,* a casual grace. The range of their poetry is deliberately narrow: poems of praise and admonition, a running commentary on moves and stances in the game of love, sometimes extending to events that touch on the court society. Their poems are composed with a keen sense of audience and of occasion—characteristically, a poem is directed to a particular end, its argument tailored for its presumed recipient and simultaneously aimed at the approval of a small circle of cognoscenti through whose hands the manuscripts circulated.

Their poetry is far less ambitious and less personal than that of Donne and Herbert. They do not seek "the six-daies-world transposing in an houre," bringing man to God and God to man by the immediate fiat of the imagination, nor do their poems represent a spiritual and intellectual auto-biography. Herbert's description of "the many spiritual Conflicts that have past betwixt God and my soul," with only a slight adjustment in wording, can fit secular meta-physical poetry as well as religious.[17] When we turn to the Cavaliers, we are aware of severe limitations in intellectual and emotional range. When Waller calls his mistress' girdle "my heaven's extremest sphere," the hyperbole can in some

---

17. "Prayer," 7, in *The Works of George Herbert,* ed. F. E. Hutchinson (Oxford, 1941); Izaak Walton, "The Life of Mr. George Herbert," in *The Lives of John Donne, Sir Henry Wotton, Richard Hooker, George Herbert, and Robert Sanderson,* ed. George Saintsbury (London, World's Classics, 1927), p. 314.

ways be taken literally. The poems of the Cavaliers express
an intellectual quietism, a recurrent emphasis on retreat,
on rejection, on limitation and exclusion. They are constantly drawing magic circles that will shut the world out,
seeking to find an autonomous realm of love and art, a court
immune to change. The great poignancy of Lovelace's "To
Althea, from Prison" comes from our awareness (and the
poet's) that he is *not* free. Donne wills impossibilities in
"The Canonization" and "The Sunne Rising" and carries
conviction; he seeks not only to convince his mistress of the
genuineness of his passion but to illuminate the nature of
love and beyond that, to give the universe meaning through
his verse.

> She' is all States, and all Princes, I,
> Nothing else is.

> And thus invoke us; You whom reverend love
> Made one anothers hermitage . . . [18]

In the Cavaliers there is a diminishing of the possibilities
of belief—partly through the pressure of historical circumstances, partly through the poet's conscious choice. When
Carew writes "In Answer of an Elegiacall Letter from
Aurelian Townshend" nearly ten years before the outbreak
of the Civil War, his choice is not transcendence of the outer
world, a microcosm that contains all the macrocosm has and
infinitely more, but exclusion, denial. The gesture is hollow
and futile; what is left is the charm of patterned unreality,
the glamour of a lost cause.

> Tourneyes, Masques, Theaters, better become
> Our *Halcyon* dayes; what though the German Drum
> Bellow for freedome and revenge, the noyse
> Concernes not us, nor should divert our joyes;

---

18. "The Sunne Rising," 21–22, and "The Canonization," 37–38, in *The
Poems of John Donne,* ed. Herbert J. C. Grierson (2 vols. London, Oxford
University Press, 1912).

> Nor ought the thunder of their Carabins
> Drowne the sweet Ayres of our tun'd Violins.[19]

Lovelace, in "To Lucasta. From Prison," canvasses the possibilities for belief and rejects them all. Peace, War, Religion, Parliament, Liberty and Property, Reformation, the Public Faith all have proved chimerical or unreliable:

> Since then none of these can be
> Fit objects for my Love and me;
> What then remaines?

Not much does remain—the options are painfully narrow, particularly when we consider how feeble is the one object of faith he can find: "th' only spring / Of all our loves and joys [,] The King."

> Oh from thy glorious Starry Waine
> Dispense on me one sacred Beame
> To light me where I soone may see
> How to serve you, and you trust me.[20]

Though the lines are moving, they would convince more if their object were God and not Charles I. When Vaughan and Milton use similar imagery of light and darkness to deal with the relationship of God and man, the problem of uncomfortable fact does not enter in. The ultimate tone, not quite, I think, what Lovelace intends, is pathos, a forlorn and flickering hope. Lovelace's "The Grasse-hopper," again a defiance of fate, carries more conviction. The movement of the verse, the modulations in tone, and the rich metaphorical texture are reminiscent of Donne. In this poem Lovelace moves away from the pole of song and toward the pole of thought, discourse, and precise analysis. Here the poet does not exclude the outside world but faces it squarely; we are aware both of the moment of warmth and

---

19. Lines 95–100, in *The Poems of Thomas Carew*, ed. Rhodes Dunlap (Oxford, 1949).

20. Lines 41–44, 53–56, in *The Poems of Richard Lovelace*, ed. C. H. Wilkinson (Oxford, 1930).

the coldness outside. The wish is still a wish, but it stands on more solid foundations; the affirmation seems earned.

> Thou best of *Men* and *Friends!* we will create
>   A Genuine Summer in each others breast;
> And spite of this cold Time and frosen Fate,
>   Thaw us a warme seate to our rest.
>
> Our sacred harthes shall burne eternally
>   As Vestal Flames; the North-wind, he
> Shall strike his frost-stretch'd Winges, dissolve and flye
>   This *AEtna* in Epitome.   (21–28)

Yet even here the options of faith and hope are narrowed: the emphasis is entirely on the earthly, the here and now, to the exclusion of any possible transcendent supernatural realm. Lovelace's ideals—and he is the idealist among the Cavaliers—are honor, loyalty, friendship, beauty, and the pleasure of the moment, all highly subjective and highly transitory.

Suckling's attitude is simpler: these ideals are frauds, and so are all others. Beauty is entirely in the eyes of the beholder, and honor and loyalty are equally products of self-delusion.

> I must confess those perfumes, Tom,
> I did not smell; nor found that from
> Her passing by ought sprung up new:
> The flowers had all their birth from you.

Man is entirely a creature of "flesh and blood," a congeries of appetites. "Sonnet II" supports its thesis that "there's no such thing as . . . beauty" with a series of reductive comparisons. The final stanza of the poem goes beyond the earlier, cheerfully cynical arguments for the relativity of beauty and the naturalness of inconstancy: the universe is mechanical, all idealization is a lie, and nothing exists beyond the self.

> And if I like one dish
> More than another, that a pheasant is;

> What in our watches, that in us is found;
> So to the height or nick
>   We up be wound,
> No matter by what hand or trick.[21]

The options have been narrowed still further: we are left with an impotent solipsism, where even choice (for whose priority Suckling is presumably arguing) is essentially meaningless. The sexual act has seldom been made to look less attractive.

The path presented here is of course an impasse, and the other Cavalier poets do not abandon idealization. But they are wary, and the strategy of limitation is in part self-protective.

> A little streame best fits a little Boat;
> A little lead best fits a little Float;
> As my small Pipe best fits my little note.[22]

Herrick is a special case in several ways, but many of his essential qualities and beliefs are characteristic of the Cavalier poets: a certain fastidiousness, a predilection for miniatures, a striving toward a craftsman's perfection, a retreat into art. The Cavalier poets are dandies, creators of secular rituals. Perfection of form in life and art becomes all-important.

The world of art for Waller is not quite autonomous; art is invariably associated in his poems with earthly beauty and with the social realm in which that beauty moves. In "To the Servant of a Fair Lady," he asks his "fair fellow-servant," Sacharissa's waiting-maid, what presents are most likely to move her mistress:

> You, her priest, declare
> What offerings may propitiate the fair;

21. "Upon my Lady Carlisle's Walking in Hampton Court Garden," 10–13; and "Sonnett II," 19–24, in *The Works of Sir John Suckling*, ed. A. Hamilton Thompson (London, 1910).

22. "A Ternarie of littles, upon a pipkin of Jellie sent to a Lady," 13–15, in *The Poetical Works of Robert Herrick*, ed. L. C. Martin (Oxford, 1956).

> Rich orient pearl, bright stones that ne'er decay,
> Or polished lines, which longer last than they. (25–28)

The materials of the poem are entirely conventional: in addressing the poem to Sacharissa through her servant, he is imitating Ovid's poem to Corinna's servant Nape (*Amores*, I.xi). The idea that poems rather than gems are the poet's appropriate gift is a commonplace of love poetry, and so of course is the assertion of art's enduring power.[23] As one might expect, the poet finds a work of art a greater gift than mere bits of rock. Supreme beauty requires its match, and things of the mind excel those of the body:

> But since her eyes, her teeth, her lip excels
> All that is found in mines of fishes' shells,
> Her nobler part as far exceeding these,
> None but immortal gifts her mind should please. (33–36)

Only the work of art can do such beauty justice and preserve the memory of departed loveliness. Troy has long since burned and Helen is long dead: "Her beauty, too, had perished, and her fame, / Had not the muse preserved them from the flame" (41–42).

Other poems which similarly ally art with earthly beauty are more skeptical of art's ability to endure. "Of English Verse" argues that time obliterates all things. Poets dream of immortality, but their prophecies die in the very telling, betrayed by the unstable medium of language. All a poet can reasonably hope for is that his love songs received an appropriate reward when he wrote them, that the women to whom he wrote, "hoping they should immortal prove, / Rewarded with success his love" (23–24).

> Verse, thus designed, has no ill fate
> If it arrive but at the date
> Of fading beauty; if it prove
> But as long-lived as present love.   (29–32)

23. See e.g. Ovid, *Amores*, I.iii.7–26, or Propertius, *Elegies*, III.ii (or for an ironic version, Ovid, *Amores*, I.viii.57–62).

No other of Waller's poems is quite this pessimistic, but others are equally tentative in their claims of what art can accomplish. As celebrant of beauty, the poet is limited to the material before him; all he can hope to do is pay tribute to what he sees by copying it as well as he can. The earthly manifestation of beauty is treated as though it were the platonic form of beauty, and the effort of the artist to embody this beauty in his work is at best a clumsy approximation. Thus Sacharissa, Sir Philip Sidney's niece, easily surpasses the heroines of the *Arcadia,* or indeed any products of her uncle's imagination:

> This glorious piece transcends what he could think.
> So much his blood is nobler than his ink!
> ("On my Lady Dorothy Sidney's Picture," 19–20)

Waller's poem "To Vandyck" begins as though it were praising the artist for his ability to create beauty, move the emotions, stir the imagination. The realm of art and the imagination appears to be entirely independent. "Onely the Poet," Sidney wrote, "disdeining to be tied to any such subjection, lifted up with the vigour of his own invention, doth grow in effect an other nature: in making things either better than nature bringeth foorth, or quite a new."[24]

> From thy shop of beauty we
> Slaves return, that entered free.
> The heedless lover does not know
> Whose eyes they are that wound him so;
> But, confounded with thy art,
> Inquires her name that has his heart.   (3–8)

But we learn before long that Vandyck's secret simply lay in his choice of model. The artist can produce beauty, but only by imitation, which again is no more than approximation. Perfection resides only in Sacharissa.

---

24. "The Defence of Poesie," in *The Complete Works of Sir Philip Sidney,* ed. Albert Feuillerat (Cambridge, 1922–23), *3,* 8.

Yet who can tax thy blameless skill,
Though thy good hand had failed still,
When nature's self so often errs?
She for this many thousand years
Seems to have practised with much care,
To frame the race of woman fair;
Yet never could a perfect birth
Produce before to grace the earth,
Which waxed old ere it could see
Her that amazed thy art and thee.   (35–44)[25]

In poems like this, Waller paradoxically uses the imagery
of platonic idealism to cast doubt on the existence of a transcendent realm. His emphasis is entirely upon things of this
world. A specialist in compliment must necessarily treat
truth as relative—indeed, the reader of Waller's lyrics is
rarely expected to believe a word the poet says in any literal
fashion, but, as often as not, he is simply to admire the wit
with which the poet turns the compliment. Each poem is a
performance, a game, and the aesthetic perspective is pre-
dominant. In his lyrics Waller has passed beyond the abra-
sive cynicism of Suckling and the defensive idealism of
Lovelace to a state of untroubled indifference (not unlike
the state in which the Epicurean gods are depicted). The
amused skepticism and poise these poems show are mirrored
in several anecdotes that have been preserved about the man
and snippets of his conversation. The sallies of wit, like
many of the poems, are intended to persuade and to turn
away possible criticism, justifying some behavior that might
appear questionable. All turn on the relationship between
life and art, and all deny moral absolutes. The most famous
is his explanation for the superiority of his poems written
for Cromwell to his poems celebrating Charles II: poets

25. Cf. "To a Lady, from whom he received the foregoing copy" (Thorn-
Drury, 2, 69): "The picture of fair Venus (that / For which men say the
goddess sat) / Was lost, till Lely from your look / Again that glorious image
took. / If Virtue's self were lost, we might / From your fair mind new copies
write" (7–12).

succeed better in fiction than in truth. In similar fashion, "upon sight of the Duchess of Newcastle's verses on the death of a Stag, he declared that he would give all his own compositions to have written them; and being charged with the exorbitance of his adulation, answered, that 'nothing was too much to be given that a Lady might be saved from the disgrace of such a vile performance.' "[26] Waller is at all times a rhetorician: the primary criterion for any statement is not truth but usefulness. The concentration on elegance of form and appropriateness to the situation, verbal and rhetorical effectiveness, to the exclusion of all other considerations, allows the poet to say whatever he likes and yet preserve an inner core of skepticism.[27]

26. Johnson, *Lives of the Poets*, *1*, 271, 280–81. The story may be apocryphal; Katharine Philips, its source, disliked Waller. See *Letters from Orinda to Poliarchus* (2d ed., London, 1729), pp. 189–90.

27. What is acceptable in poetry is not always acceptable in life. Lady Ranelagh, annoyed at the discrepancy between Waller's "fine sayings" addressed to her (perhaps protestations of love or perhaps simply of friendship) and his entire indifference to her in her absence, writes her brother Robert Boyle in 1660:

> For Mr. *Waller,* I never heard one word from him, since I left him. . . . I know his calling as a poet gives him license to say as great things as he can, without intending they should signify any more, than that he said them, or have any higher end, than to make him admired by those, whose admirations are so volatile, as to be raised by a sound of words; and the less the subject he speaks of, or the party he speaks to, deserves the great things he says, the greater those things are, and the greater advance they are to make towards his being admired, by his poetical laws. . . . I could never give my self a reason, why he, who can say such things upon things that so little deserved them, should be so unwilling to apply that faculty to those subjects, that were truly excellent, but this, that there his subject would have been debased by his highest expression, and he humbled in the exercise of his wit; but where he has employed it, his subjects have been raised by his fancy, and himself by reflecting upon it (Robert Boyle, *Works,* ed. Thomas Birch [5 vols. London, 1749], 5, 556–57).

The criticism is a shrewd one, interesting in its application to his poetry and his life.

The process we have been tracing, a shrinking of belief, finds its logical conclusion in Waller. In Lovelace, Carew, and Suckling there is an element of yearning, of intellectual questioning, a desire to prove or deny the existence of ideals; in their way, they are concerned with the metaphysical problem of the one and the many, the individual and his universe. The narrowing of Waller's horizons, intellectual and aesthetic, is apparent in the limited range of his poetry, with its heavy emphasis upon compliment, and in the hard, unsentimental realism that sometimes shows through the surface. In 1680 the sixty-two-year-old Countess of Sunderland, the Sacharissa of forty-odd years before, asked the seventy-three-year-old Waller when he would write some more "beautiful verses" to her. Waller replied, "When, Madam, your Ladyship is as young and as handsome again."[28]

It is in his exclusive concentration on what is immediately before him, the denial of transcendence or of metaphysical significance, that Waller differs most profoundly from the great writers of the beginning of the century. His "Song" ("Stay, Phoebus! stay"), for example, is based on a conceit familiar in Donne: the sun commanded by a lover to stop in its tracks. But Waller's poem is far simpler, more impersonal, and less ambitious than "The Sunne Rising." The conceit has been softened and trivialized, the diction and rhythm (appropriately for a song) are uncomplicated and reiterative, and the poem is concerned with nothing more than turning a graceful compliment. It is not a love poem, but a poem of praise, whose fair recipient has been so little immortalized by the poet's words that no one quite knows who she was. [29]

28. Thorn-Drury, *1, lxvii*.

29. Mlle. de Mornay has generally been identified as one of Queen Henrietta Maria's attendants; see e.g. Fenton, lxi; and Anne Ferry, ed., *Seventeenth Century English Minor Poets* (New York, Dell, 1964), p. 191. MS. Eng. 703 in the Houghton Library, Harvard University (Sir Henry Cholmley's commonplace book, dated before 1641) identifies her as "a Lady of the Queene Mothers Trayn 1638"; the poem then was occasioned by the visit of Marie de Medicis in 1638.

> Stay, Phoebus! stay:
> The world to which you fly so fast,
> Conveying day
> From us to them, can pay your haste
> With no such object, nor salute your rise,
> With no such wonder as De Mornay's eyes.

Whatever effect the poem has depends upon our not taking its statements seriously. In the second stanza, Waller lets us know that the sun has not stopped after all, and that he did not really expect it to do so. The wit of the first stanza is based on Ptolemaic, that of the second on Copernican astronomy; his advocacy of one hypothesis over the other is based entirely on the use to which he can put them. All ideas in Waller's lyrics are in a sense provisional, and their truth or falsity to him lies wholly in their rhetorical efficacy.

> Well does this prove
> The error of those antique books,
> Which made you move
> About the world; her charming looks
> Would fix your beams, and make it ever day,
> Did not the rolling earth snatch her away.

The conscious and consistent narrowing of scope in Waller's lyric verse, the tailoring of a poem to fit the social situation, the retreat from emotion, seriousness, and ideas, if accepted as aesthetic ideals, are potentially impoverishing. Such lyrics approach the condition of pure mindless song: we can see Ned Softly just around the corner. The general mediocrity of Restoration and early eighteenth-century lyric poetry comes in large part from the crippling aesthetic assumptions under which much of it was produced. Waller's example here was a dangerous one, and his successors imitated his weaknesses along with his virtues. An art of limitation, of exclusion, of control, can only work when there is something to be controlled. The Augustan compromise insisted on order *and* energy, reason *and* passion; the bit is useless when there is no horse.

Self-love, the spring of motion, acts the soul;
Reason's comparing balance rules the whole.
Man, but for that, no action could attend,
And, but for this, were active to no end;
Fix'd like a plant on his peculiar spot,
To draw nutrition, propagate, and rot;
Or, meteor-like, flame lawless thro' the void,
Destroying others, by himself destroy'd.[30]

The major Augustan poets and critics were not in general
interested in lyric poetry. Ambrose Philips' discussion of
the lyric in *Guardian,* No. 16 shows none of the sensitivity
or critical intelligence of Dryden and Pope; instead it
applies neoclassical criteria in a thoroughly unimaginative
way. Its aesthetic is suitable for Philips' own poetry, a pre-
scription for fops. The emphasis falls entirely upon simplicity, regularity, purity, delicacy, and ease. The poet
should avoid saying too much and should concentrate on
small effects; he should polish and refine.

> These little compositions . . . do not require an eleva-
> tion of thought, nor any extraordinary capacity, nor an
> extensive knowledge; but then they demand great
> regularity, and the utmost nicety; an exact purity of
> style; with the most easy and flowing numbers; an
> elegant and unaffected turn of wit, with one uniform
> and simple design. Greater works cannot well be with-
> out some inequalities and oversights, and they are in
> them pardonable; but a song loses all its lustre if it be
> not polished with the greatest accuracy. The smallest
> blemish in it, like a flaw in a jewel, takes off the whole
> value of it. A song is, as it were, a little image in enamel,
> that requires all the nice touches, a gloss and a smooth-
> ness, with those delicate finishing strokes, which would
> be superfluous and thrown away upon larger figures.[31]

30. *An Essay on Man,* II.59–66, in Butt, *Poems of Alexander Pope.*
31. *Guardian,* No. 16, Mar. 30, 1713, in *The British Essayists,* ed. A.
Chalmers, *13* (London, 1823), 88. The essay is attributed to Philips in M. G.

Addison's Ned Softly is ruled by similar criteria: "Pray how do you like that *Ah!* Doth it not make a pretty Figure in that Place? *Ah!* It looks as if I felt the Dart, and cried out at being pricked with it, 'For Ah! it wounds me like his Dart.' My friend *Dick Easy* . . . assured me, he would rather have written that *Ah!* than to have been the Author of the Aeneid."[32]

Philips is as concerned with unity of structure as he is with the "nice touches" of detail. Earlier writers, he complains, err through "a redundancy of wit" in that they "generally crowd into one song, materials enough for several; and so they starve every thought, by endeavoring to nurse up more than one at a time." Even "Mr. Waller (whose beauties cannot be too much admired)" is sometimes guilty of this fault. The main culprits are Donne and Cowley: "in them, one point of wit flashes so fast upon another, that the reader's attention is dazzled by the continual sparkling of their imagination; you find a new design started almost in every line, and you come to the end without the satisfaction of seeing any one of them executed."[33] The process of simplification, limitation, and retrenching which Philips is

---

Segar, ed., *The Poems of Ambrose Philips* (Oxford, 1937), p. xxxvii. Cf. Boileau, *L'art poétique*, II.82–102, and John Sheffield, Earl of Mulgrave, "An Essay upon Poetry" (1682), in J. E. Spingarn, ed., *Critical Essays of the Seventeenth Century* (3 vols. Oxford, 1908),2, 288. Mulgrave's remarks on the song, themselves adapted from Boileau, appear to be Philips' primary source: "Though nothing seems more easy, yet no part / Of Poetry requires a nicer Art; / For as in rows of richest Pearl there lyes / Many a blemish that escapes our Eyes, / The least of which Defects is plainly shewn / In some small Ring, and brings the value down; / So Songs should be to just perfection wrought" (ibid 2, 288, 9-15). For further discussion, see Catherine Walsh Peltz, "The Neo-Classic Lyric 1660–1725," *ELH*, *11* (1944), 92–116; and Herbert M. Schueller, "The Renaissance Forerunners of the Neo-Classic Lyric," *Modern Language Notes*, *62* (1947), 310–16.

32. *Tatler*, No. 163.

33. *Guardian*, No. 16. Mulgrave in his "Essay upon Poetry" praises the unity and "just coherence" of Waller's "Elegies" in couplets; see Spingarn, *3*, 289.

urging here helps define the difference between Waller and his successors and the lyric poets of the beginning of the century. Waller has gone halfway along the path Philips is describing. Indeed, I suspect that it is the fact that he has gone thus far and no farther that makes his poems worthy of serious critical interest. Waller's best lyrics succeed through a perfect adaptation of form to content: they are precise, witty, carefully constructed, and make a point neatly and effectively. His failures occur when he has nothing to say.

The peculiar interest of Waller is that he is poised so precisely between two ages. His poetry points the way from Donne to Dryden and Pope. This double allegiance to the aesthetic assumptions of an earlier and a later age enables us to trace in his poems the changes which the idea of wit underwent in the course of the seventeenth century.

Wit, the central tradition in seventeenth-century lyric poetry, is essentially metaphorical. To the Italian and Spanish baroque poets (and by extension to the English poets of the same period), metaphor is important precisely because it seeks out the hidden resemblances of things and illuminates some aspect of the pattern of the universe. The conceit, according to the Spanish critic Baltasar Gracián, is "an act of the imagination that expresses the correspondence which exists among objects."[34] In such a theory the poet

---

34. Treatises by Gracián (*Agudeza y Arte de Ingenio*, 1642), Emanuele Tesauro (*Il Cannocchiale Aristotelico*, 1654), and other continental theorists are quoted at length and discussed in important articles by S. L. Bethell and Joseph A. Mazzeo. See S. L. Bethell, "The Nature of Metaphysical Wit," in Frank Kermode, ed., *Discussions of John Donne* (Boston, D. C. Heath & Co., 1962), pp. 136–49 (originally published in *The Northern Miscellany of Literary Criticism, 1*, [1953], 19–40). Mazzeo's articles, "A Seventeenth-Century Theory of Metaphysical Poetry," *Romanic Review, 42* (1951), 245–55, and "Metaphysical Poetry and the Poetic of Correspondence," *Journal of the History of Ideas, 14* (1953), 221–34, are reprinted in his *Renaissance and Modern Studies* (New York, Columbia University Press, 1964), pp. 29–59; for the passage quoted, see ibid., p. 32.

does not create the correspondences but discovers them; he is in a sense a licensed interpreter of the emblematic universe, revealing to men what they were unable to see for themselves:

> We say amisse,
> This or that is:
> Thy word is all, if we could spell.[35]

Since the universe is essentially metaphorical, the poet must communicate through metaphor. Emanuele Tesauro writes:

> If wit consists (as we say) in binding together the remote and separate motions of the proposed objects, that is exactly the function of metaphor, and not of any other figure; since, drawing the mind, and not only the word, from one genus to another, it expresses one concept by means of another very different one; finding similarity in things dissimilar. . . . The metaphor is more witty and acute when the notions are very remote.

Certain concepts can only be expressed by metaphor, and others are most effectively expressed by metaphor. To these writers, as to most Renaissance literary theorists, poetry is the best teacher and obscurity a path to ultimate clarity: "For if a certain metaphor is not perhaps easy for you to penetrate at first sight, as enigmas and laconisms, nonetheless, when you have penetrated it, you see that conceit [i.e. idea or concept] more clearly and have it more fixed in mind than if it had been spoken to you in ordinary words."[36]

There are certain problems implicit in this "poetic of correspondence" or in its application to poetry, and these are particularly relevant to a poet like Waller. In a sense, such a poetic carries within it the seeds of its own destruction. Robert M. Adams has put the point well: we are conscious, in reading Donne and other metaphysical poets, of a sense of "stress and strain." Much of the power of Donne's

---

35. Herbert, "The Flower," 19–21.
36. Bethell, pp. 141, 145–46.

verse comes from our awareness of tensions partially resolved and partially unresolved because unresolvable; the
same thing is true, in different ways, of Herbert, Crashaw,
and Marvell. The poet is forced, as it were, to hold the universe together by an act of the will.

> The analogical universe, which is implicitly a descrip-
> tion of the universe as it ought to be, not as it is, was the
> origin of the metaphysical style; and that style was born
> with a built-in sense of strain. 'Wit,' which in its early
> meanings is not often far removed from general in-
> tellectual energy, was conceived of as doing its best to
> hold this elaborate structure together, extending it
> through unexpected and daring lines of thought or
> reinforcing it in surprising ways by noting unfamiliar
> correlations between familiar things. Their style is
> metaphysical precisely as it juxtaposes points of view
> which are in some ways compatible, in other ways not
> —as it carries out a juxtaposition which involves a
> strain.[37]

Donne *wants* his poems to appear to be composed of "hetero-
geneous materials yoked by violence together"; the hetero-
geneity, the dissonances, are emphasized in order to make
the poet's triumph all the more dazzling. Lovers and a
drawing compass, sick men and maps, tears and worlds, the
soul and a besieged town do not at first glance appear to have
anything in common, but the poet proves to us that our first
assumption was wrong. In Helen Gardner's words, "we are
made to concede likeness while being strongly conscious of
unlikeness."[38] Herbert's tone may be quieter, but he is even
more concerned with the reconciliation of apparently discordant opposites. Nothing is too great or too small to escape
his net; all things are subject to the transformations of wit

---

37. Robert M. Adams, *Strains of Discord: Studies in Literary Openness*
(Ithaca, Cornell University Press, 1958), pp. 107–08.
38. Introduction, *The Metaphysical Poets* (London, Penguin Books, 1957),
p. 19.

and faith. Waller and the Cavaliers, as we have seen, are less ambitious. Waller's conceits are muted; they do not call attention to themselves and are (or appear to be) far less daring.

Wit, according to Tesauro, employs falsehood in the service of truth. In its highest form, the conceit is an argument "urbanely fallacious"—in other words, deliberate sophistry. The two souls of the lovers are not in fact together when they are apart, "one little room" is not in fact "an everywhere," the poet has not in fact been reduced to the quintessence of nothingness after the death of his beloved— all these things are literally impossible. And yet the assertions are all emotionally true, convincing in their poetic context. The poet is conscious of the literal falsehood along with the figurative truth. The poetic conceit "imitates the false in such wise as the truth appears by way of it as through a veil: so that from what is said you quickly understand what is not said."39 The conceits of religious poetry are not fallacious in this sense, but they exemplify the paradox of truth in falsehood in another way. The religious poet is both God-regarding and self-regarding, attempting to speak of (or to) the divine in earthly terms. To the devout man all earthly things must be regarded with some suspicion or at least ambiguity; there is always the danger that the poet is expressing pride rather than devotion, thinking more of his wit than of its supposed object. The poet's "sweet phrases, lovely metaphors," the "curious frame" he weaves in his poetry, the very medium with which he works, are in themselves corrupt and are loved too much. The conflict here, unlike that in the secular love poems, cannot be resolved— at least not by man:

> But thou who only could'st the Serpent tame,
> Either his slipp'ry knots at once untie,
> And disentangle all his winding Snare:
> Or shatter too with him my curious frame

39. Bethell, pp. 144–45.

> And let these wither, so that he may die,
> Though set with Skill and chosen out with Care.[40]

There are several possible responses to the paradox of truth inseparable from falsity. One possibility is silence, a refusal to meddle with what is hopelessly impure. A second possibility is to divorce rhetoric from dialectic entirely and assume that ideas are irrelevant to poetry or merely instruments to manipulate for persuasive ends. One subject is as good as any other, and a poem becomes an exercise. A third possibility is to attempt to separate the true from the false and the knowable from the unknowable; render to God what is God's, but the proper study of mankind is man. "The ideas of Christian Theology," Johnson argues, "are too simple for eloquence, too sacred for fiction, and too majestick for ornament; to recommend them by tropes and figures is to magnify by a concave mirror the sidereal hemisphere."[41] English neoclassical literature concentrating its attention on the world of man, is consistently critical, analytic, normative; the criteria of rhetorical efficacy and "truth to the subject" remain,[42] but they are subordinated to explicit didacticism. Both the surprising reconciliation of apparent opposites and their unresolved tension are foreign to the Augustans, who prefer sharp, clearly marked contrasts; wit must work in conjunction with judgment. George Williamson has argued that paradox is the heart of poetic wit in the first part of the seventeenth century and antithesis in the last part of the century—"contraries are reconciled in the one, and opposed in the other."[43]

The locus classicus arguing the separation of wit from judgment and the necessity for clear and precise discriminations is Locke's *Essay Concerning Human Understanding.*

40. Andrew Marvell, "The Coronet," 19–24; cf. Herbert's "The Forerunners," esp. line 13.

41. Johnson, *Lives of the Poets, 1,* 292–93.

42. See Rosemond Tuve, *Elizabethan and Metaphysical Imagery* (Chicago, University of Chicago Press, 1947), p. 189.

43. *The Proper Wit of Poetry,* p. 95.

77

Locke associates wit with metaphor and is unsympathetic toward both:

> For *wit* lying most in the assemblage of ideas, and putting those together with quickness and variety, wherein can be found any resemblance or congruity, thereby to make up pleasant pictures and agreeable visions in the fancy; *judgment,* on the contrary, lies quite on the other side, in separating carefully, one from another, ideas wherein can be found the least difference, thereby to avoid being misled by similitude, and by affinity to take one thing for another. This is a way of proceeding quite contrary to metaphor and allusion; wherein for the most part lies that entertainment and pleasantry of wit, which strikes so lively on the fancy, and therefore is so acceptable to all people; because its beauty appears at first sight, and there is required no labor of thought to examine what truth or reason there is in it.[44]

The requirements of truth are all-important, and truth depends upon the ability to "distinguish one thing from another" with precision. The heirs of Bacon believed it essential to free the mind from those things which tended to mislead it; truth is discernible, but to free truth from bondage "the several classes of Idols, and their equipage ... must be renounced and put away with a fixed and solemn determination, and the understanding thoroughly freed and cleansed."[45] Metaphor is one of the chief misleaders, to Thomas Sprat as well as Locke:

> Who can behold, without indignation, how many mists and uncertainties, these specious *Tropes* and *Figures* have brought on our Knowledg? ... And, in few words,

44. Bk. II, chap. XI, par. 2, ed. Alexander Campbell Fraser (Oxford, 1894).

45. Francis Bacon, *Novum Organum,* Bk. I, lxviii, in *The Works of Francis Bacon,* ed. James Spedding, Robert L. Ellis, and Douglas D. Heath (London, 1859–74).

> I dare say; that of all the Studies of men, nothing may
> be sooner obtain'd, than this vicious abundance of
> *Phrase,* this trick of *Metaphors,* this volubility of
> *Tongue,* which makes so great a noise in the World.[46]

Faced with a widespread lack of sympathy with metaphor
and a belief in the primacy of judgment and common sense
over the erratic flights of the imagination, the Augustan
poets strove to produce a poetry that had the virtues of
prose.

Waller's poetry, as the previous pages have suggested,
represents less a break with earlier poetry than a development out of it. Metaphor is central in all his poems; both his
early lyrics and his later public verse depend heavily on conceits. There are differences between the two kinds of poems,
and Waller's virtual abandonment of the lyric in his later
career brings about a shift of emphasis in his treatment of
metaphor. The lyrics, like most poems of their kind in this
period, tend to be built around a central pattern of imagery,
with a clear structure. In the more discursive state poems,
the metaphors normally play around a surface of statement.
Such poems are more in accordance with the standard neoclassical view of metaphor as essentially ornamental, serving
to clothe, color, or embellish the thought—as Samuel H.
Monk puts it, the poet finds "aptly *illustrative* imagery
which is *applied* to statement."[47] Yet even in these poems
the metaphors are in no sense separable; much as in Waller's
speeches in Parliament, the conceits, analogies, and allusions
which dot the page work hand in hand with nonmeta-
phorical statement to embody the substance of his argument
and make his practical points for him. The quality of reti-
cence and understatement in Waller's imagery links him in
yet another way to the Augustans, whose poetry, in the words

46. Thomas Sprat, *History of the Royal Society* (1667), ed. Jackson I. Cope
and Harold Whitmore Jones (St. Louis, 1958), p. 112.

47. Samuel Holt Monk, "From Jacobean to Augustan," *Southern Review,*
7 (1941–42), 383.

of Maynard Mack, is "signalized not by the absence of metaphorical effects, but by their use in such a way that they do
not disturb a logical surface of statement."[48]

The poems to be discussed in the rest of this chapter all
display, despite their surface simplicity, a complex pattern
of imagery. All, in varying degrees, combine praise and argumentation, utilizing compliment as one element subservient
to an overall rhetorical purpose.[49] The particular methods
of organization differ: "On a Girdle," a lover's cry of triumph, is praise without overt persuasion (since the persuasion has apparently already succeeded); "The Story of
Phoebus and Daphne, Applied" is a narration, a farewell to
love, an applied myth, and in a sense a definition; "Go,
Lovely Rose" is a persuasion to love. But in each case the
materials of the poem and the pattern of imagery are largely
determined by the poem's occasion in conjunction with its
rhetorical end. The wit in these poems lies not only in the
careful elaboration of the central images, but in the grace
with which the poet makes the most of his self-imposed
limitations.

"On a Girdle" resembles a good many poems of the early
seventeenth century in its form, the development of a single

48. Maynard Mack, " 'Wit and Poetry and Pope': Some Observations on
his Imagery," in James L. Clifford, ed., *Eighteenth-Century English Literature: Modern Essays in Criticism* (New York, Oxford University Press, 1959),
p. 22; the essay was originally published in *Pope and his Contemporaries:
Essays Presented to George Sherburn* (Oxford, Clarendon Press, 1949). Cf.
Earl Miner, "Some Characteristics of Dryden's Use of Metaphor," *Studies in
English Literature, 2* (1962), 309–20.

49. Renaissance critics point out two rhetorical ends particularly appropriate to lyric poetry: to praise (or dispraise) and to plead, *laudare* and
precari (roughly equivalent to the distinction between epideictic and deliberative oratory). See Tuve, *Elizabethan and Metaphysical Imagery*, pp.
85–86; and O. B. Hardison, Jr., *The Enduring Monument: A Study of the
Idea of Praise in Renaissance Theory and Practice* (Chapel Hill, University
of North Carolina Press, 1962), pp. 95–103. In lyric poetry as in panegyric,
a poet like Waller will frequently combine the two ends, deploying praise
toward a persuasive purpose; see chap. 3 for a further discussion of the
relationship between praise and persuasion in Waller's political verse.

conceit, its use of witty hyperbole, its choice of theme, and even its choice of central image. But Waller does not aim at the ingenuity, variety of tone, or passionate intellectuality of Donne's poems, which assert the exclusiveness of a lovers' world. Instead, he opts for clarity, neatness, symmetry, and ease. The structure of "On a Girdle" is simple. The poem consists of a succession of circles, variations upon the theme of surrounding, enclosing, encircling, encompassing. I quote the poem in full: note how the circle metaphor finds its way into virtually every line.

> That which her slender waist confined,
> Shall now my joyful temples bind;
> No monarch but would give his crown,
> His arms might do what this has done.
>
> It was my heaven's extremest sphere,
> The pale which held that lovely deer,
> My joy, my grief, my hope, my love,
> Did all within this circle move!
>
> A narrow compass! and yet there
> Dwelt all that's good, and all that's fair;
> Give me but what this ribband bound,
> Take all the rest the sun goes round.

In the first stanza, Waller emphasizes the smallness and flimsiness of the girdle (praising by implication the lady's delicacy and grace): the ribbon once "confined" her waist, now "bind[s]" his temples. The monarch's crown (another circle, another way of binding the temples) and the "arms" of a warrior are insignificant to the lover; he is not misled by false appearances. In the second stanza, the circle expands to encompass vast spaces. The bit of cloth is equated with the outermost of the spheres, the primum mobile. By another variant upon the central conceit, it becomes the enclosure which "held that lovely deer." The comparison of the mistress with a lovely animal, the pun on "deer" and "dear" are both, of course, conventional. But the terms the

81

poet uses—"pale" with its suggestion of private ownership, "move" which suggests the motion of the spheres and the movement of the deer within the pale, as well as the movement of the lady herself—help tie the poem still more closely together. In the second couplet, the paradox of all in little is made more explicit: the lover's feelings have been entirely determined within this circle, his universe.

Where stanza one emphasizes the smallness of the lover's world and stanza two its breadth, the third stanza places the two ideas side by side. The circle is narrow and yet contains everything of value within it. Balance and syntactical parallelism in the two phrases of line 10 ("all that's good, and all that's fair"), with the parallelism and contrast in the concluding couplet, reinforce the impression of finality, of all-inclusiveness. In its context, the statement in the last two lines justifies itself—the lover's world is worth all the rest put together; the circuit of the sun does not exceed that of love.[50]

Waller likes to work his metaphors out in detail. He is particularly fond of mythological conceits and extended similes, both of which are classicizing stylistic devices tending toward elaboration and dignity. Neither is a device common in metaphysical poetry.[51] As a rule, Waller's metaphors tend to assume the explicitness of simile even when they do not use the "like," "as," or "so" form. Metaphors will apply in detail to the literal situation that is described, with correspondences (as A and B, so A' and B') worked out fully. An extended simile at the beginning of a poem will normally impart to the poem a circumstantial, ceremonious quality. The reader of such a poem is as conscious of the way

50. There are good discussions of this poem in Monk, "From Jacobean to Augustan," pp. 371–72, and Williamson, *The Proper Wit of Poetry*, pp. 103–04.

51. Donne, Carew wrote, had "purg'd" the "Muses garden" of "Pedantique weedes," "banish'd . . . the goodly exil'd traine / Of gods and goddesses" which had served to "swell the windy Page" ("An Elegie upon the death of the Deane of Pauls, Dr. John Donne," 25–27, 61–70).

it does not begin—direct address, syllogistic logic—as of the way it does. A simile at the end of the poem is used not to set the tone but to make a pointed application of what the poem has been saying.

"To Chloris," a short poem addressed "to a Lady, more affable since the war began," or as the 1645 edition more bluntly puts it, "upon a favour received," provides a convenient illustration of the way Waller uses the device:

> Chloris! since first our calm of peace
> Was frighted hence, this good we find,
> Your favours with your fears increase,
> And growing mischiefs make you kind.
> So the fair tree, which still preserves
> Her fruit and state while no wind blows,
> In storms from that uprightness swerves,
> And the glad earth around her strows
> With treasure, from her yielding boughs.

Even in a witty Cavalier lyric like "To Chloris," Waller takes care that his language is dignified, "poetic." The poem is full of the kind of noun-epithet combinations that are so common in Virgil and in English neoclassical poetry: "fair tree," "glad earth," "yielding boughs." It is not simply the elaborateness of the simile that marks Waller as Augustan as well as Cavalier, but the diction and syntax. The concluding lines of the poem resemble the classical epic simile as much as the metaphysical conceit. Yet the simile is witty and is deployed toward a rhetorical end familiar in Waller —explaining and justifying behavior. The girl's surrender is presented as natural and inevitable, the product of forces beyond her control. Many of the terms ("uprightness," "yielding," "treasure") bear double meanings, applying wittily to the metaphorical situation and to the literal one. Wit and dignity work together to create the poem's tone of sophisticated poise.

Waller's showpiece for the witty use of mythology is "The Story of Phoebus and Daphne, Applied." In form the poem is a brief allegorical narrative, built on a single extended comparison; the metaphor is the poem. The twenty lines develop in careful detail a parallel between Apollo's pursuit of Daphne and Waller's own unsuccessful courtship of Sacharissa. The poet Thyrsis (Waller) courts "the flying nymph" with "numbers" (i.e. poems), pursuing her over mountains and meadows.

> Such is the chase when Love and Fancy leads,
> O'er craggy mountains, and through flowery meads;
> Invoked to testify the lover's care,
> Or form some image of his cruel fair. (7–10)

In the story of Apollo and Daphne, the scenery is literal, while for Waller it applies to the poems he has written for Sacharissa and their scenic background.[52] The poetic imagination creates its own world. Despite the poet's efforts, "all his charms could not incline" the maiden "to stay." And yet, again like Apollo

> What he sung in his immortal strain,
> Though unsuccessful, was not sung in vain. (15–16)

His poems, the by-products of his love, survive their occasion. The god of poetry brings his own consolation.

> All, but the nymph that should redress his wrong,
> Attend his passion, and approve his song. (17–18)

The consolation, as the poem presents it, is unexpected and in a sense unwelcome; the poet is focusing his attention on Sacharissa, not on any onlookers. With dexterous wit, Waller gives the metaphor one further turn and makes the final application of the myth of Phoebus and Daphne. Without the final couplet, the lines quoted immediately above would simply mean "everybody who knew of his suit

---

52. See e.g. the two poems entitled, "At Penshurst" and "To my Lord of Leicester."

of Sacharissa favored it and thought he deserved to win her."
But the last lines give "approve his song" a second meaning:

> Like Phoebus thus, acquiring unsought praise,
> He catched at love, and filled his arm with bays. (19–20)

Poems on Apollo and Daphne are common in the Renaissance, but none is quite like Waller's. Giambattista Marino's "La Trasformazione di Dafne," perhaps the best-known seventeenth-century treatment of the theme, was translated or adapted by Thomas Stanley (1651) and Philip Ayres (1687). Douglas Bush suggests that Waller is imitating Marino; yet the two poems differ in that Waller's is an application of the myth, not just a retelling. Though both Waller and Marino end with a conceit representing the lover's frustration ("se'l frutto no, coglie le fronde"—in Stanley's version, "Thus this disdainful Maid his aim deceives, / Where he expected Fruit he gathers Leaves"), in Waller the apparent frustration is the lover's triumph.[53] Marvell's witty use of the myth of Apollo and Daphne in "The Garden" resembles Waller in some ways:

> When we have run our Passions heat,
> Love hither makes his best retreat.
> The *Gods*, that mortal Beauty chase,
> Still in a Tree did end their race.
> *Apollo* hunted *Daphne* so,
> Only that She might Laurel grow,
> And *Pan* did after *Syrinx* speed,
> Not as a Nymph, but for a Reed. (25–32)

Both poets deal with a form of sublimation, treating the god's failure to catch the nymph as fortunate. But the two poems are quite different both in form and in the point the

53. See Giambattista Marino, *Poesie Varie*, ed. Benedetto Croce (Bari, 1913); Galbraith M. Crump, ed., *Poems and Translations of Thomas Stanley* (Oxford, 1962), pp. 29, 383; and Douglas Bush, *Mythology and the Renaissance Tradition* (Minneapolis, 1932), pp. 216–18.

poets are making. Marvell uses the myth of Phoebus and Daphne as one of a string of related conceits to support his case for asexual retirement and solitude. Waller's form is the extended conceit, and his theme is the relationship between life and art, the world a poet inhabits and the world he creates.

By presenting the praise given his poetry as "unsought," Waller maintains the parallel with the Ovidian metamorphosis; all the poet-lover is interested in, he protests, is Sacharissa. But the protests are clearly disingenuous—it is clear that Waller is happier with the poems (and the praise) than he would have been with the girl. Faced with a choice between love and art, he chooses art; the poem is by implication a palinode, a farewell to love. Much of the charm of the poem resides in the impersonality, the objectivity, with which Waller treats his material. As F. W. Bateson has observed, though by implication the poet is "blowing his own trumpet," the tone of the poem absolves him from possible charges of egoism. Indeed, an air of detachment and formality (as exemplified in the diction of the last six lines —"attend his passion, and approve his song") is necessary for the success of the poem. Waller cannot spring the surprise at the end as effectively, or work his metaphors out in as full detail, if he speaks of himself in the first person; as Bateson says, the lover, his mistress, and their relationship have been "abstracted out of their human context."[54]

Each of the poems I have been discussing depends for its central point upon the exploitation of a metaphor or series of metaphors implicit in the poem's occasion. The conceit is necessarily interpretive and serves in some way to transform the materials to which it is applied. Its existence is not

---

54. F. W. Bateson, *English Poetry: A Critical Introduction* (New York, Barnes and Noble, 1966), p. 119. Bateson's essay, "A Word for Waller," pp. 116–22, is illuminating in its treatment of this poem and in its general remarks on the poet. Another good discussion of the poem may be found in Williamson, *The Proper Wit of Poetry*, pp. 104–05.

obvious; the author has to find it and apply it. Ideally, the conceit will seem both surprising and inevitable. The author's ingenuity is limited by the requirements of the initial situation and by such imponderables as tact. This quality of restraint amid the proliferations of wit is what separates Waller from his contemporary John Cleveland, who is equally fond of the occasional subject. Waller, as we have seen, is both idealist and realist. His poetry reflects a particular social scene and in a very real sense is confined within that social context and the values it implies; at the same time, he characteristically subjects his material to metamorphoses and is constantly escaping into a golden world. The ultimate reality in the poems is the figure of the poet, master of the puppets, unmoved mover.

"Of the Last Verses in the Book," which Waller wrote in the last months of his life, differs from the other poems I have been discussing in several clearly marked ways. In these grave and measured lines on the subject of old age, there is nothing of the playfulness of the earlier poems; grace has been replaced by sobriety. The poem's aim, simply, is truth; its only persuasion lies in the force of its convictions and the power of its verse.

The form of this late work is equally unlike anything among the love lyrics. "Of the Last Verses" has three six-line stanzas, each stanza consisting of three heroic couplets. Each couplet is complete in itself, but the three couplets in a stanza develop a common theme. Only rarely are the couplets linked syntactically; each contains a clear, carefully rounded generalization and ends unequivocally with a full stop. Metrically, "Of the Last Verses" is far from the flowing couplets of "The Story of Phoebus and Daphne, Applied," with its carefully modulated argument.

Each couplet in "Of the Last Verses" is constructed around one or more antitheses, all of which turn on the basic paradox implicit in the poem's occasion. Waller had undertaken in his old age and in ill health a project larger than anything he had done in years, a series of Divine

Poems.[55] "Of the Last Verses" begins with the specific (his ability to write poems on that subject at that time) and moves from this to general questions of age and mortality.

> When we for age could neither read nor write,
> The subject made us able to indite.   (1–2)

The rest of the first stanza, taking up the hint in the second line, explains the paradox that enables the poet to write in spite of decrepitude.

> The soul, with nobler resolutions decked,
> The body stooping, does herself erect.
> No mortal parts are requisite to raise
> Her that, unbodied, can her Maker praise.   (3–6)[56]

---

55. Except for "Of the Last Verses" itself, the *Divine Poems* are indifferent as poetry. I quote a sample:

> The fear of hell, or aiming to be blessed,
> Savours too much of private interest.
> This moved not Moses, nor the zealous Paul,
> Who for their friends abandoned soul and all;
> A greater yet from heaven to hell descends,
> To save, and make his enemies his friends.
> What line of praise can fathom such a love,
> Which reached the lowest bottom from above?
> ("Of Divine Love," II.1–8.)

This is sluggish and thin; there is virtually no forward movement in the lines, no overall organization. These lines are the mere shell of poetry, antitheses without real substance, without music, without force.

56. The best passages in the *Divine Poems* deal with the paradox of the poet's "second birth" in old age. Cf. "Of Divine Love," VI.19–38; or "On the Fear of God," II.47–54:

> Wrestling with death, these lines I did indite;
> No other theme could give my soul delight.
> O that my youth had thus employed my pen!
> Or that I now could write as well as then!
> But 'tis of grace, if sickness, age, and pain,
> Are felt as throes, when we are born again;
> Timely they come to wean us from this earth,
> As pangs that wait upon a second birth.

The central terms ("soul," "body"; "mortal," "unbodied"; "stooping," "erect") are parallel and antithetical, as rhetorical structure reinforces meaning. "Of the Last Verses" relies, far more than the earlier poems, on the devices that characterize Augustan poetry. It also differs from them in its attitude toward its occasion. In "To Chloris," "The Story of Phoebus and Daphne, Applied," and even "On a Girdle," any generalizations about love, art, or human nature to which the poem gives rise grow out of the particular situation of the poem and are inseparable from their context. In "Of the Last Verses," the occasion is no more than an excuse to get the poem started. The composition of the divine poems serves only as a concrete illustration of the general truths that are the poem's main concern.

Throughout the poem, the generalizations are expressed metaphorically. The antitheses, particularly when they are paradoxical in form ("The soul . . . / The body stooping, does herself erect"; "stronger by weakness") are, in the manner of much Augustan poetry, subdued metaphors. But more often, as in the first and last couplets of stanza two, Waller's thought finds expression in language which is explicitly figurative.

> The seas are quiet when the winds give o'er;
> So, calm are we when passions are no more!
> For then we know how vain it was to boast
> Of fleeting things, so certain to be lost.
> Clouds of affection from our younger eyes
> Conceal that emptiness which age descries. (7–12)

Each point is reinforced by balance and antithesis. In the first couplet, the parallel between winds and passions, sea and man, is made even more explicit by the strict parallelism of the lines. Waller is not leaving anything to chance; any suggestiveness inherent in the image is limited by its form, that of a simile with explicit and literal application carefully pointed out. The middle couplet is straightforward statement, not primarily metaphorical, though "fleeting" and "lost" in line 10 contain subdued metaphors. The effectiveness of the couplet comes to a large degree from the interplay between the opposed terms, "fleeting" and "certain," "certain" and "lost"—things which slip by, whose only certainty is that of being lost. In the final couplet, statement and metaphor interact most effectively. Suggestions spawned by the image enrich the prose meaning—fog that surrounds us, perhaps not wholly to our detriment; clouds in the vast, cold emptiness of the sky. Knowledge of "emptiness," the vanity of all mortal things, knowledge attained through nearness to death, is not a pleasant knowledge.

The final stanza caps this powerful image with another:

> The soul's dark cottage, battered and decayed,
> Lets in new light through chinks that time has made;
> Stronger by weakness, wiser men become,
> As they draw near to their eternal home.
> Leaving the old, both worlds at once they view
> That stand upon the threshold of the new.   (13–18)

All three couplets work with antitheses (dark and light, strength and weakness, old and new), and all are essentially metaphorical. But except for the opening couplet, the metaphors are subdued and are conventional in nature. On the whole, the power of the poem comes not so much from its few vivid images as from its evenness of tone, the sense of conviction generated by the steady roll of somber generalizations. The images, the chastened wit, in this Augustan poem serve primarily to convey the lesson the poem teaches, and, even more important, its dominant feeling.

The highly conventional nature of Waller's poetry creates certain problems for the reader. His verse is deliberately unambitious, impersonal, restrained, classical; he did not seek to open up new ground but consistently chose to work in themes and forms that other writers had cultivated before him. In Waller's aesthetic, the poet is not an explorer of the frontiers of sensibility, but a craftsman. For all the efforts of

Eliot, Ransom, and others to promulgate a new classicism, it is difficult for a twentieth-century reader to escape wholly certain post-romantic preconceptions about poetry—the feeling that in one way or another lyric poetry involves a direct expression of emotion and of personality, that immediacy, the impression of sincerity, and above all originality are major poetic virtues. Waller held a very different view of imitation and originality. His poems imply comparison with classical, continental, and earlier English poems even where they are not explicitly indebted to an earlier source. Waller was steeped in Latin poetry, and the influence, direct or indirect, of Ovid, Horace, Virgil, Propertius, Tibullus, Catullus, and Martial is inescapable in his works. It is not always possible to distinguish specific debts, since similar *topoi* and motifs recur in a number of writers; Horace and English Horatianism, the Latin elegy and lyric and their modern imitators, blend together.

Waller's classical affinities were generally recognized in his time. St. Evremond in 1671 praises Waller as a connoisseur of "the delicacy of . . . past ages":

> Of all the men I ever knew, Antiquity is the most indebted to Mr. *Waller:* he lends it his beautiful Imagination, and his nice and delicate Judgment; so that he enters into the genius of the Antients, not only to understand rightly what they thought, but still to embelish their thoughts.[57]

The Sacharissa poems are particularly reminiscent of the Latin elegists, and neoclassical critics frequently take Waller's poetry as a model for elegy in English.[58] Among the elegists, he resembles Propertius in his fondness for com-

---

57. Hayward, *The Letters of Saint Evremond*, p. 127.

58. See e.g. Mulgrave's "Essay upon Poetry," in Spingarn, 2, 288–89; and *The Works of Tibullus*, tr. John Dart (London, 1720), ix-xiii. Some echoes of the elegists in Waller's poems are listed in Pauline Aiken, *The Influence of the Latin Elegists on English Lyric Poetry, 1600–1650,* University of Maine Studies, 2d ser., No. 22 (Orono, Me., 1932), pp. 40–42.

plimentary mythological comparisons and Ovid in his preference for the occasional subject, his witty insouciance, his
employment of verbal schemes in the couplet, and his occasional tour de force of arguing several sides of the same
question in different poems. Specific echoes of Virgil are
largely confined to Waller's longer poems, but the presence
of Virgil hovers over much of Waller; the general influence
of the *Eclogues* upon his lyrics is only slightly less pervasive
than that of the *Georgics* and *Aeneid* upon his public verse.
Pastoral and elegy are closely related genres in form and
subject matter. Dryden and Pope frequently associate
Waller with Virgil, and Pope's *Pastorals* are full of echoes
of Waller.[59] The epigrammatic quality in Waller (though
not his dislike of obscenity and love of euphemistic gallantry) ally him to Martial and even more to the *Greek
Anthology*. Perhaps the most pronounced influence on the
lyrics is that of Horace. The poet's one extensive foray into
literary theory was occasioned by a translation of the *Ars
Poetica,* and he shared the Horatian aesthetic wholeheart-
edly. The characteristic tone and persona of Waller's lyrics
resemble Horace more closely than any other classical
author, and Waller's care in placement of words and calcula-
tion of small effects is Horatian.

Poetry like Waller's is ordinarily the product of a sophisticated civilization, conscious of a decline of primal fresh-
ness, a loss of vigor, and seeking to make it up by turning to
art. Style, in life and literature, becomes an end in itself;
the poet's task is not so much discovery as refining, consolida-
tion. Addison writes:

> Wit and fine Writing doth not consist so much in ad-
> vancing things that are new, as in giving things that are
> known an agreeable Turn. It is impossible, for us who

59. See Ker, *Essays of Dryden,* 2, 29, 108–09, 214–16; and Joseph Spence,
Anecdotes, Observations, and Characters, of Books and Men, ed. S. W. Singer
(2d ed. London, 1858), pp. 18–19. Waller's Virgilian qualities are discussed
further in chap. 5.

live in the latter Ages of the World, to make Observations in Criticism, Morality, or in any Art or Science, which have not been touched upon by others. We have little else left us, but to represent the common Sense of Mankind in more strong, more beautiful, or more uncommon Lights.[60]

Yet the implications of Addison's statement are perhaps unduly pessimistic. Neither the earth nor the world of art has yet entered its old age, nor is either likely to do so; a classical, imitative art is not necessarily based on the assumption that there is nothing left to be said. Indeed, literary creation rests on several relativistic assumptions—that the stock of art is not limited, that an idea, form, or motif has not one ideal manifestation but a number of potential manifestations, some of which may be equally viable, and that imitation can be creative.

The case for classical art has beeen most persuasively stated in Eliot's "Tradition and the Individual Talent":

> The historical sense involves a perception, not only of the pastness of the past, but of its presence; the historical sense compels a man to write not only with his own generation in his bones, but with a feeling that the whole of the literature of Europe from Homer and within it the whole of the literature of his own country

---

60. *Spectator*, No. 253. A second contemporary statement of similar principles exudes an even wearier tone, mingled with petulance. The hack writer John Oldmixon writes in *The Arts of Logick and Rhetorick* (London, 1728), p. 63: "It would be a hard Matter to say nothing but what's new. 'Tis sufficient that Thoughts, in all Writing witty and ingenious, shou'd not be worn out; that if the Invention be not entirely new, the Manner of Expression be so, and the Turn that's given it be uncommon; or if such a Turn be wanting, there must be something in its Place, which raises both Admiration and Delight. Most of our Poetry has lately been made up of common Thoughts, without any more Turn than Rhime or Numbers can give them. Our Satyrs, Panegyricks, Epistles, and other Poems are eternal common Place; and how can it be otherwise? Genius being in a great Measure lost, the Poets must trade on other Mens Stocks, having little of their own."

> has a simultaneous existence and composes a simultaneous order. . . . No poet, no artist of any sort, has his complete meaning alone. . . . What happens when a new work of art is created is something that happens simultaneously to all the works of art which preceded it. The existing monuments form an ideal order among themselves, which is modified by the introduction of the new (the really new) work of art among them.[61]

Eliot's remarks perhaps apply more exactly to ambitious poets like Donne, Milton, and Pope (or Eliot himself), who seek new grand syntheses, remaking tradition, than to more modest poets like Carew and Waller, content to work within a tradition. A poem by Waller is not a challenge directed at the earlier poetry—"my advent'rous Song / That with no middle flight intends to soar / Above th'*Aonian* Mount, while it pursues / Things unattempted yet in Prose or Rhyme."[62] He seeks not to outdo, but to renew, to apply traditions to practical use. Drawing from a stock of conventional materials, he seeks to form single poems that are both individual and representative, both traditional and new.

"To Phyllis," a *carpe diem* poem generally Epicurean in its philosophy, in some ways provides a paradigm of Waller's method. Each of its details is conventional, yet the poem as a whole is an original creation; its originality lies in the way in which the details are welded into a unity. As "a bee gathers wax and honey out of many flowers, and makes a new bundle of all" (Burton's description of his method in *The Anatomy of Melancholy*),[63] Waller draws his materials from a number of places: Lucretius, Ovid, Catullus, Tibullus, Anacreon, and Renaissance libertine and naturalist lyrics. He does not aim to compete with the earlier writers (it

---

61. *Selected Essays*, pp. 4–5.

62. *Paradise Lost*, I.13–16, in Helen Darbishire, ed., *The Poetical Works of John Milton* (London, 1961).

63. Robert Burton, "Democritus to the Reader," *The Anatomy of Melancholy* (London, Everyman's Library, 1932), pp. 24–25.

would be absurd, for instance, to claim that "To Phyllis" was a better poem than "Vivamus, mea Lesbia") but to create an independent poem within the tradition.

> Phyllis! why should we delay
> Pleasures shorter than the day?
> Could we (which we never can)
> Stretch our lives beyond their span,
> Beauty like a shadow flies,
> And our youth before us dies.
> Or would youth and beauty stay,
> Love hath wings, and will away.
> Love hath swifter wings than Time;
> Change in love to heaven does climb.
> Gods, that never change their state,
> Vary oft their love and hate.
>   Phyllis! to this truth we owe
> All the love betwixt us two.
> Let not you and I inquire
> What has been our past desire;
> On what shepherds you have smiled,
> Or what nymphs I have beguiled;
> Leave it to the planets too,
> What we shall hereafter do;
> For the joys we now may prove,
> Take advice of present love.

"To Phyllis" combines topoi from two conventional types of poem: the persuasion to love and the justification of inconstancy. The starting point of the poem, as in the best-known classical and Renaissance carpe diem poetry, is the inescapable fact of transiency. Our time on earth is short, and all things die; the laws of nature are immutable. Catullus' statement of the theme is famous: "soles occidere et redire possunt: / nobis cum semel occidit brevis lux, / nox est perpetua una dormienda" (in Ben Jonson's paraphrase, "Sunnes, that set, may rise againe: / But if once we loose this light, / 'Tis, with us, perpetuall night").[64] Though Waller does not use the specific metaphor of day and night, his opening lines, like "Vivamus, mea Lesbia" and Marvell's "To his Coy Mistress," depend upon the contrast of the fact of time fleeting and the hope of time suspended.

Not only are beauty and youth perishable, but love is equally fleeting. With line 7, the direction of the argument shifts, and so does the tone. Here Waller is drawing not on Catullus but on Lucretius and on the principle of universal mutation. Change is the only certainty in the universe, governing both gods and men. The ultimate source of this *topos* is Lucretius, but we find it as well in many Renaissance authors—for example, Donne:

> The heavens rejoyce in motion, why should I
> Abjure my so much lov'd variety,
> And not with many youth and love divide?[65]

The argument in Donne's "Variety" and other libertine poems of its kind is partial and sophistical; the principle of change is urged in support of a particular form of behavior, in support of human fickleness. So it is in Waller.

One classical precedent for the combination of the two

---

64. Catullus, V.4–6, in F. W. Cornish, ed., *Catullus, Tibullus, and Pervisilium Veneris*, Loeb Classical Library (London and New York, 1914); "To Celia," 6–8, in C. H. Herford, Percy and Evelyn Simpson, eds., *Ben Jonson* (11 vols. Oxford, 1925–52), *8*. Propertius' version of the topos *(Elegies*, II.xv.23–24) is equally memorable: "dum nos fata sinunt, oculos satiemus amore: / nox tibi longa venit, nec reditura dies" (while the Fates grant it, let us glut our eyes with love: the long night hasteneth on for thee who knows no dawning)—*The Elegies of Propertius*, tr. H. E. Butler, Loeb Classical Library (London and New York, 1929).

65. "Variety," 1–3. Donne treats similar ideas in "A Defense of Woman's Inconstancy" *(Paradoxes and Problems)*, in the elegy "Change," and in such lyrics as "The Indifferent" and "Goe, and catch a falling starre." In similar terms Spenser's titaness Mutability claims sway over the universe: "Proud Change (not pleased, in mortall things, / beneath the Moone, to raigne) / Pretends, as well of Gods, as Men, / to be the Soueraine" (Argument to Bk. VII, Canto VI, *The Faerie Queene*, in Edwin Greenlaw et al., eds., *The Works of Edmund Spenser* [9 vols. Baltimore, 1932–49]).

themes, mortality and fickleness, is an elegy of Tibullus. The gods, themselves subject to time and to mutation, hold lovers' inconstancy to be no sin; the law governing lovers is the knowledge that time is pressing, that a day once lost can never be recaptured.

> nec iurare time: veneris periuria venti
> inrita per terras et freta summa ferunt.
> gratia magni Iovi: vetuit Pater ipse valere,
> iurasset cupide quidquid ineptus amor
>
> . . .
>
> at si tardus eris errabis. Transiit aetas
> quam cito! non sequis stat remeatve dies
>
> . . .
>
> crudeles divi! serpens novus exuit annos:
> formae non ullam fata dedere moram.
> solis aeterna est Baccho Phoeboque iuventas:
> nam decet intonsus crinis utrumque deum.[66]

The Latin poet, unlike Waller, does not work out logical connections between the ideas. The individual statements, each of them within its own couplet, are entirely separate. Declarative verbs state irrefutable facts of nature (time fleeting, vows carried away on the winds), imperatives and conditionals the suggested consequences in behavior (don't be afraid to swear, if you delay you'll be lost).

"To Phyllis," on the other hand, is built around an explicit structure of argument, in the typical manner of seventeenth-century lyric poetry. The first two lines state the theme of the poem directly in a question that implies its

---

66. "Be not afraid to swear. Null and void are the perjuries of love; the winds bear them over land and the face of the sea. Great thanks to Jove! The Sire himself has decreed no oath should stand that love has taken in the folly of desire. . . . But if thou art slow, thou wilt be lost. Youth fleets how quickly! Time stands not idle, nor returns. . . . Cruel gods! The snake sheds his years, and is young: but the Fates grant no respite to beauty. Only Bacchus and Phoebus have youth everlasting; of either god are unshorn tresses the glory" (Tibullus, *Elegies*, I.iv.21–38, tr. J. P. Postgate, in *Catullus, Tibullus, and Pervigilium Veneris*).

own answer: if the condition of life is such that pleasures are "shorter than the day," it is foolish to "delay" in snatching these pleasures. In working out the implications of that initial statement, the poet makes use of syllogistic reasoning. We cannot extend our lives; even if we could, youth and beauty would die while our mere bodies remained alive; even if youth and beauty were to stay, love would fly. The argument continues by analogy: change in love is universal, and what is true of the gods is certainly true of man. The second half of "To Phyllis" moves from general principles to particular cases. If change is a universal principle, the poet argues, it should and does govern love. The argument is a buried syllogism (containing, I might add, the fallacy of equivocation): if the present moment is the only reality, then by definition the past has neither meaning nor effect, nor has the future. Man is the creature of forces far stronger than he, and one should not question fortune's gifts.

In depending upon the appearance of logical argumentation, "To Phyllis" follows the example of a great many poems of its period: "To his Coy Mistress" provides an obvious analogue, as do such poems of Donne as "A Valediction: forbidding Mourning," "The Undertaking," "Communitie," "Loves Infiniteness," "The Dissolution," "The Flea," and "A Lecture upon the Shadow." In all these, as in "To Phyllis," the materials of the poet are, in Tesauro's terms or those of Aristotle's *Rhetoric*, rhetorical enthymemes, intended to convince even though they may not in fact be logical proofs and may even be literally fallacious; their truth is probable and emotional, though it may pretend to be more.[67] The distinguishing characteristic of "To Phyllis" is the cool suavity with which the argument is conducted. Other treatments of the theme are marked by passion, or immediacy, or cynicism, or melancholy, Waller's by a calm unruffled precision of language and argument, a tone of one civilized person talking to another.

---

67. Bethell, pp. 144–45; Aristotle, *Rhetoric*, I.ii; II.xxii–iv.

The three poems to be discussed in the remainder of the chapter, "To a Very Young Lady," "To a Lady in Retirement," and "Go, Lovely Rose," are typical Cavalier lyrics in their directness and in their structure of argument. All of them are short lyrics addressed to a person and toward a particular end; in each, the central metaphors are embodied in a clearly articulated logical structure. Yet in their elegance, lucidity, and symmetry, they resemble Augustan verse. All three poems, typically for Waller, are characterized by a subtle interplay between the particular and the general, between formality and simplicity.

The three poems center on analogies, which bring the truths of nature to bear on the world of man, or, more accurately, on the little world of lovers and courtiers with which Waller's poetry is concerned. Waller's natural metaphors, like most of the materials of his poems, are conventional. There is ample literary precedent, English, continental, and classical, for the likening of a young beauty to a rose, the morning, or the spring, as there is for the comparison of love to a fire, or of a king or mistress to the sun. Waller's poems depend upon a network of shared assumptions, accepted truths, which he deploys toward his persuasive ends. There is, as it were, a double view: each individual faces the transience of life and pleasure as a problem fresh to him, but the allusive, conventional quality of the poems suggests that other people have faced the problem before and that the answers have been satisfactorily worked out. The poet, experienced in the ways of the world, seeks to impart his knowledge to those who have not yet become aware of the applicability of those truths to them. The poem seeks, through wit and persuasion, to bring the general truths to bear upon the particular instance.[68]

"To a Very Young Lady," like several poems of this and the next age, adapts the language of love to a poem in praise of a beautiful child. Waller has several classical precedents

68. I am indebted to Professor David Vieth for several of the points made in this paragraph.

for the central situation of his poem, the older man's address to a young girl. An epigram by Antiphilus in the *Greek Anthology* will indicate the tradition in which Waller is working: "I said even formerly, when Tereina's charms were yet infantile, 'She will consume us all when she grows up.' They laughed at my prophecy: but lo! the time I once fore-told is come, and ... I suffer myself from the wound. What am I to do?" Anacreon has several poems on the general theme, including one arguing that love between an old man and a young girl is not unnatural:

> Though my aged head be gray
> And thy youth more fresh then May,
> Fly me not; oh rather see
> In this wreath how gracefullie
> Roses with pale Lillies joyne:
> Learn of them, so let us twine.

In these two poems we see two separate aspects of the theme which Waller will combine in his poem: in the first, the idea of time's inevitable ripening process, the movement from youth to maturity; in the second, the contrast of youth and age. Two poems of Horace also supply material to Waller and other later poets who treat the topic—*Odes,* IV.i, where he complains that he is too old for love to bother him once more, and *Odes,* II.v, which deals with a girl too young as yet to love, whom time will eventually bring around:

> tolle cupidinem
> immitis uvae. iam tibi lividos
> distinguet autumnus racemos
> purpereo varius colore.
>
> iam te sequetur (currit enim ferox
> aetas, et illi, quos tibi dempserit,
> apponet annos), iam proterva
> fronte petet Lalage maritum.

(Away with desire for the unripe grape! Soon for thee shall many-coloured Autumn paint the darkening clusters purple. Soon shall she follow thee. For Time courses madly on, and shall add to her the years it takes from thee. Soon with eager forwardness shall Lalage herself make quest of thee to be her mate).[69]

In each of these poems, the relationship between older man and young girl is explicitly sexual. All four view man as largely determined by powerful natural forces within and around him. The anti-idealizing tendency in these poems is most pronounced in a two-line epigram in the *Greek Anthology:* "When you were a green grape you refused me, when you were ripe you bade me be off, at least grudge me not a little of your raisin" (V.304). Renaissance treatments of the theme sometimes share this tone of realism or even cynicism; Marvell's "Young Love" is an example. But more often than not, English poets reinterpret the tradition to desexualize the relationship, placing greater emphasis on praise and on admonition and eliminating the idea of seduction. Marvell's "The Picture of Little T. C. in a Prospect of Flowers" and Matthew Prior's charming "To a Child of Quality" both are addressed to children, while Waller's poem is directed at a girl on the borderline between childhood and adulthood. Love in all three poems is entirely innocent.

The primary difference between "To a Very Young Lady" and the two closely related poems by Marvell and Prior is one of tone. Waller limits the seriousness of his poem; his tone of elegant gallantry and the poem's burden of direct praise lead him on the whole to leave out the less pleasing aspects of the idea of time. For Marvell, time may bring conquests, but it also brings death and uncertainty; Prior wryly thinks of his own aging and of the undignified helplessness of the human condition. One poet ends his poem

69. *Greek Anthology*, V.111, tr. W. R. Paton, Loeb Classical Library (London and New York, 1916); *Anacreontea*, XXXIV, tr. Thomas Stanley, in Crump, *Poems and Translations of Thomas Stanley;* Horace, *Odes*, II.v.9–16, tr. C. E. Bennett, Loeb Classical Library (London and New York, 1918).

with the thought of sudden and early death, the other with a picture, both witty and touching, of eternal frustration:

> For as our diff'rent ages move,
>   'Tis so ordain'd, wou'd fate but mend it,
> That I shall be past making love
>   When she begins to comprehend it.[70]

In their ways, Marvell and Prior are as realistic as the Greek or Latin treatments of the theme. For Waller, on the other hand, the year stops after spring and summer; the truths he considers are just those useful to the occasion, appropriate for praise.

In the first stanza, the poet laments having been born out of his time, so far removed in years from the young beauty he is celebrating.

> Why came I so untimely forth
> Into a world which, wanting thee,
> Could entertain us with no worth
> Or shadow of felicity,
> That time should me so far remove
> From that which I was born to love?   (1–6)

The stanza's dignified movement is partly a function of its formal, abstract diction ("untimely," "entertain," "worth," "felicity"), but it is primarily a matter of syntax. The sense is drawn out within the individual line and over the stanza. "Untimely," the key word in the first line, is set off by the word order, with its multiple inversions, and anticipates the key word in the stanza, "time." Similarly, "wanting thee" receives special emphasis by its placement in the line and its suspension of the meaning of the sentence. Time in this stanza is primarily a principle of frustration and separation.

So far Waller has worked mostly with abstractions. In the

---

70. "To a Child of Quality, Five Years Old," 25–28, in Matthew Prior, *Dialogues of the Dead and Other Works*, ed. A. R. Waller (Cambridge, Eng., 1907).

second stanza, he praises young Lady Lucy Sidney through natural analogies.

> Yet, fairest blossom! do not slight
> That age which you may know so soon;
> The rosy morn resigns her light,
> And milder glory, to the noon;
> And then what wonders shall you do,
> Whose dawning beauty warms us so?   (7–12)

The advice of the first two lines and the lesson conveyed by the natural analogies are complementary; indeed, the phrase "fairest blossom," with its connotations of growth and ripening, anticipates the metaphor of the unfolding day. The metaphor is applied directly to the girl in the phrase "dawning beauty," and in the speculation on what her noonday will be like.

The last stanza continues the use of natural analogies.

> Hope waits upon the flowery prime;
> And summer, though it be less gay,
> Yet is not looked on as a time
> Of declination or decay;
> For with a full hand that does bring
> All that was promised by the spring.   (13–18)

The stanza provides a final answer to the girl's fears: time brings summer out of spring, fulfills all promise. In the first four lines of the stanza, the language recognizes that the young girl may not want to grow any older than she is and hints very lightly at the less desirable aspects of time. Summer is "less gay" than spring, maturity than youth; decay may be a fact, but it is not one the girl has to worry about now. The concluding couplet carries the argument to its final step, going beyond the earlier qualifications and balancings to a clear affirmation. Once again the natural analogy is developed in terms that praise young Lady Lucy while they state a general truth.

The poem's structure is carefully worked out. The first

stanza raises a question, lamenting the fact of time; the second introduces a different perspective upon time's power; and the third reaches a triumphant conclusion. To put it another way, the poem moves from the primarily negative and abstract language of stanza one ("so untimely," "wanting thee," "no worth," "shadow," "so far remove"), through the second stanza's balance of negative and positive terms, taking into account the girl's worries about the actions of time ("slight," "resigns," "that age which you may know so soon") while trying to counteract them ("fairest blossom," "rosy morn," "glory," "wonders," "dawning beauty," "warms"), to conclude with the assurances of the last stanza.

"To a Lady in Retirement" again uses natural analogies to point a lesson, showing the coy lady of the title the error of her ways.[71] The association of flowers with transiency is ubiquitous in classical and Renaissance poetry, as is the use of the topos to point a carpe diem moral. H. M. Richmond, in *The School of Love,* compares Waller's poem and Herrick's "To the Virgins, to Make Much of Time" in some detail with such predecessors as Ausonius' "De Rosis Nascentibus" and Ronsard's ode "A sa Maitresse" ("Mignonne, allons voir si la rose . . .").[72] I have nothing to add to Mr. Richmond's excellent discussion, except to remark that Waller's approach is once again characteristic. In his poem, there is none of the sense of death and decay at the heart of Marvell's "To his Coy Mistress," nor is there anything like the appeal to passion at the end of Marvell's poem. Nor does "To a Lady in Retirement" show the piercing consciousness of the fragility and beauty of perishable things we often find in Herrick. In Waller's poem all is subordi-

71. The title of the poem in the 1664 edition, the first after the Restoration, is "To a Lady in a Garden," and this is the title adopted by Thorn-Drury. But the title of the earliest editions (1645) and Fenton, "To a Lady in Retirement," with its emphasis on the lady's character rather than her physical surroundings, seems to me to describe the poem more accurately.

72. *The School of Love,* pp. 59–65; see also Richmond's article, "The Fate of Edmund Waller," *South Atlantic Quarterly, 40* (1961), 230–38.

nated to persuasive effectiveness: beauty, mutability, and passion are facts that have their place in the argument, and nothing more.

The diction throughout the poem is a combination of formality and ease, of the abstract and the concrete.

> Sees not my love how time resumes
> The glory which he lent these flowers?
> Though none should taste of their perfumes
> Yet must they live but some few hours;
> Time what we forbear devours! (1–5)

Latinate words like "resumes" (used in its literal sense, *re-sumere*, "take back") and "forbear" help give the lines a marmoreal finish and remoteness, while short, direct verbs of action ("sees," "lent," "taste," "must . . . live") bring us down to earth. A word like "devours" combines the two qualities: it is Latinate in form, strong and direct in meaning.

Each stanza follows the same pattern: even if A, yet B. Whatever we may wish, time will have its way. Suavely Waller dismantles any objections the lady may raise.

> Had Helen, or the Egyptian Queen,
> Been ne'er so thrifty of their graces,
> Those beauties must of length have been
> The spoil of age, which finds out faces
> In the most retired places. (6–10)

The opposing terms in the second stanza do not clash but qualify one another. Beauty is normally not doled out a piece at a time; the term "thrifty" limits the romantic and complimentary connotations in "graces" and in the names of Helen and Cleopatra (both of whom, indeed, were famous not for thrift, but for prodigality). The understatement of the last line conveys the sense of inevitability, the impossibility of escaping time, more fully than anything else in the stanza, at the same time that it comments both on the lady's sense of dignity and on her affectation of retirement.

The third stanza shows the same careful control over diction, syntax, and stanza movement.

> Should some malignant planet bring
> A barren drought, or ceaseless shower,
> Upon the autumn or the spring,
> And spare us neither fruit nor flower;
> Winter would not stay an hour.   (11–15)

The facts of nature are inescapable; whatever the earlier seasons were like, winter is sure to come. After the exhaustive catalog of patterned desolation in lines 12–14, the bare finality of the last line seems all the more emphatic.

In the final stanza, the general truths about time, beauty, and retirement are applied specifically, not merely inferentially, to the lady. Yet the language, even more than before, is formal and distant.

> Could the resolve of love's neglect
> Preserve you from the violation
> Of coming years, then more respect
> Were due to so divine a fashion,
> Nor would I indulge my passion.   (16–20)

Nearly all the major terms are Latinate: "resolve," "neglect," "preserve," "violation," "respect," "divine," "fashion," "indulge," "passion." More than this, nearly all the nouns are potential verbs. "The resolve of love's neglect" is less forceful and far less colloquial than "I swore never to love anyone," but it is much more elegant and has the compression of wit; one could say virtually the same thing about "violation," "respect," "fashion," and "passion," and their possible verb alternatives. "To a Lady in Retirement" is a singularly unpassionate love poem; the restraint and formality of its language are appropriate to the retired lady to whom it is addressed. The language, in this stanza and throughout the poem, may be said to reflect or define the lady's attitude, while at the same time the poem's argument is busy undermining her position. Marvell uses a similar

device in the first paragraph of "To his Coy Mistress," as
he presents through a series of spacious conceits a parody
version of the kind of world the lady would like to have.[73]
One index to the superiority of Marvell's poem over Waller's is that one poet's starting point is the other's conclusion:
Marvell uses the lady's terms only to refute them, where
Waller gracefully tailors his argument to fit the preferences
of his audience. Waller may be more tactful (and indeed
here as elsewhere control and limitation are the keys to his
success), but Marvell has created a great poem, Waller only
a good one.

Waller's most famous poem, "Go, Lovely Rose," preaches
a similar message to another lady in retirement. I quote the
poem in full.

> Go, lovely Rose!
> Tell her that wastes her time and me
> That now she knows,
> When I resemble her to thee,
> How sweet and fair she seems to be.
>
> Tell her that's young,
> And shuns to have her graces spied,
> That hadst thou sprung
> In deserts, where no men abide,
> Thou must have uncommended died.
>
> Small is the worth
> Of beauty from the light retired;
> Bid her come forth,
> Suffer herself to be desired,
> And not blush so to be admired.

73. We need not assume any direct influence in either direction. The
probable date of "To a Lady in Retirement" is the mid-1630s, while Marvell
(born in 1621) probably wrote the bulk of his lyrics in the late 1640s and
early 1650s. H. M. Richmond considers Marvell's possible indebtedness to
Waller in *The School of Love*, p. 64, and "The Fate of Edmund Waller,"
pp. 235–36.

> Then die! that she
> The common fate of all things rare
> May read in thee;
> How small a part of time they share
> That are so wondrous sweet and fair!

The poem's argument is extremely clear; the central conceit is not a complex one, and it is presented with a charming ingenuousness. The poem's quality of poise and restraint comes in part from its origin in a social gesture, the lover's gift of a flower. The fiction of addressing the insentient rose rather than the lady enables the poet to be both pointed and indirect. In a sense, he takes dead aim on his object, directing his arguments against the lady's coyness. Yet by using the rose as intermediary, he maintains a certain distance. Again Waller is writing in a familiar classical tradition. Martial's "I, felix rosa" *(Epigrams,* VII.lxxxix) is similarly a love poem addressed to a woman through a flower, and so is Herrick's imitation, "To the Rose" ("Goe happy Rose, and enterwove / With other Flowers, bind my Love, / Tell her too she must not be, / Longer flowing, longer free . . ."). Neither of these poems combines the rose motif with a carpe diem theme, as Waller does, but here, too, Waller has numerous classical precedents. One of many is Rufinus' epigram in the *Greek Anthology:*

> I send thee this garland, Rhodoclea, that with my own hands I wove out of beautiful flowers. There are lilies and roses and dewy anemones, and tender narcissus and purple-gleaming violets. Wear it and cease to be vain. Both thou and the garland flower and fade. (V.74)

Waller is aware that logic alone will not convince a lady; throughout the poem he seasons his advice with praise. The first stanza, in spite of its note of criticism in the second line, is primarily devoted to praise of the lady's loveliness. In the two middle stanzas the parallel with the rose is less purely complimentary, yet the poet continues to praise her youth and graces, even while he reprimands her for keeping them hidden. The last stanza, characteristically, ends not with the fact of mortality, but with the loveliness, now shown to be more lovely in its perishability, with which the poem began. The words echo the first stanza: "so wondrous sweet and fair."

"Go, Lovely Rose" is built upon a series of key terms, repeated with subtle variations in meaning: not only "sweet and fair" (the definition of the lady and key to her fate), but "die," "small," and "time." Waller's wit does not call attention to itself, but his "turns" help provide structural backbone: the general fact of death (conditional—"Thou must have uncommended died") is brought home by the particular death (imperative—"Then die!"), time as a succession of moments ("wastes her time") is brought into juxtaposition with time as eternity ("how small a part of time"). Waller uses his witty devices sparingly, and this makes them all the more effective. Thus the inversions slow down the movement of the lines and cause individual words to stand out ("uncommended," "small," "rare"), while the compressed syntax in some of the short lines (especially lines 3, 6, and 8) help make the lines seem both simple and remote, crisp and suggestive. Line 3, for example, uses only the simplest words, but the dislocation of syntax, the ellipsis, causes the reader to slow down and look at the words more carefully than he otherwise might. The occasional Latinate words fit in with the dignified movement of the lines and are placed for maximum effect. There are various neoclassical tricks of style at work in the lines: for example, the use of zeugma in line 2 ("wastes her time and me," with the pun on the two meanings of "waste," squander and consume), or the interplay of balanced and contrasted terms throughout the third stanza. Line 17 balances its antithetical elements as in a mirror, using the device of chiasmus, and the witty contrast of "common" and "rare," two terms with double meanings ("common" meaning ordinary and universal, "rare" meaning unusual and valuable), makes the line more suggestive and moving.

F. W. Bateson has argued that there are in fact "two Wallers—a minor Renaissance poet and a major Augustan poet."[74] The point requires some restatement, assuming as it does that the Renaissance and Augustan characteristics are entirely separable and that one is to be applauded and the other condemned. But Bateson's remark reflects a central truth. What distinguishes Waller from other minor mid-seventeenth-century poets is his anticipation of the neo-classical aesthetic, his foreshadowing of a new age while he reflects the old.

Most critics, if they deal with Waller at all, treat his work as evidence of a sad decline or simply profess amazement that such a poet could ever have been popular. But to treat Waller as an oddity, a curious; inexplicable phenomenon like Isaac Watts or Mrs. Hemans, or as an example of degenerating literary standards, seems to me both to falsify literary history and to fail to do justice to the writer. The myth of the dissociation of sensibility, a lesser version of the myth of the fall of man or the golden age, reflects a reality more psychological than literal: its point of departure is a sense of loss, a feeling that things must have been better once. If, the argument goes, we could only get back to the prelapsarian days of Shakespeare and Donne (or the early middle ages, or the agrarian economy, or the literal belief in the Eucharist, or healthy paganism—the number of versions is limitless), then we could find out where we took the wrong turn and avoid making the mistake a second time. But the course of literary history is not a straight one, and in an objective sense there are no wrong turnings. Each age and each major writer reinterprets the previous age and the entire course of relevant literary history, rejecting certain practices and adopting others. As readers or writers we may

74. *English Poetry*, p. 117.

prefer the aesthetic of Wordsworth or Eliot or William Carlos Williams or Dryden, or we may make up one of our own, but in all cases we choose from the past what is significant to us and reinterpret it and value it according to our own needs and interests. Waller's particular significance is that, as the author singled out from the "former age" by the Augustans as precursor, he shows both the continuity of seventeenth-century wit and its redefinition to fit new aesthetic standards.

If we see Waller solely in the light of his relationship to the past, he is likely to appear a sadly shrunken figure. We prefer Donne, and with good reason. To J. B. Broadbent, Waller, Cowley, and the Cavalier and Restoration poets in general are all "decadent": "Decadence in art is a blurring of the original vision, a smoothing of the uncomfortable knobbliness of genius, so as to make it viable to a wider audience who already have some second-hand idea of what the original was like and now need never have more than that."[75] In some ways this argument is unanswerable. Yet like all versions of the dissociation of sensibility, it is exclusive and backward-looking, committed to the belief in a single true vision which has somehow been lost. Dryden viewed the literary history of the seventeenth century in a very different way. Although in his remarks on Shakespeare, Donne, Oldham, and many other writers, he pays tribute to the "knobbliness of genius," Dryden is committed to an ideal of creative imitation. A poet can learn from other poets; he can and should choose from the writers of previous ages what appears to him viable and reject what is less useful. To Dryden, Donne was "the greatest Wit, though not the best Poet of our Nation."

> Would not Donne's *Satires*, which abound with so much wit, appear more charming, if he had taken care of his words, and of his numbers? . . . And I may safely

75. *Poetic Love* (London, Chatto and Windus, 1964), pp. 243–44.

say it of this present age, that if we are not so great wits as Donne, yet certainly we are better poets.[76]

It is through Waller that the wit of Donne is accommodated to the developing neoclassical ideal with its emphasis upon order, clarity, and harmony. The very limitations of scope and ambition that make Waller a less exciting poet than Donne are the qualities that make him particularly useful to Dryden, and they are the preconditions of his art.

Even those critics who recognize Waller's historical importance as a precursor of Augustanism are likely to speak only of what he does not do. Alexander Ward Allison's *Toward an Augustan Poetic,* though full of careful analysis of the technique of Waller's verse, is essentially negative in its judgments, especially when comparing the poet with his predecessors or contemporaries:

> His poems are not so much sequences of thought as aggregations of pleasantries. . . . He is more interested in an agreeable modulation of sentiments than in the logical texture of his verse. . . . He was blander than most of his contemporaries, and less earnest. . . . Ethical discriminations, being at least potentially invidious, were not allowed to disturb the even tenor of his praise.[77]

To Robert L. Sharp, Waller brought to poetry "regularity and common sense," a "saner imagination" to suit "the reader weary of bombast, complexity and wit." His verse is "not entirely free of conceits," but conceits are "so toned down . . . as to be inconspicuous and unmetaphysical." By his conscious avoidance of metaphysical "extravagance, harshness, and obscurity," Sharp claims, he helped bring about "a technical reformation in English poetry."[78]

76. Ker, *Essays of Dryden,* 2, 102; Kinsley, *Poems of Dryden,* 2, 583.

77. Pp. 13–15. The portions of Allison's book which deal with Waller's language and versification are excellent, and I have relied on them heavily in chap. 5.

78. *From Donne to Dryden* (Chapel Hill, University of North Carolina Press, 1940), pp. 111–12.

To these critics, Waller is a poet of trivial subject matter and simple, unmetaphorical style. Given their descriptions, one can see why Waller has had so few defenders; he appears to violate two primary modern prerequisites for poetic merit, seriousness (in subject matter and in approach) and complexity. Yet the character of his poetry is due neither to an inability to write like his predecessors nor to a conscious abandonment of their poetic techniques. Waller, admittedly, is a lesser figure than the poets he learned from or those who learned from him. Standing between Donne and Dryden, he has neither the brilliance and passion of one nor the authority of the other. But his lyrics have a special quality of their own; though his subjects are slight, and deliberately so, in the very pose he adopts, combining worldliness, tolerance, and gallantry, there is both strength and charm. His ease is the result of a great deal of care; he paints his miniatures with great delicacy. His is an art which depends upon the prior limitation of materials, upon the cultivation of an illusory transparency.

In the quality of grace, social and aesthetic, that marks Waller's verse, he resembles other Cavalier poets. He seeks to write an efficient and economical verse, working through surprising and yet inevitable juxtapositions, parallels, and contrasts. The element of surprise in Waller is subordinate to the element of inevitability; unlike many of his predecessors, he prefers the explicitness of simile to the sudden thrust and chooses metaphors where the terms dovetail easily, rather than those where the gap between tenor and vehicle is a wide one. His conceits tend to be drawn from conventional literary sources, rather than from science or metaphysics; their art lies in the precision with which they are developed and applied, rather than in suggestiveness or originality. Metaphor works together with generalization; even in his lyrics, Waller is a poet of aphorisms and sententiae, in whom the specific is always threatening to become the general. In his later verse, the generalizations become dominant. Yet even in this "poetry of statement," as in most good Augustan verse, there is a metaphorical richness and complexity below the surface.[79]

79. The term "poetry of statement" was used by Mark Van Doren in *John Dryden, A Study of his Poetry* (3d ed. New York, Holt, Rinehart and Winston, 1946), and redefined by Maynard Mack in " 'Wit and Poetry and Pope.' "

3 Heroic Praise

It can be argued that Waller's most significant poems are not his lyrics, but the panegyrics to which he devoted most of his attention in the later part of his career. Roughly half of the collected edition of his poems (130 out of 272 pages of text) is taken up by formal occasional poems, written for the most part in commemoration of state events, and usually composed in heroic couplets. There is very little panegyric written today, and what little exists is not taken seriously. But in the seventeenth and eighteenth centuries, a different view of poetry prevailed. Jonson's poetry is largely occasional in nature, as is much of Donne's. Dryden and Addison both came into prominence as writers of formal state panegyric. In the political controversies of the seventeenth and eighteenth centuries, poetry played an important role in rallying forces; Cavaliers and Roundheads, Whigs and Tories had their poets.

In the years following the Restoration, Waller was commonly recognized as the king of panegyrists. His metier, Dryden and Sir William Soame write in their translation of Boileau's *L'art poétique,* was to "extol . . . a Hero's mighty Acts." The Earl of Rochester describes him in similar terms:

> *Waller,* by Nature, for the Bays design'd,
> With force, and fire, and fancy unconfin'd
> In *Panegyricks,* does excell *Mankind.*
> He best can turn, enforce, and soften things,
> To praise great *Conquerors,* or to flatter *Kings.*[1]

1. *The Art of Poetry . . . Made English,* I.17, in Kinsley, *Poems of Dryden;* "An Allusion to Horace: The 10th Satyr of the 1st Book," 54–58, in Vivian de Sola Pinto, ed., *Poems by John Wilmot, Earl of Rochester* (London, 1953).

The conventional accounts of Waller during his life and in the years shortly after normally speak of him as excelling in two kinds of poetry: the soft, melting phrases of love and the "nobler Panegyrick Strain." "No satyr lurks within this hallow'd ground, / But nymphs and heroines, kings and gods abound; / Glory, and arms, and love, is all the sound."[2] There were panegyrists before him, but, as the Augustans saw it, Waller was Virgil to the other poets' Ennius. He brought to the form a high gloss, a classical elevation and distancing, and a single-minded consistency in approach, for which he may be said to have made it anew.

Panegyric, elaborate praise of heroes, statesmen, or men of wealth and power, has always been a staple of literature.[3] Classical and Renaissance literary theorists, speculating upon the origins of poetry, have frequently suggested that hymns and encomia were the first poems. According to Aristotle, early poetry, beginning with simple improvisation, "soon broke up into two kinds according to the differences of character in the individual poets; for the graver among them would represent nobler actions, and those of noble personages; and the meaner sort the actions of the ignoble. The latter class produced invectives at first, just as others did hymns and panegyrics."[4] Puttenham's *Arte of English Poesie* gives the praise of God and of noble men as the first two subjects (in value, if not in time) for poetry: "But the chief and principall [matter or subject of Poesie] is: the laud honour and glory of the immortal gods. . . . Secondly the worthy gests of noble Princes: the memoriall and

2. George Granville, Lord Lansdowne, "To the Immortal Memory of Mr. Edmund Waller, upon his Death," in Robert Anderson, ed., *A Complete Edition of the Poets of Great Britain* (London, 1793–1807), 7, 697. Similar terms recur throughout the memorial volume, *Poems to the Memory of that Incomparable Poet Edmond Waller Esquire* (London, 1688).

3. Two recent works are extremely helpful on the history and importance of panegyric, especially in the Renaissance and seventeenth century: Hardison, *The Enduring Monument,* and Nevo, *The Dial of Virtue.*

4. *Poetics,* 4, tr. Ingram Bywater, in *The Works of Aristotle,* ed. W. D. Ross (12 vols. Oxford, 1910–52), *11,* 1448b.

registry of all great fortunes, the praise of vertue and re-
proofe of vice."[5]

In classical rhetoric, the epideictic or panegyrical is, along
with the deliberative and judicial, one of the three classes of
oratory.[6] There is a great deal of panegyrical oratory in
Greek and Latin—in the works, for example, of Isocrates,
Gorgias, Cicero, and Pliny the Younger. Panegyric is equally
common in classical poetry. Pindar's work is largely panegyrical, while Virgil, Horace, and Ovid, indebted as they
were to imperial patronage, wrote poetry that is full of
praise, direct and indirect. In the decadent literature of the
third and fourth centuries, both poetry and oratory had
become primarily instruments of panegyric in the works of
Claudian and the Gallic orators represented in *XII Panegyrici Latini*.[7]

Panegyric flourishes under a system of patronage of the
arts. Fifteenth-century Italy, John Addington Symonds
tells us, teemed with "eulogies of petty patrons transformed
into Maecenases, of carpet knights compared to Leonidas,
of tyrants equalled with Augustus, of generals who had
never looked on bloodshed tricked out as Hannibals and
Scipios."[8] Louis XIV of France was possibly the most

5. George Puttenham, *The Arte of English Poesie* (1589), ed. Edward
Arber (London, 1895), p. 39. Puttenham argues that satire, comedy, and
tragedy, in all of which "the evill and outrageous behaviours of Princes"
and common men "were reprehended," came into being after hymn and
before panegyric (pp. 45–51). With Puttenham, as with Aristotle, the poetry
of praise and the poetry of blame grew up together.

6. Aristotle formulated the threefold division of oratory in *Rhetoric*,
I.3, and he was followed by Quintilian, Cicero, and many other rhetoricians.
See Theodore Burgess, *Epideictic Literature*, University of Chicago Studies
in Classical Philology, 3 (Chicago, 1902), 91–97.

7. Examples of the elaborate epideictic oratory popular in the third
and fourth centuries have been preserved; see *XII Panegyrici Latini*, ed.
R. A. B. Mynors (Oxford, 1964). There is an excellent discussion of the
panegyrical poetry and oratory that flourished in late antiquity and the
middle ages in E. R. Curtius, *European Literature and the Latin Middle
Ages*, tr. Willard R. Trask (New York, 1953), pp. 154–66, 174–82.

8. *Renaissance in Italy*, (7 vols. London, 1875–87), 2, 512.

copiously celebrated king in history; patriotic sentiment
provides a partial explanation, but the likelihood that well-
turned praise would be rewarded spurred the poets more.
Elizabethan literature abounds with praise of the Queen,
straightforward or in one or another mythical or allegorical
guise, in poems of all kinds, masques, and broadside
ballads.[9] Many of Elizabeth's panegyrists wrote in hope of
patronage. Yet, as the example of Spenser would indicate,
the poet's vision was not always limited to court concerns,
fixed on "who's in, who's out," reward and punishment. In
the course of the seventeenth century, the court world grew
more and more isolated, and panegyric became more and
more openly party verse.[10] Under Charles II and his successors, party allegiances to a large extent determined the
course of a poet's career, and poetry was used extensively
as a political instrument.

A comparison between Waller and representative panegyrists of the preceding two generations can be illuminating
—not least for the capsule literary history it provides. Early
Renaissance panegyric tends to be an idealizing poetry,
highly ornate in its language, full of Ovidian decorative
mythology turned to the praise of the ruler. William
Drummond's *Forth Feasting: A Panegyricke to the Kings
most excellent Majesty* (1617), not very distant from the
earliest poems of Waller in time, is aeons removed in its
essential nature. Like many of Drummond's poems, *Forth
Feasting* is indebted to models of the French and Italian
Renaissance; here he draws heavily on Ronsard and
Marino.[11] The author proceeds by piling up details, by

9. Elkin Calhoun Wilson, *England's Eliza* (Cambridge, Harvard University Press, 1939), is a thorough survey of the literature in praise of
Elizabeth.

10. See Nevo, *The Dial of Virtue*, pp. 24-25, 138-63, 264-65; and C. V.
Wedgwood, *Poetry and Politics under the Stuarts* (Cambridge, Cambridge
University Press, 1960), pp. 44-70, 207-08. See also John Loftis, *The Politics
of Drama in Augustan England* (Oxford, 1963), pp. 1-34.

11. *The Poetical Works of William Drummond of Hawthornden*, ed. L. E.
Kastner (2 vols. Edinburgh, 1913), *I*, 242. The title and the central fiction of

musical repetition and embellishment, the free play of
fancy. His ideal is the Elizabethan one of copiousness, and
he strews mythological compliments over the page with
abandon:

> Let Heavens weepe Rubies in a crimsin Showre,
> Such as on *Indies* Shore they use to powre:
> Or with that golden Storme the Fields adorne,
> Which *Jove* rain'd, when his *Blew-eyed Maide* was borne.
>
> (35–38)

In twenty-six lines, Drummond manages to work in eleven
figures from classical mythology ("Each circling Flood to
Thetis tribute payes, / Men heere (in Health) out-live old
Nestors dayes") and seven citations from exotic geography,
along with a full complement of hawks, hounds, hares, harts,
reeds, lilies, incense, and altars. (357–92).

Forth Feasting, unlike the state poems of Waller and the
Augustans, is remote from the concerns of practical politics.
It does not provide along with its praise a point-by-point
commentary upon a particular situation. The first 116 lines
of the poem say only that James has been away and has
returned; the interest lies not in the prose kernel, but in the
embellishments. In the central part of the poem, we are
given a highly stylized account of James I as an ideal prince,
conforming very closely to the topoi for poems on great men
listed in the Renaissance rhetorical treatises.[12] After a
manner thoroughly conventional in Renaissance poetry,
English and continental, the poem surveys the prince's
birth, his youth (the account of James as youthful hunter
and lover of knowledge is largely translated from Ronsard),

---

the poem (in which the poet feigns to speak in the voice of the river Forth,
celebrating James I's return to the land of his birth) are imitated from
Marino's congratulatory poem *Tebro Festante.*

12. For a good brief account of such conventions, see A. L. Bennett, "The
Principal Rhetorical Conventions in the Renaissance Personal Elegy,"
Studies in Philology, 51 (1954), 107–26, esp. 110–14; see also Curtius, *European Literature and the Latin Middle Ages,* pp. 174–79; and Burgess, *Epideictic Literature,* pp. 122–27.

his maturity, with its great deeds, and his future greatness. In the latter part of the poem, the praise is more narrowly applicable to James' circumstances. The King's peace policy is praised, and the King is urged to make his visits annual. Yet even here the ideas are treated fancifully, used primarily as occasions for graceful, witty, metaphorical elaboration: "Now, where the wounded Knight his Life did bleed, / The wanton Swaine sits piping on a Reed" (219–20).

The work of Ben Jonson had a more direct influence on Waller than did Drummond or continental Renaissance panegyric. Waller did not know Jonson personally,[13] though he contributed verses to the memorial volume *Jonsonus Virbius.* But in his occasional poetry as in his lyrics, he is a "son of Ben." Waller's poetry, like Jonson's, is characterized by classicism and restraint; both poets are highly conscious of writing in a tradition, and both believe strongly in economy. Waller follows the Cavalier poets in general in giving poetry a social context, and Jonson in particular in making it essentially public.

Jonson's belief in the Horatian virtues of clarity and regularity, the ideal of craftsmanship in verse, is amply testified to in the critical comments recorded in the *Discoveries* and *Conversations.*[14] He imitates classical models and prefers classical forms. Yet his own style is far rougher than that of his Cavalier or Augustan successors. His first collection of poems, the *Epigrammes,* is in many ways typical of all his verse; he is concerned above all with brevity, with masculine force and pungency, with packing the maximum of meaning into a small space. He is predominantly a poet of "strong lines" and often sacrifices smoothness and clarity for concision.

13. See Aubrey, *Brief Lives,* p. 308.

14. E.g. "That Done for not keeping of accent deserved hanging. That Shaksperr wanted Arte. . . . That Done himself for not being understood would perish" *(Ben Jonson's Conversations with William Drummond of Hawthornden,* in Herford and Simpson, *Ben Jonson, 1,* 132–38). Cf. Jonson's famous characterization of Shakespeare in *Discoveries,* ibid., *8,* 583–84.

If we look at Epigram XXXV, "To King James," we can see Jonson's method in panegyric:

Who would not be thy subject, *James*, t'obay
A prince, that rules by'example, more than sway?
Whose manners draw, more than thy powers constraine.
And in this short time of thy happiest raigne,
Hast purg'd thy realmes, as we have now no cause
Left us of feare, but first our crimes, then lawes.
Like aydes 'gainst treasons who hath found before?
And than in them, how could we know god more?
First thou preserved wert, our king to bee,
And since, the whole land was preserv'd for thee.[15]

The poem is built upon a series of antitheses: the King rules by the example of his character rather than by force, through law rather than fear and coercion. The parallel elements are sometimes balanced within a single line ("Whose *manners draw*, more than thy *powers constraine*"), sometimes over two lines (lines 9–10), sometimes into a phrase, crowded (line 6) or leisurely (line 2). Jonson is careful to vary the placement of the caesura in order to avoid monotony in his handling of the antitheses. But he is not particularly concerned with smoothness or sweetness,[16] and the elliptical, packed quality of the lines makes them far from clear. "Crimes" in line 6 is contrasted with "lawes," yet both are contrasted with earlier causes for fear (arbitrary rule, or no rule, chaos). Lines 7–8, somewhat elliptically, praise James' laws as instruments by which the diseases of

15. In Herford and Simpson, *Ben Jonson, 8.* This poem is singled out as typical of Jonson in its antithetical rhetoric by Felix E. Schelling, "Ben Jonson and the Classical School," *PMLA, 13* (1898), 242–43.

16. See Jonson's scornful comment on poets whose primary concern is smoothness, in the *Discoveries,* ibid., *8, 585.* The synaloepha (T'obey, by'example), the abundance of monosyllables, and the cacaphonies in lines 5–8 are all contrary to the practice of Waller and the Augustans. The best treatment of Jonson's style is Wesley Trimpi, *Ben Jonson's Poems, A Study of the Plain Style* (Stanford, Stanford University Press, 1962).

the commonwealth have been cured[17] and present the King as the representative of the divine order, God's vice-regent. But Jonson's tone is hardly one of easy flattery; we are conscious (by the tone as much as by anything Jonson says) that problems remain.

Jonson writes a bare, sinewy verse; when he writes praise, he does not strive for grandeur or for the soft insinuating phrase. Even in praising, he preserves the character of the plain blunt man who will not flatter, the enemy of cant, the satirist and critic of society. He ends a complimentary epigram to Mary Lady Wroth: "My praise is plaine, and where so ere profest, / Becomes none more then you, who need it least" (Epigram CIII, 13–14). Criticism of the surrounding world outweighs praise of the subject in many of his complimentary epigrams. An epigram, he tells us in Epigram CII, "To William Earle of Pembroke," should be directed "against the bad, but of, and to the good." The good man, in Jonson's view, is "besieg'd with ill," surrounded by "ambition, faction, pride . . . envie," in a society where everything has its price: "They follow vertue, for reward, to day; / To morrow vice, if shee give better pay" (3, 9–10, 14–16). Probably the least crabbed, most elegant of Jonson's panegyric epigrams is the poem addressed to the Countess of Bedford; Jonson is concerned here with presenting an ideal of perfection in woman (or in a patroness):

> I meant the day-starre should not brighter rise,
> Nor lend like influence from his lucent seat.
> I meant shee should be curteous, facile, sweet,
> Hating that solemne vice of greatness, pride.
>
> (Epigram LXXVI, 7–10)

Yet even here the ideal is measured by its opposite. We are not allowed to forget that worldly greatness normally brings pride in its wake and that social position is not normally a guarantee of virtue.

17. Herford and Simpson find in the lines a specific reference to laws enacted at James' request in 1604 and to plots against the King in the two or three previous years. See ibid., *11*, 7.

Jonson may be thought of as the father of the strain of occasional poetry that came to dominate the later seventeenth century, culminating in its greatest practitioner, Dryden.[18] Both men conceive of poetry after the manner of Horace: both are highly civilized poets, whose work is a commentary upon society, fixing praise and blame. Both require an external occasion to set them off. Jonson worked many of the same fields that Dryden was later to cultivate: prologues and epilogues, epistles of various kinds (dedicatory and commendatory poems published at the head of a volume, and discursive Horatian epistles), epitaphs and funeral elegies, state panegyrics. Where Jonson sets forth examples of good and bad in epigrams (and plays), Dryden writes topical satires.

Waller is a central figure in the line that leads from Jonson to Dryden. He serves Dryden as an example in devoting most of his poetic output to occasional verse and in dedicating himself to a classical ideal of style. He does not have the range of either Jonson or Dryden: he writes less, and what he does write shows far less variety in form or ideas. But by cultivating a single variety of occasional poetry, the grand, elaborate, and ceremonious, he makes it his own. Jonson, in his panegyric epigrams, epistles, and masques, is, for all the moral weight he can bring to bear, conscious of working in minor forms. His poems are "Sylvae" (a term used for a collection of small occasional pieces), "Underwoods," a pendant to his dramas. Waller is the first English poet for whom panegyric is the very center of his poetry.

In our own age, few modes of poetry are as unfashionable as panegyric. For all the attention Donne has received in recent years, his *Epicedes and Obsequies* and his *Epithalamions* are generally treated with embarrassed silence. The

18. Schelling's essay, "Ben Jonson and the Classical School," though in some ways dated, is the best available treatment of Jonson as an occasional poet and forerunner of Augustanism. See also Van Doren, *John Dryden*, pp. 107–12.

old line about Augustan satire has passed out of currency; no one nowadays speaks of Pope as a horrible little man ladling out boiling oil or an uninspired artisan of rocking-horse couplets. But panegyric has not shared in the rehabilitation of its sister form, satire; praise, we feel, is suspect, fraudulent, where scorn must be sincere. Thus Robin Skelton characterizes Waller as "a good politician, representative of the 'top people,' " who is "more interested in displaying his craftsmanship and in flattering the influential, than in exploring his perceptions." To C. V. Wedgwood, Waller "spreads flattery like butter; it is the very best butter, but that hardly justifies it." His poems of praise are "altogether too brisk and professional," "art . . . debased to unworthy uses." Dr. Johnson, in a passage quoted earlier, states the case against the panegyrist crushingly: "He that has flattery ready for all whom the vicissitudes of the world happen to exalt must be scorned as a prostituted mind that may retain the glitter of wit, but has lost the dignity of virtue."[19]

The charges against panegyric are insincerity and predictability. To Johnson, any occasional poet is damned before he begins:

> In an occasional performance no height of excellence can be expected from any mind, however fertile, and however stored with acquisitions. . . . The occasional poet is circumscribed by the narrowness of his subject: whatever can happen to man has happened so often that little remains for fancy and invention. We have all been born; we have most of us been married; and so many have died before us that our deaths can supply but few materials for a poet.[20]

Yet an occasion can stimulate a poet's imagination as well as choke it. It can offer a poet something to build on, some-

---

19. Skelton, *Cavalier Poets*, pp. 35–36; Wedgwood, *Poetry and Politics under the Stuarts*, pp. 122, 146, 207; Johnson, *Lives of the Poets, 1*, 271.
20. "Life of Dryden," *Lives of the Poets, 1*, 424.

thing which can give his poetry substance. The panegyrist's job is to turn historical fact into symbol, to do justice to his occasion and yet transcend it, turning the local and particular into the general and universal.[21]

In all of his poems, Waller begins with the raw materials of historical accident. His method, according to his first editor, Elijah Fenton, is to "[illustrate] a plain historical fact with all the graces of poetical fiction."[22] Waller's poem on the death of Oliver Cromwell illustrates the method at its simplest and most direct. A severe storm which coincided with Cromwell's last illness is made to testify to the Protector's greatness:

> We must resign! Heaven his great soul does claim
> In storms, as loud as his immortal fame;
> His dying groans, his last breath, shakes our isle,
> And trees uncut fall for his funeral pile.

The howling of the wind is metamorphosed into Cromwell's "dying groans," the falling of trees into a massive funeral pyre: all things mourn his death. Similarly, in the poem's closing lines, the poet attributes motivation where, in the gray world of fact, none can exist. Nature, "sighing,"

> Swell'd the sea with such a breath,
> That to remotest shores her billows rolled,
> The approaching fate of her great ruler told.[23]

21. Recent books on Dryden place especial emphasis on the relationship between occasion and imagery in Dryden's poems. Arthur Hoffman's remarks on the ways in which the occasional poet can give universal significance and convincing form to "complex sequences and tangles of history" are illuminating—see *John Dryden's Imagery* (Gainesville, University of Florida Press, 1962), pp. 13, 161–63, and passim. See also Alan Roper, *Dryden's Poetic Kingdoms* (London, Routledge and Kegan Paul, 1965), esp. p. 189.

22. Fenton, p. iv.

23. *Upon the Late Storm, and of the Death of His Highness Ensuing the Same,* 1–4, 32–34. Notice how explicitly the title (used in the original broadside publication of the poem) identifies the occasion.

What is especially significant here is not the pathetic fallacy, which after all is conventional in funeral elegies. The storm, the falling trees, the swollen seas are all "plain historical fact," which characteristically have been transmuted into heroic fiction. The death is explicitly the death of a hero; the imagery is as much epic as funereal. The emphasis throughout the poem falls upon his "glory," on the "empire" he brought the nation. Cromwell is likened to Romulus and to Hercules both in his greatness and in the circumstances of his death, just as in other poems the Duke of Monmouth leading an army against Scotland is like Mercury, Jove's messenger, the Duchess of York visiting the fleet is another Thetis and another Venus, and Charles I in rebuilding St. Paul's is a second Solomon.[24] History and literature provide a storehouse of heroes to serve as a constant reminder to the present of what greatness is.

The earlier figures with whom the poet compares or identifies his hero are promiscuously classical and biblical, historical and literary; what matters is not their provenance but their nature. Such comparisons are by no means merely decorative: each serves to illuminate the character and circumstances of Waller's central figure. Past and present are shown as connected, and the same ethical characteristics are shown to apply in modern times as in the heroic ages of the past. Indeed, the identification of new-style and old-style hero (where the two are presented almost as *figura* and fulfillment) suggests kinship to the biblical tradition of typology as well as the neoclassical doctrine of imitation.[25]

To Waller, as later to Dryden, panegyric is one of the

24. "On the Duke of Monmouth's Expedition into Scotland," 1–4; *Instructions to a Painter*, 81–84; "Upon His Majesty's Repairing of Paul's," 43–46.

25. Cf. Erich Auerbach, "Figura," in *Scenes from the Drama of European Literature* (New York, 1959), pp. 11–76. For a good summary of the tradition of figural interpretation, especially as applied to panegyric and related genres, see Joseph A. Mazzeo, "Cromwell as Davidic King," in *Reason and the Imagination: Studies in the History of Ideas 1600–1800* (New York and London, 1962), pp. 29–32.

"branches" of "the epic poesy."[26] Waller is the father (or at least the main popularizer) of a major neoclassical genre: the heroic occasional poem, which attempts to join topical directness and epic dignity. He has ample theoretical sanction for his development of the genre. Epic poetry traditionally contains topical elements, and this aspect of the epic is especially stressed by neoclassical critics. Dryden's remarks on the *Aeneid*, for example, dwell at great length on the poem's practical political usefulness to the newly crowned Augustus, and his own unwritten epic was to have included "many beautiful episodes . . . wherein, after Virgil and Spenser, I would have taken occasion to represent my living friends and patrons of the noblest families."[27] It is a short step from the theory of the specific topical applicability of epic poems to the application of epic devices to other poems. What Waller does (and Dryden after him) is to give his occasional materials the form of a heroic myth, maintaining historical and circumstantial specificity while interpreting his materials in a manner controlled by his heroic imagery. Whether a particular poem is a straightforward panegyric, a funeral elegy, a "prospect" poem, or a narrative "historical" poem (like his two poems on naval battles, *Of a War with Spain, and a Fight at Sea* and *Instructions to a Painter*), all are variants upon his central formula: topical detail treated in an epic manner, with a strong element of praise.

In such poetry, facts exist in order to be interpreted. Aristotle makes it clear in his discussion of epideictic rhetoric that the panegyrist must select, arrange, and display his materials to his subject's advantage:

> We take our hero's actions as admitted facts, and our business is simply to invest these with dignity and nobility. . . . We can always idealize any given man by drawing on the virtues akin to his actual qualities; thus

26. Preface to *Annus Mirabilis*, in Ker, *Essays of Dryden, 1*, 18.
27. Ibid., 2, 38, 168–73.

we may say that the passionate and excitable man is
"outspoken"; or that the arrogant man is "superb" or
"impressive." . . . We must also take into account the
nature of our particular audience while making a
speech of praise. . . . If the audience esteems a given
quality we must say that our hero has that quality, no
matter whether we are addressing Scythians or Spartans
or philosophers. . . . Since we praise a man for what he
has actually done, and fine actions are distinguished
from others by being intentionally good, we must try to
prove that our hero's noble acts are intentional. . . .
Therefore we must assert coincidences and accidents to
have been intended.[28]

One of Waller's earliest poems, addressed to Henrietta
Maria, deals with the rather ignoble maneuvering by which
a French match supplanted a proposed Spanish marriage for
Charles I (then prince). In a "factual" account, especially
one written by an unsympathetic chronicler, Charles, his
father, the Duke of Buckingham (promoter and go-between
in both proposed marriages), and the French and Spanish
princesses would all come out as fools, dupes, or knaves. In
the poem, all is transformed into a heroic romance:

> Like a lion, finding, in his way,
> To some intended spoil, a fairer prey,
> The royal youth pursuing the report
> Of beauty, found it in the Gallic court;
> There public care with private passion fought
> A doubtful combat in his noble thought.[29]

28. *Rhetoric*, I.9, tr. W. Rhys Roberts, in *Works, 11,* 1367a-b, 1368a.
29. "To the Queen, Occasioned upon Sight of Her Majesty's Picture,"
41–46. Epic similes are among Waller's pet heroicizing devices; other noble
lions roar and stalk their prey in "To my Lord of Falkland," 37–40, *Panegyric to my Lord Protector,* 165–68, *Instructions to a Painter,* 23–24, and *Of
a War with Spain, and a Fight at Sea,* 40–42. The final couplet is imitated
from Edward Fairfax's translation of Tasso *(Godfrey of Bulloigne, or the
Recouerie of Ierusalem* [London, 1600], VI.70); see Thorn-Drury, 2, 156.
The conflict between love and honor, the demands of the individual and

In writing *Of a War with Spain, and a Fight at Sea* (1658), Waller was faced with the problem of finding something to say about an uneventful six-month blockade. The British fleet had set forth expecting a battle, but the Spaniards refused to sail out of port; both sides were dissatisfied. But when he translated the facts of the blockade into poetry, Waller made it seem a resounding English victory, through his selection and interpretation of these facts:

> And now some months, encamping on the main,
> Our naval army had beseiged Spain;
> They that the whole world's monarchy designed,
> Are to their ports by our bold fleet confined;
> From whence our Red Cross they triumphant see,
> Riding without a rival on the sea.   (19–24)[30]

If truth for the panegyrist is infinitely flexible in this way, it is only to be expected that he can have his own words turned against him. An unfavorable interpretation of events is as legitimate as a favorable one (as the traditional coupling of panegyric and satire, praise and blame, would indicate). A surprisingly large number of Waller's poems called forth printed or unprinted answer poems; one such is Sir William Godolphin's detailed refutation of the funeral poem on Cromwell, "An Answer to Mr. Waller's Poem on Oliver's Death, called the Storm." Godolphin takes the same facts and gives them an exactly opposite interpretation:

> Winds pluck up Roots and fixed Cedars move,
> Roaring for Vengeance to the Heavens above;
> From Theft, like his, great *Romulus* did grow,
> And such a Wind did at his Ruin blow
>
>   .   .   .

---

those of the state, is of course the central theme of French and English heroic drama.

30. The blockade is described in C. H. Firth, *The Last Years of the Protectorate 1656–1658*, (2 vols. London, 1909), *1*, 46–47.

> Wherever Men, wherever Pillage lies,
> Like ravenous Vultures our wing'd Navy flies
>
> . . .
>
> Nor would Domestick Spoil confine his Mind,
> No Limits to his Fury but Mankind.
>
> . . .
>
> Nature her selfe rejoiced at his Death,
> And on the Waters sung with such a Breath,
> As made the Sea dance higher than before,
> While her glad Waves came dancing to the Shore.[31]

Godolphin's poem may be seen as an attack not only upon Cromwell (and Waller), but upon panegyric itself. He is not arguing that truth is relative, but that *his* truth is right and Waller's is wrong; his refutation is intended to set matters straight, to show things in their proper light. Yet his reinterpretation of historical fact follows Aristotle's precepts for epideictic writing ("eulogy or censure") in the same way Waller's does. The juxtaposition of the two opposite truths suggests that one is as valid as the other.

What all this indicates is that the panegyrist (or satirist) is arguing a case. The test is not objective standards of truth so much as skill—what does the poet do with his materials, how good a case does he make, are his arguments convincing? The poems, if they are any good at all, will not be confined within their circumstances or their role as instruments of persuasion, but these things determine the content and direction of each poem. The occasional nature of the poem

31. *Poems on Affairs of State: From the Time of Oliver Cromwell, to the Abdication of K. James the Second* (5th ed. London, 1703), *1,* 246–47. Godolphin's poem is at all times extremely close to Waller's original; most of the time he simply inverts Waller's imagery to turn it to dispraise, and he even uses many of the same rhymes. At times he extends his parody to Waller's earlier poem on Cromwell, *A Panegyric to my Lord Protector.* The middle four lines above are a parody of *Panegyric,* 33–34: "Fame, swifter than your winged navy, flies / Through every land that near the ocean lies"; and *Upon the Late Storm,* 17–18: "The ocean, which so long our hopes confined, / Could give no limits to his vaster mind."

gives it specificity, while the heroic and artistic qualities—
the existence of the poem as poem and as part of a poetic
tradition—seek to give it universality.

The chief prerequisites for a panegyrist are delicacy and
tact—in choosing his materials, in finding the proper approach, and, hardest of all, in sustaining his poem (which is
likely at any point to soar off into the blue or settle numbly
into the mud). Bloated fustian and insipidity are not the
only dangers that threaten the panegyrist; his topical materials constantly supply him with problems in practical
politics. A poem written to the new King in 1660, for example, would have to take into account its hero's having as
yet "done little" except suffer in exile. "A life of escapes and
indigence," Johnson remarks, "Could supply poetry with
no splendid images."[32] Yet poverty and disgrace, "escapes
and indigence," play no part in Waller's account of the
King's exile *(To the King, upon His Majesty's Happy Return)*. Charles in exile is no homeless wanderer, but the true
prince awaiting his call. He has the virtue, the beauty, the
civility of the ideal prince, but the power is not yet his; his
time has not come.

> Naked, the Graces guarded you from all
> Dangers abroad; and now your thunder shall.
> Princes that saw you, different passions prove,
> For now they dread the object of their love;
> Nor without envy can behold his height,
> Whose conversation was their late delight.   (27–32)

The complete prince must first be a complete man. Hitherto
Charles has excelled in the private sphere; now he is to
assume the near-divinity of kingship. His exile has served as
his education, teaching him those things a prince must
know.

> Yet does this absence gain
> No small advantage to your present reign;

32. *Lives of the Poets, 1,* 271–72.

> For having viewed the persons and the things,
> The councils, state, and strength of Europe's kings,
> You know your work; ambition to restrain,
> And set them bounds, as Heaven does to the main.
> We have you now with ruling wisdom fraught,
> Not such as books, but such as practice, taught.
>
> (39–46)

What Charles has learned, Waller suggests several times, is self-control, gentleness, mercy; hardship has taught him to be patient and to forgive. The praise is highly pointed and particularly suited for a nation which, after a long interregnum, had without conditions called back its king. Waller's poem seeks to reassure Englishmen about the intentions of the King and to urge a policy of toleration and general amnesty (along the lines of the Declaration of Breda) upon the King. The poet has an especially delicate task here, since he and a great many other Englishmen had gone over to the support of Cromwell's regime. He is forced to write as a suitor to the King rather than an adviser.

> All are obnoxious! and this faulty land,
> Like fainting Esther, does before you stand,
> Watching your sceptre. The revolted sea
> Trembles to think she did your foes obey. (15–18)

He solves his problem by praising the King for possessing the virtues that serve his own purposes best and by clothing the King in imagery which inescapably suggests a pattern of behavior.

> Thus patience crowned, like Job's, your trouble ends,
> Having your foes to pardon, and your friends;
> For, though your courage were so firm a rock,
> What private virtue could endure the shock?
> Like your Great Master, you the storm withstood,
> And pitied those who love with frailty showed. (89–94)

The King is above "private virtue" not merely in his public position, as embodiment of the state, but because he is infused with a heavenly light. The wisdom and mercy he has learned through suffering identify him with the prototype of all sufferers. Like his "Great Master," Waller says, Charles can (and will) understand and forgive the weakness of others. The advice is sound as ethics and as practical politics appropriate to the situation.[33]

Panegyric, like satire, deals with ideals of conduct, measuring human behavior against a norm. To equate the one with empty flattery is akin to dismissing the other as the product of ill temper. Waller's statement of the proper "Use of Poetry" is both a definition and an implicit defense of his own work.

> Well-sounding verses are the charm we use,
> Heroic thoughts and virtue to infuse
>
> . . .
>
> Where a brave, a public action shines,
> That he [the poet] rewards with his immortal lines.
> Whether it be in council or in fight,
> His country's honour is his chief delight;
> Praise of great acts he scatters as a seed,
> That may the like in coming ages breed.[34]

That is, the poet's job is to praise virtuous public acts where he finds them and by praising to provide models of conduct; this is of course standard Renaissance epic theory. Panegyric thus is prescriptive; teaching by delight, it seeks to "fashion a gentleman or noble person in vertuous and gentle disci-

---

33. The last couplet quoted alludes to Matt. 14:31. Other poems written on the occasion of the King's return inevitably make use of similar materials. The closeness of Dryden's political and aesthetic views to those of Waller, along with the shared persuasive purpose of the two poems, makes the similarities between Waller's poem and *Astraea Redux* particularly striking. See H. T. Swedenberg, Jr., "England's Joy: *Astraea Redux* in its Setting," *Studies in Philology, 50,* (1953), 30–44, esp. 38–39; and Hoffman, *John Dryden's Imagery,* pp. 10–18.

34. "Upon the Earl of Roscommon's Translation of Horace, 'De Arte Poetica'; and of the Use of Poetry," 23–36.

pline."[35] In praising a ruler for virtues he may or may not have, the poet is in fact recommending a particular course of action or outlook. In the words of Erasmus: "No other way of correcting a prince is so efficacious as presenting, in the guise of flattery, the pattern of a really good prince. Thus do you instill virtues and remove faults in such a matter that you seem to urge the prince to the former and restrain him from the latter."[36] There is a similar passage in Queen Elizabeth's *Entertainment at Warwick*, 1572: "In ... *panegyricae* ... were sett fourth the commendacions of Kings and Emperors, with the sweet sound whereof, as the ears of evil Prynces were delightid by hearing there undeservid praises, so were good Princes by the pleasant remembrance of their knowen and true vertues made better, being put in mynde of their office and government." Queen Elizabeth answered: "I now thank you for putting me in mind of my duety, and that should be in me."[37]

Waller's political poems must ultimately be judged not as politics but as poetry. Political verse rarely has any marked effect in bringing into being the policies for which it argues —any more than political prose does. And in the long run it hardly matters. Milton's sonnets and *A Modest Proposal* reflect their circumstances as they transcend them; so, ideally, should Waller's poems. If they do not, much of the

35. "A Letter of the Authors," in Greenlaw, *Works of Edmund Spenser, 1,* 167. The Renaissance belief in the didactic nature of epic poetry is discussed in Hardison, *The Enduring Monument,* and E. M. W. Tillyard, *The English Epic and its Background* (London, 1954); see also Nevo, *The Dial of Virtue,* pp. 27–30.

36. Tr. Lester K. Born, in "The Perfect Prince According to the Latin Panegyrists," *American Journal of Philology, 55,* (1934), 35. The passage in its original Latin can be found in *Opus Epistularum Erasmi,* ed. P. S. Allen (Oxford, 1906), *1,* 397.

37. John Nichols, ed., *The Progresses and Public Processions of Queen Elizabeth* (London, 1823), *1,* 311. The passage is quoted in Ernest W. Talbert, "The Interpretation of Jonson's Courtly Spectacle," *PMLA, 61,* (1946), 457. Talbert's essay emphasizes the preceptive side of the two related genres, masque and panegyric. See also Hardison, *The Enduring Monument,* pp. 30–31.

time, their failure is artistic as well as persuasive. Where they succeed, it is because they have endowed some more or less perishable particulars with the solidity of well-wrought argument and well-wrought verse.

There is little development in Waller's career; I suppose this is one of the things that makes him a minor poet. The only development that can be traced through the early "Of the Danger His Majesty (while Prince) Escaped . . . at St. Andere" (1624), "To the King, on his Navy" (1636), *A Panegyric to my Lord Protector* (1655), *Instructions to a Painter* (1666), and "Of the Invasion and Defeat of the Turks" (1683) is that of a young and uncertain poet, a mature poet, and a tired poet working on the same kind of materials in the same way. The early poems tend to be relatively short and to be organized around a central metaphor or an antithesis (both methods of associating, linking, defining). Thomas Rymer says of "To the King, on his Navy," "the first line, with all that follow in order, leads to the conclusion, all bring to the same point and centre," the successful union in Charles I (and his navy) of "power" and "piety."[38] Waller's later poems, when they are not mere jeux d'esprit, tend to be elaborate public performances. Some are heroic narratives, the kind of poem Dryden refers to (speaking of his *Annus Mirabilis*) as the "historical" poem, which fails to qualify fully for the title of epic only because its scope is limited, its "action is not properly one," and its contents are "tied too severely to the laws of history."[39] Others combine praise of a person with description of a place *(On St. James's Park, as Lately Improved by His Majesty)*, or, like *A Panegyric to my Lord Protector,* are primarily persuasive in their intent.

There is no cut-and-dried division either in category or in time—for example, the very first of his poems, "Of the

38. *A Short View of Tragedy* (1692), in *Critical Works of Thomas Rymer,* p. 127.
39. Ker, *Essays of Dryden, I,* 11.

Danger His Majesty Escaped," is a clumsy attempt at heroic narrative. But it is possible to make a general distinction between simple eulogy (the dominant form of Waller's pre-1645 panegyrics) and longer discursive poems. The second group of poems cannot receive their unity and organization from the development of a central metaphor: they simply are too long. Throughout his career Waller was plagued with the problem of unity and coherence in the larger forms. One possibility is to make the genre the source of whatever unity and progression of effects the poem possesses: narrative tells a story, georgic-descriptive describes and generalizes. But this does not solve the problem of coherence of parts or guarantee that the unity will be anything more than a matter of historical accident (a succession of events connected with the battle of Lowestoft, or a succession of objects in the vicinity of St. James' Park).[40] Waller is most successful in improvising a structure in the *Panegyric* to Cromwell, and here the structure is essentially an extension of that in his shorter poems. The historical occasion, and along with it, as in all successful pieces of rhetorical persuasion, the audience, provide him both materials and an approach. The historical narrative the poem contains, the imagery, the allusions to the classical and British past, the local effects of wit, the elegant praise—all subserve the poem's essentially persuasive purpose and as such find their artistic justification.

An extended analysis of several poems may show more clearly how Waller puts his poems together, as well as the range of effects of which he is capable. His poem on the assassination of the Duke of Buckingham in 1628 illustrates how his occasions are simultaneously historical and symbolic, how he can weld a series of classical and biblical allu-

---

40. Cf. Aristotle's definition of unity of action, *Poetics*, 8, in *Works*, *11*, 1451a. "Of the Danger His Majesty Escaped," *Of a War with Spain, and a Fight at Sea*, and *Instructions to a Painter* all grew by accretion from fragments composed at various times and reflecting various circumstances. In all three poems, the patchwork construction creates problems in unity and coherence.

sions into a unified structure, saying something which is appropriate to the occasion while going beyond the occasion. Yet "Buckingham's Death," though it serves as a paradigm of Waller's method and though it handles its hyperbole elegantly, somehow lacks resonance. It is a nicely turned piece of praise, but that is all; its existence is, as it were, contingent, mechanical, willed. In "To the King, on his Navy," and the *Panegyric*, style and subject matter are fused in perfect harmony. Occasion, rhetorical purpose, and purely artistic qualities are inseparable. Here the occasion not only serves as a stimulus for composition and source of materials but gives the poem a raison d'être in persuasion and provides a springboard for the expression of deeply held ideals, political, ethical, and aesthetic.

When the news of Buckingham's murder was brought to Charles, he was at public prayers. His reaction was unexpected. According to Clarendon's account, he "continued unmoved, and without the least change in his countenance, till prayers were ended." Though his later, private reaction was different ("much passion and . . . abundance of tears" in the privacy of his chamber, "melancholic and discomposure" for several days), his initial reception of the news caused talk, and indeed "made many men to believe that the accident was not very ungrateful" to him.[41] These circumstances inspired Waller's poem. Its subject is not the death of the reigning favorite but, as the title indicates, the King's reaction: "Of His Majesty's Receiving the News of the Duke of Buckingham's Death." The poem has a practical impulse behind it—in part it is intended to scotch rumors that the King had turned against Buckingham. Waller interprets the King's behavior in a manner favorable to the pro-Buckingham faction, praising Charles not only for his self-control but for his generosity, his advancement, after Buckingham's death, of the Duke's kinsmen and allies.[42]

41. Clarendon, *History of the Rebellion, 1*, 37–38.
42. See contemporary comments quoted by Thorn-Drury, 2, 157–58. In quoting the poem, I depart from Thorn-Drury's text in lines 24 and 31,

> Where thy immortal love to thy blest friends,
> Like that of Heaven, upon their seed descends,
> Such huge extremes inhabit thy great mind,
> God-like, unmoved, and yet, like woman, kind.
>
> (31–34)

As the passage quoted indicates, the imagery makes large claims. Panegyric inhabits such spheres as these. Yet all these soaring flights find their origin in the poem's occasion, the particular circumstances from which it arises. The accident that led Charles to be at prayers when the news of Buckingham's death was brought to him dictates the heroic-religious imagery of the poem, the celebration of the King as Christian hero. Church and state are run together; the secular and religious are allowed first to interpenetrate, finally to fuse.

The picture of the King at prayers suggests a biblical parallel. Charles heroically praying is like Jacob wrestling, undaunted, with the angel.

> So earnest with thy God! can no new care,
> No sense of danger, interrupt thy prayer?
> The sacred wrestler, till a blessing given,
> Quits not his hold, but halting conquers Heaven;
> Nor was the stream of thy devotion stopped,
> When from the body such a limb was lopped,
> As to thy present state was no less maim,
> Though thy wise choice has since repaired the same.
>
> (1–8)

The correspondences between the passage and the biblical account are complex. On the simplest level, Charles does not stop praying, as Jacob does not stop wrestling. Charles can be spoken of as "halting" because he is wounded by the death of Buckingham (the term, of course, applies to Jacob literally). A limb of the body politic has been cut away.

---

following Fenton and the best of the 1645 editions, *Poems of Edmond Waller, Esq.*, printed by I. N. for Humphrey Mosley.

The King's being at prayers is a different matter from an ordinary man's being at prayers. The King is head of the Church of England; there is in the lines at least a hint of Charles as biblical leader of his people, as Jacob prototype. Religion and policy are separate things, "devotion," on the one hand, and, on the other, "state," "thy wise choice," appointments to fill Buckingham's posts. But devotion and state are part of the same body (the body politic; the King): devotion carries over into the political sphere, and a state may be a state of mind. The dual, indivisible nature of kingship creates a constant strain. As man, the King may show emotion, as King he may not.

In the next lines, we move to another kind of heroism. The rest of the poem consists of a string of "outdoing" comparisons, which contribute to build up a picture of the ideal hero. Such comparisons, in which the subject is shown not only as equal to the heroes of antiquity but as excelling them in their own sphere, are staples of panegyric verse and epideictic oratory and are among Waller's favorite devices of heroic amplification.[43] Rarely does he make as full use of them as he does in this poem.

> Bold Homer durst not so great virtue feign
> In his best pattern: for Patroclus slain,
> With such amazement as weak mothers use,
> And frantic gesture, he receives the news.
> Yet fell his darling by the impartial chance
> Of war, imposed by royal Hector's lance;
> Thine in full peace, and by a vulgar hand
> Torn from thy bosom, left his high command.
>
> (9–16)

---

43. The fullest discussion of the "outdoing" topos is Curtius, *European Literature and the Latin Middle Ages,* pp. 162–65; see also Aristotle, *Rhetoric,* I.9, in *Works, 11,* 1638a, and Hardison, *The Enduring Monument,* p. 31. For examples of "outdoing" comparisons in Waller, see *Panegyric,* 69–78; "Of the Danger His Majesty Escaped," 77–100; "Upon His Majesty's Repairing of Paul's," 57–60.

Achilles, like any epic hero, is a "pattern" for princes—in this case a pattern not only to be emulated, but to be surpassed. He is, as it were, an unsatisfactory prefigurement of Charles.

What Charles is particularly praised for is the royal, heroic "virtue" he displays at this time of crisis. In the lines just quoted, as in the allusion to Jacob wrestling with the angel, the imagery suggests emotional strain: such virtue is not easily won. The fairly heavy dose of love imagery ("his darling," "thy bosom") evokes the emotion the hero is repressing. In saying Charles is not like (i.e. better than) a lover, the poet is saying that he is like a lover, comprehends all the virtues of a lover.

The next lines continue to find precedents for Charles in the classical world:

> The famous painter could allow no place
> For private sorrow in a prince's face:
> Yet, that his piece might not exceed belief,
> He cast a veil upon supposed grief.   (17–20)

The allusion, according to Thorn-Drury's note, is to Timanthes' portrait of the sacrifice of Iphigenia, which, after expressing "various degrees of grief" in the onlookers, shows "Agamemnon, the father of the victim, with his face buried in the folds of his drapery."[44] Waller's version of this familiar classical exemplum is not the standard one. He is not interested in the decorum of grief, or the inexpressible, but in kingship. There is, in Agamemnon as in Charles, a separation between the man and the office, Charles Stuart and Charles Rex.

For all the seriousness of the metaphor, the lines contain an element of audacity, of playful wit. It would not do for Charles to surpass Achilles and not Agamemnon.

---

44. Thorn-Drury, 2, 157. Fenton compares the hidden face of Agamemnon with the silence of Ajax and of Dido in Hades, "far more eloquent" than any speech (xv).

'Twas want of such a precedent as this
Made the old heathen frame their gods amiss.
Their Phoebus should not act a fonder part
For the fair boy, than he did for his hart;
Nor blame for Hyacinthus' fate his own,
That kept from him wished death, hadst thou
    been known.   (21–26)

Waller is being fairly cavalier, towards both the classical authors and his own poem. He is doing arabesques around his central metaphor, but he still maintains it. (It is only fair to point out that the lines—easily the weakest in the poem—are strained, obscure in syntax, and cacaphonous in a way Waller's later verse rarely is.) Apollo was represented in *Metamorphoses,* X, as having grieved immoderately for the fair youths Cyparissus and Hyacinthus; if Ovid had known of Charles, he would not have framed his gods so ill. We may note that we have moved imperceptibly from pagan kings to pagan gods. The dividing line between the two is indefinite (especially since both are made, much of the time, by poets). The hero is half god, the pagan god is half man. The Christian king, the Christian hero, participates, like them, in two worlds, and has the better of them in both.

Throughout the poem, the imagery is not simply heroic, but religious-heroic. Charles is introduced praying heroically, and a comparison between paganism and Christianity as guides to conduct is implicit throughout the poem. A pattern is intended to teach virtue, and Christian virtue. In the last twelve lines, Charles is in full religious armor:

He that with thine shall weigh good David's deeds,
Shall find his passion, not his love, exceeds:
He cursed the mountains where his brave friend died,
But let false Ziba with his heir divide.   (27–30)

The biblical king is both sacred and secular leader; in David, the heroic and religious strains come together. But Charles surpasses David, as he has the other heroes. Like them, he mingles the divine and the human. But while in

David, Achilles, or Ovid's Apollo, the divine infects the human and the human the divine *(hubris* or weakness), Charles is more consistent, every inch a king. His divinity exalts his humanity, his humanity softens his divinity.

> Where thy immortal love to thy blest friends,
> Like that of Heaven, upon their seed descends.
> Such huge extremes inhabit thy great mind,
> God-like, unmoved, and yet, like woman, kind!
> Which of the ancient poets had not brought
> Our Charles' pedigree from Heaven, and taught
> How some bright dame, compressed by mighty Jove,
> Produced this mixed Divinity and Love?   (31–38)[45]

As "Buckingham's Death" illustrates, Waller, like Dryden (and in a very different way, Milton) was concerned in all his public verse with "the accommodation of the classical and the Christian images of the hero."[46] The single overriding concern of Waller's political poetry is a secular version of Milton's central problem—not the justification of the ways of God to men, but the justification of earthly power, the attempt to show that the de facto state of affairs is in accordance with abstract standards of justice. Waller's procedure is in a sense the reverse of Milton's: instead of adapting classical poetic conventions to Christian homiletic purposes, he clothes his secular materials with Christian as-

---

45. Mrs. Nevo takes Waller's characteristic hyperbole, in this poem and elsewhere, as representing "eulogistic mythology" with no relationship to "the real world of historical events" *(The Dial of Virtue,* pp. 36, 40). I would disagree and would argue that Waller's panegyrics, like *Cooper's Hill* and Marvell's poems on Cromwell, inhabit a real and ideal world at once. Though I have reservations about Mrs. Nevo's treatment of Waller, her book seems to me a fine one, indispensable for any student of the period. Along with Earl Wasserman's *The Subtler Language,* it is one of the few books to take seventeenth-century political poetry seriously and analyze it closely, while placing it firmly in the context of its time. Her readings are never strained, and the historical backgrounds she adduces illuminate the poems rather than smothering them.

46. Hoffman, *John Dryden's Imagery,* p. 17.

sociations. In reading, we correct for hyperbole. We are not expected to believe that Charles I is in a literal sense a descendent of the Olympian gods or the equivalent in action of the Christian God. Rather, the metaphorical associations serve the end of persuasion, leading us to interpret Charles' character and policies in the most favorable manner. Here and elsewhere, Waller uses biblical allusions, as he uses historical parallels and classical echoes, to set up a factitious typology, to create an atmosphere conducive for persuasion.

The imagery of "To the King, on his Navy," as in many of Waller's poems, draws upon both classical and biblical sources. Pegasus and Jupiter fulminant rub shoulders with Noah and the builders of the Tower of Babel. But the Christian imagery is primary in the poem, and the other is subsumed under it. "To the King, on his Navy," like "Buckingham's Death," presents a hierarchy of values in which Christian heroism is plainly the best kind. We do not have the sense, as in Milton, that the Christian truth supplants all other, partial truths, and that the classical version of heroic action is somehow corrupt or suspect, a matter of mere "Bases and tinsel Trappings . . . / The skill of Artifice or Office mean, / Not that which justly gives Heroic name / To Person or to Poem."[47] Waller's ends are more worldly and more limited. But the pattern of imagery suggests a Christian context by which the actions and institutions he describes can be interpreted. British power, as the poem presents it, is divinely ordained, the agent of heavenly justice. The poem's imagery constantly shows the divine type shining through the earthly manifestation. Thus contemporary events reflect not only "storms and piracy," with nature, man, and political institutions equally lawless and chaotic, but a pattern of divine providence: a second Eden, miraculously preserved, a second Noah saved from a second Deluge, a recovery of the union between God and man and a symmetry of the earthly and heavenly realms, lost with

47. *Paradise Lost*, IX.36–41.

man's fall. Each of these myths has a classical analogue: the
fortunate isles and the golden age, the story of Deucalion,
the flight and return of Astraea. The poet makes use of these
as well, but the Christian version has primacy because it
carries the most conviction toward his persuasive ends.[48]

The element of fact is much less pronounced in "To the
King, on his Navy" than in "Buckingham's Death" (or in
most of Waller's poems). We know from the title alone that
the poem will celebrate the British navy and, through it, the
King, that it will deal with the role of the navy and, by extension, England. But the poem does not, except incidentally, comment on particular deeds of the navy or go into
historical or descriptive detail. Indeed, the poem is so little
tied to clearly identifiable events that it has generally been
misdated. Thorn-Drury assigns the poem to 1627, when a
large fleet was sent unsuccessfully to besiege La Rochelle.
But internal and external evidence makes this date highly
unlikely and confirms Fenton's suggestion of 1636, when
revenues collected from ship money were used to outfit a
fleet. Waller's poem is an implicit defense of the navy and
of Charles' policies against attack. The policy he defends
is not an absurd adventure, like Buckingham's comic opera
challenge of both France and Spain, but explicitly a policy
of armed neutrality. The grounds the government used for
justifying the unpopular tax of ship money were precisely
those stated in Waller's poem:

> If we . . . defend ourselves, it would be a warning to all
> nations, and we should be the more assured to enjoy
> our peace if the wars abroad do make us stand upon our
> guard at home. Therefore no question it hath ever been
> accustomed the greatest wisdom for a nation to arm
> that they may not be enforced to fight, which is better
> than not to arm and be sure to fight. . . . The dominion
> of the sea, as it is an ancient and undoubted right of

48. Dryden and Pope similarly conflate classical and biblical myths of a
restored paradise; cf. Roper, *Dryden's Poetic Kingdoms*, pp. 104–06.

the Crown of England, so it is the best security of our land. The wooden walls are the best walls of this kingdom.[49]

The primary interest in the poem lies not in its political context, but in its qualities as a work of art. Here is the poem in full:

> Where'er thy navy spreads her canvas wings,
> Homage to thee, and peace to all she brings;
> The French and Spaniard, when thy flags appear,
> Forget their hatred, and consent to fear.
> So Jove from Ida did both hosts survey, 5
> And when he pleased to thunder part the fray.
> Ships heretofore in seas like fishes sped,

49. Lord Keeper Coventry's speech announcing the extension of ship money to all England, June 27, 1635, in Gardiner, *History of England, 8,* 79. The text of the first ship-money writ, similarly appealing to patriotism and the sovereignty of the sea, emphasizes protection from piracy more than the dangers of war (cf. "To the King, on his Navy," 7–14):

> Because we are given to understand that certain thieves, pirates, and robbers of the sea, as well Turks, enemies of the Christian name, as others, being gathered together, wickedly taking by force and spoiling the ships, and goods, and merchandises, not only of our subjects, but also the subjects of our friends in the sea, which has been accustomed anciently to be defended by the English nation . . . also the dangers considered which, on every side, in these times of war do hang over our heads . . . it behoveth us and our subjects to hasten the defence of the sea and kingdom with all expedition or speed that we can . . . forasmuch as we, and our progenitors, Kings of England, have been always heretofore masters of the aforesaid sea, and it would be very irksome to us if that princely honour in our time should be lost or in any thing diminished (Samuel R. Gardiner, ed., *The Constitutional Documents of the Puritan Revolution, 1625–1660* [3d ed. Oxford, 1906], pp. 105–06).

Additional confirmation of the 1636 date is a contemporary allusion to "Mr. Waller's verses of the navy under the E. of Northumberland" (Digby papers, Historical Manuscripts Commission, *Eighth Report,* pt. 1, p. 217). Northumberland was appointed admiral of the fleet in 1636. George Digby, 2d Earl of Bristol (1612–77), who translated Waller's poem into Latin under this heading, is, as a friend and political ally of Waller and Northumberland, unlikely to have been mistaken in his attribution.

The mightiest still upon the smallest fed;
Thou on the deep imposest nobler laws,
And by that justice hast removed the cause   10
Of those rude tempests, which for rapine sent,
Too oft, alas! involved the innocent.
Now shall the ocean, as thy Thames, be free
From both those fates, of storms and piracy.
But we most happy, who can fear no force   15
But winged troops, or Pegasean horse.
'Tis not so hard for greedy foes to spoil
Another nation, as to touch our soil.
Should nature's self invade the world again,
And o'er the centre spread the liquid main,   20
Thy power were safe, and her destructive hand
Would but enlarge the bounds of thy command;
Thy dreadful fleet would style thee lord of all,
And ride in triumph o'er the drowned ball;
Those towers of oak o'er fertile plains might go,   25
And visit mountains where they once did grow.
　　The world's restorer once could not endure
That finished Babel should those men secure,
Whose pride designed that fabric to have stood
Above the reach of any second flood: 30
To thee, his chosen, more indulgent, he
Dares trust such power with so much piety.[50]

Thomas Rymer singles out "To the King, on his Navy"
for praise as "beyond all Modern Poetry in any language."

For there, besides the Language Clean and Majestick,
the Thoughts new, and noble; the Verse sweet, smooth,
full and strong; the turn of the Poem is happy to Admiration. . . . Whoever before that time, tryed the same
thoughts in Latin and in English verse; the former
always had the advantage; the expression being more
lively, free, elegant, and easie: Whereas in the English

50. In lines 8 and 27, I have substituted the reading of Fenton and the
1645 editions for Thorn-Drury's text.

some thing or other was still amiss; force or affectation, poverty or superfluity mangling or disguising, pinching or encombring it.

The ideal behind Rymer's remarks is classical: one may note his emphasis upon care in expression, upon Latinity as an ideal, upon Virgilian smoothness, and upon unity and ordonnance. Verse should be "Majestick," "noble," yet "lively . . . elegant, and easie." Heroic poetry is the highest form, the standard against which other poetry can be measured. Rymer remarks on the concluding antithesis of "power" and "piety": "Here is both *Homer* and *Virgil;* the *fortis Achilles,* and the *pius Aeneas,* in the person he Compliments, and the greatness is owing to his Vertue."[51]

The stateliness and dignity of the poem befit the role Rymer chooses for it, that of model to succeeding poets. A heightening of tone is maintained in the ornamental periphrases ("canvas wings," "liquid main," "towers of oak") and the classical and biblical allusions. The diction and syntax, as is common in Waller, are frequently Latinate and at all times formal, sonorous; this clearly is the language of poetry and not of prose.

But the poem is witty as well as heroic, graceful as well as dignified. When John Dennis, in *The Impartial Critick* (1693), writes a critique of the poem in answer to Rymer, the wit is the source of his objections. The thoughts in Waller's poem may be "new" and "noble," but "they are not all of them true." After quoting the first two lines, he comments:

> If Mr. *Waller* had been to say that in Prose, he would have expressed himself otherwise: he would have said thus: Where e'er thy Fleet goes she carries Peace to all, and causes all to pay or do Homage to thee: for where e'er she goes she brings Homage; would not be good *English* in Prose.

51. *Critical Works of Thomas Rymer*, p. 127.

"This Metaphor *Feed,*" he says of the fourth couplet, "is too gross for a Ship, tho' I perfectly know what Mr. *Waller* means by it." Dennis' ideal of decorum is restrictive. "The word Fray is altogether unworthy of the Greatness of the Thought and the Dignity of Heroick Verse." In a similar vein he objects to "sped" and "fishes" as "too mean," not sufficiently "Heroical."

Waller's heroic diction comes equally under his fire. The poetic use of a Latinate word or construction to provide sonority or compression is to Dennis illegitimate, as, indeed, are any departures from habitual English syntax. He objects to the words "nobler laws" and "involved," and to the lines (9–12) in which they occur.

> But, pray, what is that Comparative *Nobler* referr'd to? For *Laws* are neither mention'd before nor after. . . . To involve a Man in Ruine is intelligible enough, but barely to involve a Man cannot be good *English,* methinks, because it presents no clear Notion of any thing to my Mind. . . . If any one should talk to thee of a rude Tempest, which sent upon the Ocean for Rapine, sometimes involves a very honest Fellow, would'st thou not swear, that that Man banter'd thee?

A further remark indicates his approach explicitly: "Yet this is the down-right meaning of the Couplet, or there can be no meaning at all in it."[52]

Clearly, Waller depends upon something other than "down-right meaning," and, indeed, Dennis' adverse criticisms implicitly constitute a good description of Waller's style. His language is metaphorical, he makes full use of rhetorical devices, and his poem is informed by wit. More tightly knit than most of his panegyrics, "To the King, on his Navy" builds up through the witty use of hyperbole and implied analogy an elaborate metaphorical structure which, as Rymer puts it, all "leads . . . to the same point and centre":

52. *Critical Works of John Dennis,* ed. Edward Niles Hooker, (2 vols. Baltimore, 1939–43), *1,* 24–28.

that British power is unlimited and unassailable because it is used for good. The British navy brings about the universal rule of law.

The opening lines of the poem state the theme:

> Where'er thy navy spreads her canvas wings,
> Homage to thee, and peace to all she brings.   (1–2)

By its strength, the navy causes all to do (rightful) homage to the English crown; by its presence, it imposes peace. "Canvas wings" is a heroic touch, suggesting the double function of power and protection.[53] This strength that brings peace, it is interesting to note, exists as *potential*. Waller celebrates not the exercise of power, but power held in check. English strength keeps all in equipoise.

> The French and Spaniard, when thy flags appear,
> Forget their hatred, and consent to fear.   (3–4)

The loyalties and enmities of France and Spain are here wittily shown to be no more than skin-deep; the facts of power quickly dispel such illusions. Their "consent," a fine, diplomatic Latinism, is no sooner mentioned than it is cut down to size, shown simply to be fear. In bringing the two rivals to unwilling agreement, the British navy performs its function of bringing harmony out of discord.[54]

The third couplet continues the work of building up England at the expense of its rivals; the tone is as much

53. The periphrasis "canvas wings" (for sails) is an imitation of Fairfax's Tasso *(Godfrey of Bulloigne,* XV.32), a passage which is itself probably an imitation of *Aeneid,* III.520. There may be a glancing allusion to the dove of the Holy Spirit or to the eagle often associated with Jove, in keeping with the more explicit presentation later in the poem of England's divine mission.

54. One reason Thorn-Drury assigns the poem to the year 1627 is that he finds a reference in these lines to an alliance between France and Spain. The two countries signed a treaty of peace in April 1626 and negotiated a short-lived alliance against England in March 1627. But the lines need not refer to any literal alliance. The presence of the British navy, Waller is saying, makes the French and Spanish forget for the moment their enmity; it keeps the peace between them and is more powerful than either.

mock-heroic as heroic. "When he pleased to thunder" indicates the vast superiority of the gods over mortals, England over France and Spain.[55] In addition, the phrase carries on the earlier suggestions of power held in abeyance, used only as warning. Here, as elsewhere, the wish is father to the thought: the British fleet was in no such commanding position.

The next lines of the poem develop the contrast between the ugly, indecorous actual and the ordered, perfect ideal. Heretofore, the sea had been lawless: the strong, whether pirates or navies preyed on the weak. With the coming of the British navy, the disorder stirred up by the pirates will cease, and peace will reign over the ocean.[56] In such a golden world, it is perfectly reasonable to expect the abolition of storms.

Throughout these lines, Waller has the tradition of Virgilian and biblical prophecy in mind, much as Pope does in *Windsor-Forest*. The specific literary echoes are primarily classical, but the whole has a Christian tinge. The "nobler laws" are the laws of British rule, of peace, and of God—Virgil's *pax Romana* somewhat Christianized:

> tu regere imperio populos, Romane, memento
> (hae tibi erunt artes) pacique imponere morem,
> parcere subiectis et debellare superbos.[57]

55. The passage alludes to *Iliad*, VIII.66–77, where Zeus on Mount Ida weighs the Grecian and Trojan fates and then sends thunderbolts down upon the Greeks.

56. For some years, the ravages of North African pirates had done great damage to English shipping, even within English waters. The extent of piracy was one of the ostensible reasons for Charles' demands for ship money, but ships assembled under the ship-money writs were not employed against the pirates with much success; see Gardiner, *History of England, 8,* 219–20, 270. The British invasion of the pirate stronghold Sallé in 1637 is the subject of Waller's poem, *Of Sallé*.

57. "Remember thou, O Roman, to rule the nations with thy sway—these shall be thy arts—to crown Peace with Law, to spare the humbled, and to tame in war the proud" *(Aeneid,* VI.851–853, tr. H. Rushton Fairclough, Loeb Classical Library [London, 1934]).

The ordained destiny of Britain, as Waller presents it, is imperium, and British sway will bring its universal peace to nature itself, even to the restless sea.[58] Where the Virgilian tradition associates the returned Saturnian golden age with justice and empire (foretold by the gods), in the biblical prophecies both justice and empire belong to God. The Roman parallels link the British navy with Roman power, the biblical parallels with divine law.

> For out of Zion shall go forth the law, and the word of the Lord from Jerusalem. And he shall judge among the nations, and shall rebuke many people: and they shall beat their swords into plowshares, and their spears into pruninghooks: nation shall not lift up sword against nation, neither shall they learn war any more.[59]

The celebration of England as an island in the next lines continues both the vein of hyperbolic fancy and the serious undertones. England is presented as a second Eden, peaceful and protected amidst the ceaseless turmoil of storms, battles, and piracy in the fallen world outside. This vision of the island paradise recurs again and again in Waller's poetry— most notably in *A Panegyric to my Lord Protector:*

> Whether this portion of the world were rent,
> By the rude ocean, from the continent;
> Or thus created, it was sure designed
> To be the sacred refuge of mankind.
>
> .   .   .
>
> Our little world, the image of the great,
> Like that, amidst the boundless ocean set,

58. Cf. *Eclogue* IV.38–39 (tr. Fairclough): "cedet et ipse mari vector, nec nautica pinus / mutabit merces; omnis feret omnia tellus" (Even the trader shall quit the sea, nor shall the ship of pine exchange wares; every land shall bear all fruits).

59. Isa. 2:3–4. For a discussion of how Dryden and Pope make use of similar traditions in *Astraea Redux* and *Windsor-Forest*, see Swedenberg, "England's Joy," pp. 33–34, and Maynard Mack, "On Reading Pope," *College English*, 7 (1946), 266–68.

> Of her own growth has all that Nature craves;
> And all that's rare, as tribute from the waves.[60]

England's physical status as an island becomes, as it were, the sign of a covenant with God and indicates the special role designed for her to play. Not only can no nation invade Britain except with "winged troops" (a forecast which came true with the *Luftwaffe* raids of World War II), but even a second Flood would leave Britain's power untouched. The navy will merely ride the waves.

> Should nature's self invade the world again,
> And o'er the centre spread the liquid main,
> Thy power were safe, and her destructive hand
> Would but enlarge the bounds of thy command.
>
> (19–22)

By wit, the apparent absolute extreme of disorder is calmly resolved into a manifestation of order.

Gradually the poem has moved from politics, earthly concerns, the world we all live in, to the realm of miracle. The religious imagery, explicit now, provides "reasonable colour"[61] for the hyperbolic praise, presenting the King of England as a second Noah, God's chosen. The reference to "piety" in the poem's last line is by no means a gratuitous extra compliment, thrown in at the end. In the juxtaposition of the two terms, the poem's imagery reaches its culmination: Britain's power can be as great as it is because it is combined with piety. Ordinary men and nations seek power as self-aggrandizement, attempt to impose their will,

---

60. *Panegyric*, 25–28, 49–52. Waller's most extended treatment of the motif is "The Battle of the Summer Islands," a pastoral idyll set in Bermuda. See Josephine Waters Bennett, "Britain among the Fortunate Isles," *Studies in Philology*, *53* (1956), 114–40, for a survey of the tradition associating England with the islands of the blest, the Hesperides, and the Garden of Eden. Perhaps the best-known treatment of the topos is John of Gaunt's speech in *Richard II*, II.i.40–46; cf. also Marvell's lament for the loss of paradise with the outbreak of Civil War, "Upon Appleton House," 321–28.

61. The phrase is from Rymer's comment on the lines (*Collected Works of Thomas Rymer*, p. 127).

set themselves up as rivals to God. British power, on the other hand, is exercised in the interests of justice, of divine order, of the ideal made manifest on earth.

> To thee, his chosen, more indulgent, he
> Dares trust such power with so much piety.
>
> (31–32)

A Panegyric to my Lord Protector was generally recognized in the eighteenth century as Waller's masterpiece. Johnson writes of it:

> The famous *Panegyrick* . . . has always been considered as the first of his poetical productions. . . . [It] has obtained from the publick a very liberal dividend of praise, which however cannot be said to have been unjustly lavished; for such a series of verses had rarely appeared before in the English language. Of the lines some are grand, some are graceful, and all are musical.[62]

Like most of Waller's poems, the *Panegyric* finds its origin in a particular set of historical circumstances. The poet had been allowed to return to England in 1651, after seven years of banishment for his Royalist "plot." His poem, more than a simple rendering of thanks, is a conscious political gesture. Having made his peace with the regime, he urges others to do the same. The poem is perfectly in line with Waller's monarchic principles: it is praise of Cromwell as king, as ideal monarch and promoter of the glory of England.

The *Panegyric* thus concerns itself with the most important political issue of the 1650s: the "settling" of the state, the transformation of the rule of the sword into the rule of law. Hobbes' *Leviathan* (1651) had considered the problem of de facto power philosophically. Other works, occasioned by the establishment of the Commonwealth (1649) and the

---

62. *Lives of the Poets, 1,* 269–89. The *Panegyric* has received little attention since the eighteenth century. There are good brief accounts of the poem in Nevo, *The Dial of Virtue,* pp. 116–17; Bateson, *English Poetry,* p. 168; and Ruth Wallerstein, "The Development of the Rhetoric and Metre of the Heroic Couplet," *PMLA, 50* (1935), 204.

Protectorate (1654), were more specific guides to action, and many, like the *Panegyric,* were directed at wavering ex-Royalists. Clarendon and other advisers to the exiled King greatly feared the possible establishment of a monarchy under Cromwell; perhaps that is one reason for their violent antipathy toward "turncoats" like Waller.[63] A good number of pamphlets published between 1654 and 1656 are essentially monarchical and conservative defences of Cromwell, stressing like Waller the benefits of order against factionalism and anarchy. Thus John Hall in *The True Cavalier Examined by his Principles* (1656) writes: "As I had from Scripture and Reason found Monarchy to be the best and only right form of government, so . . . it was not for any one Monarchs sake I did it; but out of a desire to maintain perpetual peace and unity amongst us, I asserted . . . obedience to be continually due to that Person which God . . . should set over us."[64]

But Waller's defense of Cromwell is not, like the pamphlet I have quoted, mere watered-down Hobbes, arguing simple submission to power. Using the interrelated appeals of patriotism and self-interest (the subtitle speaks of "the present Greatness and joint Interest of His Highness, and this Nation"), the *Panegyric* urges national unity as a prerequisite for international dominion. Approximately half

63. See Clarendon, *History of the Rebellion, 6,* 21–22, and Wormald, *Clarendon,* pp. 199–203. The possibility of Cromwell's becoming king was a main subject of debate in and outside of Parliament in 1656–57; see Firth, *The Last Years of the Protectorate, 1,* 61–67, 128–200. Waller was active in urging the crown on Cromwell at this time. *Of a War with Spain, and a Fight at Sea* (1658) ends with these lines: "Then let it be as the glad nation prays; / Let the rich ore forthwith be melted down, / And the state fixed by making him a crown; / With ermine clad, and purple, let him hold / A royal sceptre, made of Spanish gold" (106–10).

64. Perez Zagorin, *A History of Political Thought in the English Revolution* (London, 1954), p. 92. Other pamphlets of a similar import include Hall's *Of Government and Obedience* (1654), Michael Hawke's *The Right of Dominion* (1655), and Thomas White's *The Grounds of Obedience and Government* (1655); see Zagorin, pp. 87–94.

of the poem is devoted to "the greatest leader," half to "the greatest isle"; Cromwell's chief praise is the strength and prosperity of the nation.[65]

Three other celebrated panegyrics of Cromwell, roughly contemporaneous with Waller's poem, do not share Waller's royalism but agree in their persuasive purpose. Milton's *Second Defence of the People of England* (1654) and Marvell's *First Anniversary of the Government under O. C.* (1655) are arguments for the superiority of the Protectorate government over tyrannous monarchy and anarchical democracy. Like Waller's poem, they are defenses of a particular form of government, the Protectorate, which (as Waller later says of William of Orange) reconciles "empire and freedom." Such a form of government, all three men argue, brings to England the virtues of glory, order, and peace, while preserving individual liberty. Marvell's poem has been called "an argument that Cromwell accept the English crown and inaugurate a new dynasty of kings." Whether or not the *First Anniversary* specifically urges Cromwell to become king, the poem clearly is directed at the problem of succession and legitimation, "Founding a firm State by Proportions true" (248), and argues for a mixed state with a strong executive.[66] Milton's political position is

65. The subtitle in the 1655 folio edition is equally explicit about the poem's purpose: "By a Gentleman that Loves the Peace, Union, and Prosperity of the English Nation."

66. John M. Wallace, "Andrew Marvell and Cromwell's Kingship: 'The First Anniversary,'" *ELH, 30* (1963), 209–35. I agree with Wallace that the poem is persuasive in nature, but I feel he mistakes the type of government Marvell is arguing for. As a chorus of foreign princes is represented as proclaiming in unison at the end of the poem, Cromwell is not a king, but something greater: "'Abroad a King he seems, and something more, / At Home a Subject on the equal Floor. / O could I once him with our Title see, / So should I hope yet he might Dye as wee'" (389–92, in Margoliouth, *Poems and Letters of Andrew Marvell*). Cromwell's rule is God-given, as Marvell presents it, and a human crown is only a sign of human limitations. Cf. the treatment of kingship in I Sam. 8; and see Mazzeo, "Cromwell as Davidic King," pp. 29–55.

somewhat different: he praises Cromwell for rejecting the title of king and places more emphasis on the idea of liberty than Marvell or Waller does. But he agrees with them in presenting Cromwell as a natural ruler, a force for order, and an enlarger of England's dominion. The conclusion of the *Second Defence* is a particularly impressive and moving example of prescriptive panegyric, with its solemn admonition to the Lord Protector and to the English people to remain worthy of rule and of freedom, to carry out the great task for which they are ordained.[67]

A third panegyric addressed to Cromwell makes up a large part of James Harrington's *The Commonwealth of Oceana* (1656), a work which, though unsympathetic both to monarchy and to the actual government of the Protectorate, praises Cromwell as a potential force for order. The *Oceana* is a plea to Cromwell to serve as a great legislator and father of his country in setting up a permanent constitution. Like Waller's poem and Marvell's, the *Oceana* is prescriptive panegyric, with counsel (implicit and explicit) directed at Cromwell and the English people. The concluding eulogy of Cromwell makes effective use of historical analogies in pointing out the options available to the Protector:

> *Alexander* erecting Trophies common with his Sword and the Pestilence; to what good of Mankind did he infect the ayre with his heaps of carkases? . . . But if *Alexander* had restored the Liberty of *Greece,* and

---

67. See especially the long passage toward the end addressed to the citizens of England, beginning with the words, "Nam et vos, o cives, quales ipsi sitis ad libertatem vel acquirendam vel retinendam haud parvi interest," in *Joannis Miltoni Angli Pro Populo Anglicano Defensio Secunda [Second Defence of the People of England]* ed. Eugene J. Strittmatter, in *The Works of John Milton, 8* (New York, Columbia University Press, 1933), 238–41. The address to Cromwell and the English people takes up the last thirty pages of the Columbia edition (224–55); for eulogy of Cromwell as hero and emperor, see 213–25. There is an interesting discussion of the *Second Defence* in Z. S. Fink, *The Classical Republicans* (2d ed. Evanston, Northwestern University Press, 1962), pp. 104–07.

propagated it to Mankind, he had done like my Lord *Archon* [Cromwell], and might have been truly call'd the Great.[68]

Contemporary epic theory is directly relevant to the *Panegyric*. According to Le Bossu and Dryden, an epic poem, and by extension a panegyric, must always have a clear end in mind, a "moral." Such a work will achieve its ends by indirect means, clothing its "moral" in fictional or historical circumstances, suggesting its central truths through analogy and interwoven patterns of imagery (and, in epic poetry itself, through action). Dryden's account of the genesis and moral of the *Aeneid* fits Waller at least as well as it does Virgil:

We are to consider him [Virgil] as writing his poem in a time when the old form of government was subverted, and a new one just established by Octavius Caesar, in effect by force of arms, but seemingly by the consent of the Roman people. . . . Virgil having maturely weighed the condition of the times in which he lived; that an entire liberty was not to be retrieved; that the present settlement had the prospect of a long continuance in the same family, or those adopted into it; that he held his paternal estate from the bounty of the conqueror, by whom he was likewise enriched, esteemed and cherished; that this conqueror, though of a bad kind, was the very best of it; that the arts of peace flourished under him; that all men might be happy, if they would be quiet . . . these things, I say, being considered by the poet, he concluded it to be the interest of his country to be so governed; to infuse an awful respect into the people toward such a prince; by that respect to confirm

68. *The Commonwealth of Oceana*, ed. S. B. Liljegren (Heidelberg, 1924), pp. 58–59, 207–26, esp. 211–12. The political background of *Oceana* is discussed in Fink, *The Classical Republicans*, pp. 52, 61–62, 67–71; and Firth, *The Last Years of the Protectorate, 1*, 61–72.

their obedience to him, and by that obedience to make them happy. This was the moral of his divine poem.[69]

But for the lesser scope of Waller's poem, Dryden could be discussing the *Panegyric*, with its overriding political purpose, its conscious idealization of the less-than-perfect, and its preference for "the arts of peace" over those of war.

The opening lines of the *Panegyric* present a strong implicit case for accepting Cromwell's rule. The Protector is presented as a force for order, restoring the sick state to health; harmony and unity, on the one hand, are contrasted with chaos, fury, and the law of the jungle, on the other:

> While with a strong and yet a gentle hand,
> You bridle faction, and our hearts command,
> Protect us from ourselves, and from the foe,
> Make us unite, and make us conquer too;
>
> Let partial spirits still aloud complain,
> Think themselves injured that they cannot reign,
> And own no liberty but where they may
> Without control upon their fellows prey.   (1–8)

The wise, self-controlled leader, embodiment (as the very quality of the verse suggests) of the mean, must protect his factious people from their own worst qualities. Those who oppose his rule, the poem suggests, do so out of selfishness; what they really want is to exercise their appetites unchecked in a Hobbesian state of nature. Against the civil turmoil they would create, some principle of order is necessary.

> Above the waves as Neptune showed his face,
> To chide the winds, and save the Trojan race,
> So has your highness, raised above the rest,
> Storms of ambition, tossing us, repressed.   (9–12)

69. Ker, *Essays of Dryden*, 2, 168, 171–72; René Le Bossu, *Traité du poëme épique* (Paris, 1675), pp. 37–38.

The stigma of ambition is placed not on Cromwell, but on his enemies. At no point, we ought to note, does Waller praise the idea of democracy or treat the Civil War itself as anything but a disaster.[70] The war and the confusion that followed are seen as darkness ("When fate, or error, had our age misled, / And o'er this nation such confusion spread" [121–22]), finally enlightened by the coming of a single great man, through whom the world can be set right again:

> Your drooping country, torn by civil hate,
> Restored by you, is made a glorious state.   (13–14)

In these lines we have the central argument of the poem in brief. Waller poses a choice between the destructiveness of civil hate, a nation bled dry, exhausted, on the one hand, and wholeness, sanity, national glory on the other.

The next ninety-odd lines develop the theme of national glory. Under Cromwell's rule, England was becoming the "seat of empire" (15); by "[making] us unite," he had "[made] us conquer"(4):

> The sea's our own; and now all nations greet,
> With bending sails, each vessel of our fleet;
> Your power extends as far as winds can blow,
> Or swelling sails upon the globe may go.   (17–20)

Indeed, all nature serves the British vision of Empire. In sending "whole forests . . . to reign upon the sea,"[71] the British bend nature to their will: it is their mission to plant

70. Dryden presents Cromwell's rise to power in very similar terms in his *Heroique Stanzas* on Cromwell's death (esp. lines 25–56); see the editorial commentary in Edward Niles Hooker and H. T. Swedenberg, Jr., eds., *The Works of John Dryden* (Berkeley and Los Angeles, 1956–), *1*, 189–91, 197–98.

71. *Panegyric*, 42. Waller's lines are a variant upon a topos ultimately derived from Ovid, *Metamorphoses*, I.94–95: "nondum caesa suis, peregrinum ut viserat orbem, montibus in liquidas pinus descenderat undas" (Not yet had the pine-tree, felled on its native mountain, descended thence into the watery plain to visit other lands)—tr. Frank Justus Miller, Loeb Classical Library (London, 1921). Cf. *To the King, on his Navy*, 25–26.

"the world's great waste," to civilize the ocean. Here, as in "To the King, on his Navy," Waller presents British power as unlimited because it is the instrument of justice. Once again Waller is drawing on the double tradition of messianic-imperial prophecy, biblical and Roman. The classical associations call forth ideas of glory, honor, heroism, protection, law, while the biblical associations suggest a divine mission for the nation and its leader, implying that the coming of Cromwell is divinely ordained.

> Heaven (that has placed this nation to give law,
> To balance Europe, and her states to awe)
> In this conjunction does on Britain smile;
> The greatest leader, and the greatest isle!   (21–24)

Through most of the poem, Waller keeps the two strands of imagery apart, developing classical and Christian motifs independently in separate conceits. But the two burdens, glory and justice, empire and peace, are interconnected; as in Virgil, the return of the age of gold is the fulfillment of divine prophecy:

> hic vir, hic est, tibi quem promitti saepius audis,
> Augustus Caesar, Divi genus, aurea condet
> saecula qui rursus Latio regnata per arva
> Saturno quondam, super et Garamantas et Indos
> proferet imperium (iacet extra sidera tellus,
> extra anni solisque vias).[72]

The British Isles, remote from the turmoil of continental Europe, fulfill a God-given role as arbiter of European disputes and "sacred refuge" for the victims of tyranny and injustice.

---

72. "This, this is he, whom thou so oft hearest promised to thee, Augustus Caesar, son of a god, who shall again set up the Golden Age in Latium amid the fields where Saturn once reigned, and shall spread his empire past Garamant and Indian, to a land that lies beyond the stars, beyond the paths of the year and the sun" (Aeneid, VI.791–96).

Hither the oppressed shall henceforth resort,
Justice to crave, and succour, at your court;
And then your Highness, not for ours alone,
But for the world's protector shall be known.

(29–32)

This stanza turns on two puns in key words, "protector" and "court." Both terms are associated with power and justice, with imperium and the rule of law, with the earthly realm and the heavenly. Cromwell is Lord Protector, the protector of England's interests—and he is protector of the rights of the oppressed, bulwark of law, benefactor of suffering mankind. This double function of protection is hinted at in the poem's opening lines: "Protect us from ourselves, and from the foe." In a similar fashion, the double meaning of "court" conveys sentiments that are at once patriotic and moral. The influx of petitioners to Cromwell's court is an external sign of Cromwell's and England's greatness. Yet the petitioners come not only to pay tribute but to seek justice; the Protector presides over a court of law.

It is a court with ample power to execute its decisions: pirates and land pirates tremble at the thought of British retribution. The English can come and go as they will, free in their island sanctuary from any possible invasion.

Angels and we have this prerogative,
That none can at our happy seat arrive;
While we descend at pleasure, to invade
The bad with vengeance, and the good to aid.

(45–48)

The actions of the British fleet, as Waller presents them, are as impartial as divine edicts. Britain is ordained to do God's work on earth.

Throughout the first part of the *Panegyric,* Waller keeps returning to the image of the magic island, beloved of God, to which all things flow. To ordinary mortals, the sea is an emblem of inconstancy, but to the British it is an "ever constant friend," bringing an unending stream of tributes from the nations of the earth.[73]

> The taste of hot Arabia's spice we know,
> Free from the scorching sun that makes it grow;
> Without the worm, in Persian silks we shine;
> And without planting, drink of every vine.
>
> To dig for wealth we weary not our limbs;
> Gold, though the heaviest metal, hither swims;
> Ours is the harvest where the Indians mow;
> We plough the deep, and reap what others sow.
>
> (56–64)

These witty lines, playing upon a single paradox, use the facts of English trade and plantation of colonies to present England as a demi-Eden, whose inhabitants enjoy the whole world's pleasures with none of the concomitant disadvantages. In line 64 Waller manages to endow the familiar locution "plough the deep" with real force by taking its ordinarily dead metaphor literally. The phrase serves as a kind of summary—these are our fields, our resources. In the passage as a whole Waller is building upon the familiar topos of the earthly paradise, where all things grow unbidden and the destructive forces familiar in the everyday world are kept far away.

> ipsa tibi blandos fundent cunabula flores,
> occidet et serpens, et fallax herba veneni

73. Here and elsewhere the terms of the praise recall the exaltation of Zion in Isa. 60:3–9.

> And the Gentiles shall come to thy light, and kings to the brightness of thy rising. . . . The abundance of the sea shall be converted unto thee, the force of the Gentiles shall come unto thee. The multitude of camels shall cover thee, the dromedaries of Midian and Ephah: they shall bring gold and incense, and they shall shew forth the praises of the Lord. . . . Surely the isles shall wait for me, and the ships of Tarshish first, to bring their sons from far, their silver and their gold with them.

Pope makes use of the same chapter of Isaiah in *Windsor-Forest* and *Messiah;* see Mack, "On Reading Pope," pp. 267–68.

occidet; Assyrium volgo nascetur amomum

. . .

et durae quercus sudabunt roscida mella.[74]

The next stanzas continue the theme of national greatness, with a different emphasis. Religious motifs are subordinated to the classical heroic, peace and prosperity to
military glory and a parade of conquests. In a manner
typical in panegyric, the Protector is measured against the
heroes of antiquity. Alexander's victories were trifles next
to Cromwell's; Rome was never able to subdue the fierce
Scots, as Cromwell has.[75] What has been implicit in many
of the passages juxtaposing the English present and the
classical past is made explicit in lines commenting on
Cromwell's victory over the Scots:

> Preferred by conquest, happily o'erthrown,
> Falling they rise, to be with us made one;
> So kind dictators made, when they came home,
> Their vanquished foes free citizens of Rome.
>
> (93–96)

The British Empire, Waller tells us, will be a second Roman
Empire. The actions of Cromwell and the growing power of
England need such terms to describe them.[76]

74. "Unasked, thy cradle shall pour forth flowers for thy delight. The
serpent, too, shall perish, and the false poison-plant shall perish; Assyrian
spice shall spring up on every soil. . . . And the stubborn oak shall distil
dewy honey" *(Eclogue* IV.23–25, 30). Cf. Ovid, *Metamorphoses,* I.89–112. For
an analytical survey of the tradition, see A. Bartlett Giamatti, *The Earthly
Paradise and the Renaissance Epic* (Princeton, 1966), esp. pp. 3–47, 84.

75. *Panegyric,* 71–88. The claims of panegyric (especially "outdoing"
comparisons) need not, of course, be literally true; and in fact the admis-
sion of the Scots to Parliament, which Waller extols in lines 89–96, had far
less political importance than Waller gives it. See Samuel R. Gardiner,
History of the Commonwealth and Protectorate 1649–1656 (London, 1903),
2, 282–83. Obviously, a Scot would feel differently about Cromwell's conquests (as would a Mede about Alexander's).

76. A similar patriotic imperialism may be found in Harrington, Marvell,
and Milton. Harrington sees England explicitly as a second Rome; see

The two primary themes of the first half of the poem
("peace and empire," as Waller puts it in summarizing
Cromwell's career in his poem on the Protector's death)[77]
are recapitulated in the second half. In retelling recent
history, the last part of the poem presents a powerful plea
for unity.

> Your never-failing sword made war to cease;
> And now you heal us with the arts of peace;
> Our minds with bounty and with awe engage,
> Invite affection, and restrain our rage.   (109–12)

The contrast here is like that in the opening lines—war
versus peace; implacable, animal vengeance ("Tigers have
courage, and the rugged bear; / But man alone can, whom
he conquers, spare" [115–16]) versus forgiveness; sickness
versus health.

> To pardon willing and to punish loath,
> You strike with one hand, but you heal with both;
> Lifting up all that prostrate lie, you grieve
> You cannot make the dead again to live.   (117–20)

Waller is required to walk a tightrope throughout the
poem, and in a passage like this one he does so with great
skill. He is addressing his fellow ex-Royalists, urging them
to support the new regime, in effect holding out the promise
of amnesty. But he must proceed by indirection. The wit in
the lines enables him to say several things at the same time:
the lines praise Cromwell, provide a series of general statements and maxims about Christian forgiveness and the
nature of man, appeal to adamant Royalists and Roundheads to live and let live, and urge on all (but especially
wavering Royalists) the benefits of peace. By associating his

---

Oceana, pp. 82–85, 185–97, and Fink, *The Classical Republicans*, pp. 81–83.
Marvell does not use the Roman analogy, presenting the British nation as a
"new Israel" rather than a "new Rome"; cf. Mazzeo, "Cromwell as Davidic
King," p. 33 and passim.

77. *Upon the Late Storm*, 28.

hero with Christian virtues, even with the figure of Christ himself, Waller provides powerful unspoken arguments in support of the Protectorate.

The poem continues with a series of classical and biblical analogies, presenting Cromwell as a natural king. Cromwell, in Waller's account, is a solid representative of the landed gentry ("One! whose extraction from an ancient line / Gives hope again that well-born men may shine" [125–26]), in whom the ancient British virtues of self-control, piety, and frugality still live—a second Cincinnatus, called from his plough to save his country. Like Marvell in the "Horatian Ode," Waller contrasts the Protector's earlier quiet retired life with his triumphant entry upon the public scene. Yet where Marvell writes as an uncommitted, analytic observer for whom "power" is on one side, "the antient Rights" on the other, Waller is an advocate.[78] One is inspired by the muse of history, the other by the muse of rhetoric. In Waller's poem, though Cromwell begins his rise in obscurity, he is at all times the true prince, God's anointed:

> Born to command, your princely virtues slept,
> Like humble David's, while the flock he kept.
>
> But when your troubled country called you forth,
> Your flaming courage, and your matchless worth,
> Dazzling the eyes of all that did pretend,
> To fierce contention gave a prosperous end.   (135–40)

The primary problem that all who wrote in praise of Cromwell faced (particularly if they had originally been Royalist sympathizers) was how to justify his seizure of power. Waller's answer is clever and complex:

> Still as you rise, the state, exalted too,
> Finds no distemper while 'tis changed by you;

78. "An Horatian Ode upon Cromwel's Return from Ireland," 29–40. My description of course is intended to apply to the "Horatian Ode," not Marvell's later poems to Cromwell, which are nothing if not committed.

> Changed like the world's great scene! when, without
> noise,
> The rising sun night's vulgar lights destroys.   (141–44)

Cromwell's deeds and the glory reflected on the state by his actions in themselves provide partial justification. His rise is no less irresistible than the rising of the sun each day. In a man of this scale, Waller is suggesting, questions of personal ambition are meaningless. Any such questions are pushed further into the background by the standard connotations of the sun as an emblem of royalty. Cromwell's assumption of power has brought the anarchy of "fierce contention" to an end and replaced the scattered "vulgar lights" of night with the true sun.[79]

Even more powerful indirect arguments for acceptance of Cromwell's rule are provided in an extended comparison of England between the death of the King and the coming of Cromwell, and Rome after Caesar's death. Once the "bond of union," the fundamental principle upon which the state rests, is broken, chaos and violence reign:

> This Caesar found; and that ungrateful age,
> With losing him fell back to blood and rage;
> Mistaken Brutus thought to break their yoke,
> But cut the bond of union with that stroke.
>
> That sun once set, a thousand meaner stars
> Gave a dim light to violence, and wars,
> To such a tempest as now threatens all,
> Did not your mighty arm prevent the fall.

79. Johnson's remarks on the poem are relevant:

His choice of encomiastick topicks is very judicious, for he considers Cromwell in his exaltation, without enquiring how he attained it; there is consequently no mention of the rebel or the regicide. All the former part of his hero's life is veiled with shades, and nothing is brought to view but the chief, the governor, the defender of England's honour, and the enlarger of her dominion. The act of violence by which he obtained the supreme power is lightly treated, and decently justified. It was certainly to be desired that the detestable band should be dissolved which had destroyed the church, murdered the King, and filled

If Rome's great senate could not wield that sword,
Which of the conquered world had made them lord,
What hope had ours, while yet their power was new,
To rule victorious armies, but by you?   (149–60)

The Roman metaphor is a way of stating England's strength
and weakness at once—her potential greatness and her
paralysis. Parliament had found it could not rule; the
struggle between the army and Parliament had to be resolved by the reestablishment of a single supreme power. In
the next stanza, the Roman imagery reaches its logical culmination.

As the vexed world, to find repose, at last
Itself into Augustus' arms did cast;
So England now does, with like toil oppressed,
Her weary head upon your bosom rest.   (169–72)

The effect is cleverly calculated: the intimations of greatness
are flattering, and the suggestions of rest after long toil, of
peace, security, the wandering son returned to the fold,
appear to answer all questions, to impart an air of finality.
If Cromwell had brought peace and glory, does this not
legitimize his rule?

The final four stanzas provide a kind of coda, a recapitula-
tion of some earlier themes along with a quick survey of
Cromwell's achievements. To end his poem on a properly
resounding note, Waller has to move from peace back to
war, from the theme of order and serenity to the theme of
glory. Cromwell's achievements as a warrior have only been
treated indirectly, and so Waller gives us a few trumpet fan-
fares:

Then let the Muses, with such notes as these,
Instruct us what belongs unto our peace;
Your battles they hereafter shall indite,
And draw the image of our Mars in fight;

---

the nation with tumult and oppression; yet Cromwell had not the right
of dissolving them (*Lives of the Poets, 1,* 269).

> Tell of towns stormed, of armies overrun,
> And mighty kingdoms by your conduct won;
> How, while you thundered, clouds of dust did choke
> Contending troops, and seas lay hid in smoke. (173–80)

In the very last lines of the poem, we are shown a vision of England's new glory—and divine mission—under the Protector. The two streams of imagery, classical and religious, converge in the final exaltation of God's warrior, the Lord Protector, receiving his proper obeisance from the petty monarchs of the world:

> While you in triumph ride
> O'er vanquished nations, and the sea beside;
> While all your neighbour-princes unto you,
> Like Joseph's sheaves, pay reverence, and bow.
> (185–88)[80]

The effectiveness with which Waller puts his arguments across in the *Panegyric* is largely due to the poem's wit. Indeed, the political circumstances under which Waller is writing necessitate a great amount of delicacy in choosing a stance and in developing arguments suitable for an audience that could easily be at one another's throats. The poem is remarkable throughout for the control the poet exercises over its tone, for its stylistic suppleness. A discussion of the style may conveniently start with the passage at the end of the poem, quoted above. His own "low strains," Waller says, are only fit for the Protector's "milder deeds"; he cannot produce the "high raptures" Cromwell's great exploits deserve (181–83). But as he tells us he is not writing a certain kind of verse, he is providing an example of that very thing. The passage is loosely based on the conclusion to Horace's *Epistle to Augustus,* in which Horace deprecates his own "sermones," his "parvum carmen," as unworthy of the emperor, and then, in describing the kind of verse

80. The primary allusion is to Gen. 37:7, Joseph's prophetic dream of his brothers' bowing before him; the lines also reflect Isa. 66 and similar biblical visions of triumph.

proper to Augustus, ascends into epic strains: "terrarumque situs et flumina dicere, et arces / montibus impositas et barbara regna."[81] Both passages utilize the rhetorical device called *occupatio*, the pretended refusal to narrate or describe what one is in fact narrating.

The description of "our Mars in fight" is very grand indeed, but with a grandeur that is pointed, decorous, closer to Pope's Homer than to *Paradise Lost*. The actions and the way they are described are both great and neat, enclosed within a firm, balanced rhetorical structure ("Tell of towns stormed, of armies overrun"). Clouds of dust and smoke, seemingly overflowing in lines 179–80, are contained within the couplet, as meter reinforces meaning. In the phrase that concludes the stanza, "and seas lay hid in smoke," the effectiveness of the hyperbole is a function of the wit: so much is said so casually, so succinctly.

The *Panegyric* anticipates Augustan poetry in its consistent and skillful use of balance and antithesis. Indeed, the poem, in its overall structure and in each stanza, is built upon the juxtaposition and contrast of opposed and parallel terms; its central doctrine, the reconciliation of opposites in the mean, is embodied in the fabric of the verse. In this, Waller's most careful and fully realized poem, his skill in handling the couplet is often on a par with Pope's.

> Preferred by conquest, happily o'erthrown,
> Falling they rise, to be with us made one;
> So kind dictators made, when they came home,
> Their vanquished foes free citizens of Rome.
>
> (93–96)

In the first couplet, the striking oxymora, one in each half-line, are closely knit together and cumulative in effect. But the lines require some resolution in the second couplet—the superiority of the English, suggested here, needs to be proved, demonstrated, nailed down. Similarly, the nervous

81. Horace, *Epistle* II.i.250–59, ed. H. Rushton Fairclough, Loeb Classical Library (London, 1929).

bite of the first two lines, with their distinct caesuras and sharply etched phrases, is, as it were, resolved metrically and syntactically in the calm, reasonable certainty of the last couplet.

At its most successful, Waller's poetry seems pellucid, and yet there is a surprising amount going on under the surface. The stanza immediately following the one just quoted will serve as an example:

> Like favor find the Irish, with like fate,
> Advanced to be a portion of our state;
> While by your valour, and your bounteous mind,
> Nations, divided by the sea, are joined.   (97–100)[82]

The diction in this passage is typically elegant. Most of the key terms are of Latin origin, yet none is in any way obscure or unfamiliar. Once again, the versification is skillful, with its variation of caesura and of types of parallelism. The imitative effect of the divided last line and the equivalence in sense suggested by the placement and alliteration of the parallel terms in the first line are particularly handsome effects. Here as before, the suavity of the language serves to make the audacity of the wit more palatable. Read fast, the second line is patriotic English history, the march of empire, Ireland's assumption of her place in a greater whole. Read with closer attention to its component elements, however, the phrase takes on additional meaning, becomes a slur on the Irish: they are "advanced" when they become even a "portion of our state." The rhetorical device in operation here is not a pun, but it is very like one. The distance between pun and other rhetorical devices is lessened still further in the second couplet. It is possible to isolate two separate devices—the pun on "joined" (physically and politically) and the paradoxical juxtaposition of the contradictory terms, "divided" and "joined." But in

82. The last line alludes to the biblical account of the creation, Gen. 1:6–7. In line 99 (as in line 122, quoted earlier), I adopt the reading of Fenton and the 1655 quarto in preference to Thorn-Drury.

the poem, the two things work as one. The pun would be far less effective if the occasion of the poem were the dedication ceremonies of the Cromwell Bridge; its point depends upon Cromwell's not actually joining them physically, and on the impossibility of his ever doing so. Indeed, a central quality of Waller's wit, as of Augustan wit in general, is the way in which it strives to make the impossible look perfectly reasonable.

4   The Rise of Heroic Satire

Waller served as an example to his neoclassical successors in two ways—as a model for imitation, especially in panegyric and satire, and as an innovator in technique. Waller's role in the development of the heroic couplet is a subject several critics have commented upon; the only book-length study of the poet, Alexander Ward Allison's *Toward an Augustan Poetic: Edmund Waller's "Reform" of English Poetry*, devotes itself entirely to this subject. But other equally important aspects of Waller's influence, in particular the relationship between his panegyrics and Augustan verse satire, have received much less attention.

One index to the major role Waller played in forming the Augustan sensibility is the frequency with which his poems were imitated. Waller's "sweetness," as exemplified in his lyrics, gave rise to a large and undistinguished progeny of occasional love songs and jeux d'esprit by one or another young gentleman, dotting the pages of Tonson's *Miscellanies* and similar volumes. The most persistent of the epigoni was George Granville, Lord Lansdowne, who in Johnson's words "seems to have had no ambition above the imitation of Waller, of whom he has copied the faults, and very little more."[1] A more interesting group of poems is the flourishing minor genre of complimentary epistles to ladies, in which Waller's influence and that of the Ovidian elegy coalesce. Examples among the works of Dryden include his verses to Anne Hyde, Duchess of York (1665), "To the

1. Johnson, *Lives of the Poets*, 2, 294. Lansdowne's poems may be found in Anderson, *Poets of Great Britain*, 7.

Duchess on her Return from Scotland" (1682), and "To her Grace the Duchess of Ormond" (1700). Such poems, Dryden explains, are characterized by gallantry of tone and a Virgilian "softness and tenderness": "I knew I addressed them to a lady, and accordingly I affected the softness of expression, and the smoothness of measure."[2] The closest equivalents to these poems among Pope's works are the "Epistle to Miss Blount, with the Works of Voiture" (1712) and the "Epistle to Miss Blount, on her leaving the Town, after the Coronation" (1714). But the influence of Waller is strong throughout the first part of Pope's career. As love poet and stylist, he is one of the *Pastorals'* tutelary spirits, and *The Rape of the Lock* is in a very real sense a descendent of Waller's poetry of the beau monde, of gallant praise.[3]

We find a similar pattern of slavish copying and creative adaptation in the development of the heroic occasional poem, panegyric, and satire in the late seventeenth and early eighteenth centuries. Minor poets like Katherine Philips, John Hughes, and Charles Montague, Earl of Halifax, produced panegyrics that doggedly followed the earlier poet's manner; Montague's *On the Death of his Most Sacred Majesty King Charles II* (1685) is a virtual cento of passages from Waller. The heroic panegyrics of Dryden, though they owe fewer specific debts, build upon Waller's example. But by far the most significant influence Waller exerted was upon a genre he rarely practiced himself, satire.

Waller had a low opinion of satire as a literary genre. To him, the proper function of poetry was to praise; the poet should "[look] on all that err" with "silent pity." Com-

2. Ker *Essays of Dryden, 1,* 19.

3. Waller was one of Pope's "great favourites" in his youth, and among the first poems he wrote were seven imitations of Waller; see Butt, *Poems of Alexander Pope,* pp. 3–5, 12; and Spence, *Anecdotes,* pp. 6, 18–19. The notes to Alexander Pope, *Pastoral Poetry and An Essay on Criticism,* ed. E. Audra and Aubrey Williams (London and New Haven, 1961), point out a number of echoes of Waller in the *Pastorals* and other early poems of Pope. Gay, who wrote several poems in this manner, pays explicit tribute to Waller in *The Fan,* a pallid satire in imitation of both Waller and Pope.

menting, two years before *Absalom and Achitophel,* on attacks on the Duke of Monmouth, he writes: "Lampoons, like squibs, may make a present blaze; / But time and thunder pay respect to bays." His dislike of satire had both aesthetic and temperamental grounds. "Satyricall writing," he remarked in 1677, 'was downe-hill, most easie and naturall . . . . At Billingsgate one might hear great heights of such witt. . . . . The cursed earth naturally produces briars and thornes and weeds, but roses and fine flowers require cultivation."[4]

The example of Waller's poetry, tuned to praise rather than detraction, was frequently invoked in opposition to the unsparing mockery of Restoration satire. Thus Sir William Temple, in a letter written in 1667, finds "the wit [Waller] and his company spent in heightening love and friendship" vastly preferable to "what is laid out so prodigally by the modern wits in the mockery of all sorts of religion and government."[5] Fenton begins his commentary on the poet by applying to him Archbishop Tillotson's distinction between debasing and heightening wit:

> For, Wit (says he) is a keen instrument, and every one can cut and gash with it; but, to carve a beautiful image, and polish it, requires great art and dexterity. To praise any thing well is an argument of much more Wit, than to abuse: a little Wit, and a great deal of ill-nature, will furnish a man for Satire: but, the greatest instance of Wit is to commend well.[6]

4. "Upon the Earl of Roscommon's Translation of Horace," 30; "On the Duke of Monmouth's Expedition into Scotland," 37–38; *Brief Lives,* p. 310.

5. *Letters Written by Sir William Temple, Bart, and other Ministers of State* (2 vols. London, 1700), *1,* 116–17. Cf. the memorial poem by Sir John Cotton, in *Poems to the Memory of Edmond Waller:* "Thou do'st not write like those, who brand the Times, / And themselves most, with sharp *Satyrick Rhimes.* / Nor does thy *Muse,* with smutty Verses, tear / The modest Virgin's chast and Tender Ear."

6. Fenton, p. iii. The original may be found in Sermon II, "The folly of scoffing at religion," *The Works of the Most Reverend John Tillotson, Lord Archbishop of Canterbury* (12 vols. London, 1757), *1,* 91.

Yet it was precisely in satire, the genre for which he felt such contempt and instinctive opposition, that Waller's influence was most pervasive. The heroic panegyric of Waller is the forerunner of the heroic satire of Dryden. Where earlier writers had associated satire with a "low style . . . according to [the] subject," an Horatian *sermo pedestris* or a pseudo-Juvenalian or Persian harshness, Dryden considered satire, like panegyric, to be "undoubtedly a species" of heroic poetry. His comparison of Horace and Juvenal shows his preference for a "noble . . . sublime and lofty" style, in which "the majesty of the heroic" is "finely mixed with the venom of [satire]." In his view, satire, like other forms of poetry, should have its "beauties" and its "delicate touches."[7] Consistently, Dryden sought to raise satire above mere lampoon, which blazes forth and immediately sputters out. His best poems are characterized by the attempt to lend highly ephemeral particulars an air of permanence, to turn briars and thorns into fine flowers. In doing so he is directly indebted to the example of Waller, of whom he says (in another context), "unless he had written, none of us could write."[8]

Panegyric and satire, the poetry of praise and the poetry of blame, are sister forms; classical rhetoricians, as we have seen, treat them as closely associated historically and governed by similar rules. The boundary between them is not absolute. A satire generally needs to present the norms

7. Ker, *Essays of Dryden*, 2, 84–86, 108. The relationship between Dryden's theories and the style of his own satires has been discussed by a number of critics; see esp. Reuben A. Brower, "An Allusion to Europe: Dryden and Tradition," *ELH*, *19* (1952), 38–48, reprinted as the introductory chapter of his *Alexander Pope: the Poetry of Allusion* (Oxford, Clarendon Press, 1959), pp. 1–14; Ian Jack, *Augustan Satire* (Oxford, Clarendon Press, 1952), pp. 43–76; and Nevo, *The Dial of Virtue*, pp. 215–17, 240–65. Mrs. Nevo's book is the best treatment in print of the relationship between panegyric and satire in the seventeenth century; my own study, completed in its original form before publication of Mrs. Nevo's book, may serve as independent support of some of her conclusions.

8. Ker, *Essays of Dryden, 1*, 284.

whose violations it deplores; thus satire abounds in visions of the good. There are passages of direct, unironic panegyric in *Absalom and Achitophel,* as there are in Horace, Juvenal, Rabelais, Boileau, and Pope. A great many satires, of course, masquerade as panegyric *(MacFlecknoe, A Tale of a Tub, The Praise of Folly).* And in the brilliantly equivocal passages addressed to George II in Pope's *Epistle to Augustus,* the dividing line between panegyric and satire becomes paper-thin. Walleresque panegyric, like the verse satire of the Augustan age, depends on a style which is witty and flexible, capable of smoothness or bite, written in couplets in which every word counts. Both work by setting up an ideal (often associated with a classical-Christian golden age, mythical or semi-historical) against which the actual is measured; both depend heavily upon a network of allusions, explicit or implicit comparisons; both frequently present an ideal of order and sanity seriously threatened from without.

The potentialities of satire are greater than those of panegyric, the difficulties less disabling. Perhaps heroic panegyric can never entirely get around the problem of truth, the limitations imposed by the unchanging necessities of praise, support of the status quo, inflation and simplification of the dubious and problematical. Irony is a great advantage: it enables a poet to eat his cake and have it too, to echo and imitate earlier, perhaps less legitimate heroicizing while making use of it for his own purpose. If a writer is able to use comic inflation along with serious, if he is able to encompass in his poem not only heroic virtue but worldly vanity, then the way is open for great poetry.

Waller's own attempts at writing heroic satire were not entirely successful. "The Battle of the Summer Islands" (1638), an elaborate narrative poem set in far-off Bermuda and dealing with a battle between the islanders and a whale, appears to waver between a serious and a comic treatment of its subject. Dr. Johnson judges the poem harshly:

Of *The Battle of the Summer Islands* it seems not easy to say whether it is intended to raise terror or merriment: the beginning is too splendid for jest, and the conclusion too light for seriousness. The versification is studied, the scenes are diligently displayed, and the images artfully amplified; but as it ends neither in joy nor in sorrow, it will scarcely be read a second time.

But Johnson misreads the tone, which attempts to combine wonder with playful mockery. The magic land the poem describes, with its eternal spring and extraordinary fruitfulness, is presented as a place not quite believable, as the setting of a fairy tale whose characters are miniatures of men. The two elements, the marvellous and the comic, are both present throughout the work, though in different proportions. Thus the poet is able to modulate from the pastoral idyll of the first canto to the mock-heroic comedy of the rest.[9]

As praise of an ideal, the first canto resembles Waller's panegyrics. In this first section of the poem, the Summer Islands are the Fortunate Isles, where all things flourish in their original, unfallen perfection. Waller's pet theme of the "happy island," protected from the evils of the world, finds its fullest expression here:

> Bermudas, walled with rocks, who does not know?
> That happy island where huge lemons grow,
> And orange trees, which golden fruit do bear,
> The Hesperian garden boasts of none so fair.   (I.5–8)

---

9. *Lives of the Poets, 1,* 289. The only recent critic to devote any attention to the poem is Maren-Sofie Røstvig, *The Happy Man: Studies in the Metamorphoses of a Classical Ideal 1600–1700* (Oslo, 1954), pp. 150–52. Her remarks, though interesting, are limited to the idyllic first canto, ignoring the rest of the poem. She relates the poem, with its "escapist tendency," to the genre of poems contrasting rural retirement with the bustle of the city, and finds that its emphasis on "the pleasant aspects of . . . retirement" and presentation of an Earthly Paradise exemplify a "soft" Epicurean primitivism.

In this earthly paradise the trees bear gold, while pearls, coral, and ambergris deck the beaches. Even "the naked rocks" are "not unfruitful," and at certain times of the year abound "with luscious food," the eggs of birds. The very weeds are valuable: while tobacco, "the worst of things," is shipped to England in payment of rent, the islanders dine off the far more precious fruits their land freely provides them (I.25–35).

In cold England, the fallen world, spring is over almost as soon as it appears, but Bermuda is a land of eternal spring, where all potentials are fulfilled:

> For the kind spring, which but salutes us here,
> Inhabits there, and courts them all the year.
> Ripe fruits and blossoms on the same trees live;
> At once they promise what at once they give. (I.40–43)

Here as in his panegyrics, Waller draws on classical and Christian versions of paradise. Both the myth of the golden age and the biblical Garden of Eden are visions of past glory, now lost.[10] The magic island serves as a standard for judging the diminished world men inhabit—the "cold orchards" which produce a few small fruits in several years' time, the "unripe and ill-constrained notes" poets are forced to sing in the sunless north:

> Heaven sure has kept this spot of earth uncursed,
> To show how all things were created first.
>
> (I.58–59)

Waller has ample precedent, literary and other, for his characterization of the islands of the Western Hemisphere as an unfallen Eden. Captain John Smith, in his *Generall*

---

10. The word *nondum* (not yet) and other negatives echo through Ovid's account of the golden age *(Metamorphoses,* I.89–112): forts, swords, hoes, ploughs were not yet necessary. Like Milton in *Paradise Lost,* Ovid makes the alternation of seasons consequent on man's fall from perfection. The double strain of "yearning and nonpossession, desire and inaccessibility" is characteristic of nearly all versions of paradise and Elysium; see Giamatti, *The Earthly Paradise and the Renaissance Epic,* p. 84.

Historie of Virginia, New England, and the Summer Isles,
provides not only the terms of Waller's description, but
something of the same idealization:

> There seems to be a continuall Spring . . . and though
> the trees shed their leaves, yet they are alwaies full of
> greene. . . . Without plowing or much labour, they have
> two Harvests every yeere . . . and little slips of Fig-trees
> and Vines doe usually beare fruit within the yeere, and
> sometimes in lesse.[11]

The accounts of voyagers regularly described the new world
in terms of the received myths of perfection: a land of gentle
and everlasting spring, in which the earth brings forth
abundance without planting and the inhabitants "live after
the maner of the golden age."[12] The paradise can be a
secular one, or it can carry religious overtones, as in Andrew
Marvell's "Bermudas." Marvell's poem provides a particularly interesting contrast with "The Battle of the Summer
Islands," on which it draws as a direct source. To Marvell,
every detail bears religious significance. At all times we are

11. *Travels and Works of Captain John Smith,* ed. Edward Arber and
A. G. Bradley (2 vols. Edinburgh, 1910), 2, 626–27; cf. *Battle of the Summer
Islands,* I.40–55. The *Generall Historie* was published in 1624 and reached
a fourth edition in 1632. The opening section of Smith's account of Bermuda
provides Waller with most of his details about the island's natural riches—
pearls, ambergris, lemons, oranges, palmettos, figs, plantains, melons, pine-
apple, papaw, cedars, and tobacco. One unusual detail for which Smith
serves as source is the gathering of eggs off the rocks (I.25–28). A second work
by Smith, *The True Travels, Adventures, and Observations of Captaine John
Smith, in Europe, Asia, Affrica, and America* (1630), includes in its chapter
on Bermuda a brief description of a whale trapped in a bay, which may
very well have served as Waller's source for the second and third cantos
(the events, though in this case not the tone and treatment); see *Travels and
Works,* 2, 889.

12. Arthur Barlowe's account of the discovery of Virginia (1584), in
Richard Hakluyt, *The Principal Navigations, Voyages, Traffiques, and
Discoveries of the English Nation* (6 vols. London, 1907), 6, 128. More than
a dozen passages in travelers' accounts treating the Americas as a paradise
are cited in Robert Rawston Cawley, *The Voyagers and Elizabethan Drama*
(Boston and London, 1938), pp. 290–91.

aware that the gifts of nature are God's, and the poem is a hymn of thanksgiving. This element is entirely absent from Waller, even in the passages where the poets are most close.[13] Waller's paradise is a dream of innocent epicurean retreat from the cares of the world—the poet as inspired beachcomber, with nothing to do but amuse himself with thoughts of love and poetry:

> Oh! How I long my careless limbs to lay
> Under the plantain's shade, and all the day
> With amorous aires my fancy entertain,
> Invoke the Muses, and improve my vein!   (I.62–65)

His poem is a fanciful exercise in impossibilities, a dream paradise attainable only by the imagination, fated not to last.

From the beginning of the poem, we have been aware of the possibility of loss, and several details serve as foreshadowing. Wild figs which grow on the island, we are told, are the equal of those which Cato displayed to the Roman Senate in urging the destruction of Carthage, "With the rare fruit inviting them to spoil / Carthage, the mistress of so rich a soil" (I.23–24). The destructive human emotions which have been kept out of the "happy island . . . walled with rocks" are massed outside, waiting to come in—or are present in potential within the islanders themselves. In the second canto, two whales are trapped by the tide among the rocks of the island. The enormous creatures are at first a

13. "With Cedars, chosen by his hand, / From *Lebanon*, he stores the Land. / And makes the hollow Seas, that roar, / Proclaime the Ambergris on shoar. / He cast (of which we rather boast) / The Gospels Pearl upon our Coast. / And in these Rocks for us did frame / A Temple, where to sound his Name" ("Bermudas," 25–32, in Margoliouth, *Poems and Letters of Andrew Marvell*). The equivalent passage in Waller is largely secular, and any religious implications are as much pagan as Christian: "Where shining pearl, coral, and many a pound, / On the rich shore, of ambergris is found. / The lofty cedar, which to heaven aspires, / The prince of trees! is fuel for their fires" (I.9–12). Several parallels between the two poems are pointed out in Margoliouth's edition, *1*, 220.

source of terror, but then when the islanders see that they are relatively helpless, they begin to look more and more like an easy prey, and the young men of the island march forth to do battle. The child of nature we have seen in the first canto has turned into the more equivocal hero of mock-epic, the awkward knight, the representative of human folly:

> [They] Dispose already of the untaken spoil,
> And as the purchase of their future toil,
> These share the bones, and they divide the oil.
>
> (II.35–37)

The intentions of cantos two and three are plainly mock-heroic. In presenting the encounter between men and whales, the poet consistently makes use of the language and conventions of epic poetry: epithets, similes, noble-sounding sententiae, an elevated Latinate style, invocations of the gods, comparisons with earlier representatives of the epic tradition. The description of the younger whale's return after his escape, for example, consists of one amplifying comparison after another:

> Roaring she tears the air with such a noise,
> As well resembled the conspiring voice
> Of routed armies, when the field is won,
> To reach the ears of her escaped son.
> He, though a league removed from the foe,
> Hastes to her aid; the pious Trojan so,
> Neglecting for Creusa's life his own,
> Repeats the dangers of the burning town.
>
> (III.57–64)

Though the whales provide a properly heroic adversary, the knights whose task it is to slay the dragon do not measure up. Turnus usurps the role of Aeneas, and "The men, amazed, blush to see the seed / Of monsters human piety exceed" (III.65–66).

The distinguishing characteristic of the mock-heroic

approach is a conscious disproportion between material and treatment, between fact and image: the heroic emotions and attitudes evoked have no appropriate object to fasten onto, and the contrast between magniloquent language and unheroic actuality serves to refute the pretensions under attack. Where the panegyrist seeks to gloss over what is potentially embarrassing, the satirist makes these very things stand out glaringly, showing the gap between the ideal and the actual. The youths of the island make every effort to "show / What love, or honour, could invite them to" (II.44–45), but their pretentions of chivalric glory are shown to be hollow. They suffer the simplest and most direct indignity in the lexicon of knighthood, falling off a horse:

> And down the men fall drenched in the moat;
> With every fierce encounter they are forced
> To quit their boats, and fare like men unhorsed.
>
> (III.14–16)

Again and again, the great strength and courage of the whales are contrasted with the pettiness and puniness of the men. Even when the mother whale lies helpless before their assaults, the men are outclassed: "The shining steel her tender sides receive, / And there, like bees, they all their weapons leave" (III.23–24). One is reminded of Gulliver in Lilliput.

What destroys the tranquillity of the island, we come to see, is not the invasion of the whales but the vanity of man, dreaming of self-aggrandizement and instant glory. The whales, free of sin and excessive concern with self, are at one with the unfallen world of uncurbed magnanimity we have seen in the first canto; the men are not. All the human feeling in this part of the poem, as well as all the genuine courage, rests with the whales. The battle is grotesque, but the whales are not an object of ridicule; indeed, toward the end of the poem, pathos rather than humor is the prevalent mode. In describing the attack on the defenseless whale, Waller uses a straightforward, unironic rhetoric of amplification to accentuate the pity of the situation—the whale's physical greatness, the awesome power of nature, and the hubris of man, who is constantly attempting to interfere with the natural order, imposing his own rule:

> And now they change the color of the lake;
> Blood flows in rivers from her wounded side,
> As if they would prevent the tardy tide
>
> .   .   .
>
> She swims in blood, and blood does spouting throw
> To heaven, that heaven men's cruelties might know.
>
> (III.46–52)

"The Battle of the Summer Islands," then, attempts to be at one time serious and comic; idyllic, heroic, and mock-heroic; ironic and pathetic. Waller shows the way for Dryden and Pope in treating his comic material seriously, in giving his mock-heroics a dignity of utterance, in using a heroic rather than a burlesque style. Yet his poem is not really like those of the Augustan satirists—it is far gentler and far more softhearted. Perhaps, in spite of its mock-heroics, it is closer to the genre of pastoral than to satire; criticism is subordinate here to the presentation of an ideal.[14] One is reminded, particularly in the first canto, of the juxtaposition of the idyllic and comic in many pastorals, the double perspective on a world much less sophisticated, in both a good and a bad sense, than our own. "The Battle of the Summer Islands" is in many ways a Renaissance poem rather than a neoclassical one, closer to Spenser than to Pope. The flexibility of tone and the choice of subject matter, along with the machinery of cantos and arguments, indicate Waller's debt to the Renaissance epic romance; Tasso, Ariosto, and Spenser (especially those parts of Books III, IV and VI of the *Faerie Queene* that are closest

---

14. Frank Kermode's introduction to *English Pastoral Poetry* (London, George G. Harrap, 1952), esp. pp. 14–15, includes suggestive remarks on the relationship between the two genres of pastoral and satire.

to the Italianate tradition) are his models as much as the classical epic.[15]

Waller's one other mock-heroic poem, "The Triple Combat" (c. 1675), similarly tempers its satire with gentleness. The poem is a graceful account of the battle for supremacy between the recently arrived Duchess of Mazarin, the Duchess of Portsmouth, and English Chloris (identified by various commentators as Nell Gwyn and the Duchess of Cleveland). The tone is one of dignified amusement; its decorum is unruffled throughout.

> Yet like the Three on Ida's top, they all
> Pretend alike, contesting for the ball;
> Which to determine, Love himself declined,
> Lest the neglected should become less kind.
> Such killing looks! So thick the arrows fly!
> That 'tis unsafe to be a stander-by.   (33–38)

We can see in lines like this what Pope learned from Waller. A good deal more is at stake in *The Rape of the Lock,* of course, and Waller is by no means the later poet's equal in his mastery of the local effects of language or in satiric pointedness. Still, "The Triple Combat" points the way for Pope with its witty allusions to the epic tradition and with its delicate control over a complex tone. The hints of disapproval at the sexual conduct of the royal mistresses and at the world of palace intrigue they inhabit are balanced by the suave, courtly tone and the constant undercurrent of praise. What holds the various elements together is irony: the critical sharpness shows through the gallantry, especially in the witty second couplet. The same effect is at work else-

15. Ariosto provides precedent for "The Battle of the Summer Islands" in his mixture of heroic romance and comic irony, but Waller nevertheless preferred the dignity of Spenser and Tasso to Ariosto's lightheartedness. Edward Fairfax's translation of *Gerusalemme Liberata* was Waller's favorite poem. Lines imitated from Fairfax's Tasso, *The Faerie Queene,* and the *Aeneid* are sprinkled through his works, and several allusions to the events of the three poems show his detailed familiarity with them.

where in the poem. To say that "Venus had been an equal
friend to" each contestant (25) is both praise and dispraise;
the irony allows author and reader to share the joke, creat-
ing an air of civilized detachment from the spectacle of
human pretension. "The Triple Combat" is far removed
from the bluntness of most contemporary treatments of the
subject:

> Was ever prince's soul so meanly poor,
> To be enslav'd to every little whore?
>
> . . .
>
> Witness the royal line sprung from the belly
> Of thine anointed Princess, Madam Nelly,
> Whose first employment was with open throat
> To cry fresh herrings e'en at ten a groat.[16]

The Augustan satirists, in company with Waller, give their
allegiance to "fine raillery," artistic indirection, rather than
direct abuse. "How easy it is," Dryden writes, "to call rogue
and villain . . . But how hard to make a man appear a fool,
a blockhead, or a knave, without using any of those op-
probrious terms! . . . A man may be capable, as Jack Ketch's
wife said of his servant, of a plain piece of work, a bare
hanging; but to make a malefactor die sweetly was only
belonging to her husband."[17]

Dryden himself was uncertain of his ability to live up to
his ideal of heroic satire, and it is understandable that Waller, in his few attempts in the genre, should have failed to
achieve the ideal. In isolated passages both "The Battle of
the Summer Islands" and "The Triple Combat" manage
the difficult task of making "a malefactor die sweetly," succeed in holding their discordant elements in a delicate ironic
balance. But the balance is a difficult one to maintain, and
the success of both poems is limited and intermittent. Waller

---

16. "Satire" (1677), attributed to John Lacy, 7–8, 23–26, in Lord, *Poems on Affairs of State, 1,* 426.
17. Ker, *Essays of Dryden, 2,* 92–93.

THE POETRY OF LIMITATION

was not temperamentally inclined toward satire, and the poems we have been discussing have more elegance than bite. As Dryden says of Horace, "his urbanity, that is, his good manners, are to be commended, but his wit is faint; and his salt, if I may dare to say so, almost insipid."[18] If, as Northrop Frye has suggested, satire is characterized by a "double focus of morality and fantasy," with two poles of militant, purposeful attack and pure, amoral inventiveness, the free play of the imagination, Waller is more at home with the second.[19] Moreover, he reverses the ordinary proportions of satire in giving greater emphasis to the ideal than to its violation. Indeed, Waller sometimes finds the ideal where no one else would. In its closing lines, "The Triple Combat" makes a surprising turnabout. The sway of the King's mistresses, which Waller has been mildly poking fun at, and which other satirists of the time fiercely attack, suddenly and charmingly becomes an image of perfection, of the world art creates for itself.

> Our golden age,
> Where Love gives law, Beauty the sceptre sways,
> And uncompelled, the happy world obeys.
>
> (44–46)

Even in satire, the characteristic attitudes of Waller the panegyrist are not far away.

The years between 1660 and 1700 witnessed an extraordinary profusion of satire. Much of it, like much of the panegyric the period produced, is now unreadable—squibs which barely blazed up for a moment. Yet the best of the Restoration satirists, like Waller, sought a hedge against oblivion, sought in one way or another to give their poems more staying power without sacrificing their pointed topicality. In their satires, Dryden, Rochester, Marvell, Butler,

18. Ibid., p. 84.
19. *Anatomy of Criticism* (Princeton, Princeton University Press, 1957), pp. 224–25.

and Oldham were all in varying degrees concerned with form, with tradition, and with the creation of a multiple perspective. Dryden, the major figure among these satirists, owes more to Waller in his satiric method than the others do, but all dealt with a similar set of problems.

Satire, like panegyric, must be effective both as persuasion and as literature; it must convince in two different ways. The author writes as a partisan, yet in a sense he must disguise his partisanship; satire and panegyric are often most effective when they create the illusion of objectivity. Satirists are the self-acknowledged legislators of the world. Ordinarily, satire is aimed at the educable, "the more Moderate sort . . . not the Violent," those able to take the satirist's lesson to heart. Even where there is little or no hope for reforming the fools and knaves themselves, they can be branded "a public nuisance," arraigned for the benefit of others. " 'Tis an action of virtue to make examples of vicious men. They may and ought to be upbraided with their crimes and follies; both for their own amendment, if they are not yet incorrigible, and for the terror of others, to hinder them from those enormities which they see are so severely punished in the persons of others."[20] In all these cases, it is the satirist's responsibility to show that what he considers a vice is one, and that correction is possible or desirable—in other words, to validate his standards. His position is anything but detached, yet through various devices he gives his partisan arguments the objectivity of wit, point, precision, and aesthetic distance.

Heroic satire, as developed by Dryden, is fundamentally an approach to the problem of validation, an attempt to get around the inevitable subjectivity and particularity of the genre. The heroic path was not the only one for neoclassical satire, of course. But much of the experimentation in the techniques of satire which characterized the Restoration

---

20. Dryden, Preface to *Absalom and Achitophel,* in Kinsley, *Poems of Dryden, 1,* 215; "Discourse concerning Satire," in Ker, *Essays of Dryden, 2,* 80.

and early eighteenth century led similarly in the direction of art, detachment, and control. The awareness of tradition implicit in the ideal of creative imitation, the manipulation of points of view and personae, the careful maintenance and deliberate, pointed violation of stylistic decorum, the development of a network of allusions which adumbrate standards for judgment—all these things reflect the conviction that satire can be a fine art.

Waller served as a model for heroic satire in several ways—in his panegyrics, in his own heroic satires, and, by a curious irony, in a number of poems in which he was the victim of satire. The most consistent and successful application of epic devices to satire before Dryden is found in parodies of heroic panegyrics. The parodist has certain built-in advantages: problems of style, tone, and the relevance of details to the whole are to some extent solved for him. The form and direction of his work, as well as the point of view, are to a large degree determined by its relationship to an original which he can in part imitate and in part attack. In the series of anti-heroic "painter" poems which followed in the wake of Waller's *Instructions to a Painter* (1666), the assumptions and style of Walleresque panegyric are turned against their originator. At times they rely on direct parody, at times, less closely tied to a specific original, on a free ironic imitation, using the methods of panegyric to refute illegitimate pretensions of heroism. Though uneven in quality and often uncertain in approach, the best of the "painter" poems succeed in their best moments in combining in a single form the advantages of epic poetry and satire.

Waller's *Instructions to a Painter,* a highly elaborate "historical poem" praising the exploits of the Duke of York, is particularly vulnerable to attack because its insistence on epic grandeur and romantic gallantry is so relentlessly single-minded. The poem's characteristic figure is hyperbole; at all times it seeks to magnify, making the Duke of York a superior Achilles and the battle of Lowestoft (in reality rather inconclusive) a second battle of Actium:

Draw the whole world, expecting who should reign,
After this combat, o'er the conquered main

. . .

Make the sea shine with gallantry, and all
The English youth flock to their Admiral

. . .

With his extraction, and his glorious mind,
Make the proud sails swell more than with the wind.

(5–6, 9–10, 19–20)

Throughout the poem, the raw and often unlovely materials of fact are changed before our eyes into the stuff of romance, and the poet never loses his composure. One passage describes the fleet's return to port after having run out of provisions. Prosaic fact may tell us that the sailors were unpaid and that the visit of the court ladies to the fleet was mere self-indulgence and show.[21] To the poet, none of this matters:

Spreading our sails, to Harwich we resort,
And meet the beauties of the British court.
The illustrious Duchess, and her glorious train,
(Like Thetis with her nymphs) adorn the main.
The gazing sea-gods, since the Paphian Queen,
Sprung from among them, no such sight had seen

. . .

The soldier here his wasted store supplies,
And takes new valour from the ladies' eyes.   (79–90)

Three gentleman volunteers are killed at the Duke of York's side. In the heroic never-never-land of the poem, nothing in life could become them like the leaving it:

Happy! to whom this glorious death arrives,
More to be valued than a thousand lives!
On such a theatre as this to die,

---

21. See Arthur W. Tedder, *The Navy of the Restoration* (Cambridge, Eng., 1916), pp. 112—17; and Wedgwood, *Poetry and Politics Under the Stuarts,* pp. 199–200.

> For such a cause, and such a witness by!
> Who would not thus a sacrifice be made,
> To have his blood on such an altar laid?   (149–54)

Yet truth cannot be kept from breaking in. Three hundred forty lines of unabated gallantry is quite a lot; the poet's wit and grace have the difficult job of controlling the intrinsic absurdity of much of his material. The result, in lines like the "glorious death" passage, is an elegant monotony, neatly turned out, predictable and thin. The reader is surfeited with sweets—as, clearly, were several of Waller's contemporaries.

Waller's poem was greeted shortly after publication by the "Second Advice to a Painter," a biting satire on the Duke of York and the court party. The relationship between this poem and Waller's is simple and direct: the "Second Advice" is virtually a line-by-line refutation of *Instructions to a Painter,* parodying Waller's characteristic rhetoric and looking at the events Waller had described, the conventions and attitudes that inform his poetry, with the cold eye of satire: "First, let our navy scour through silver froth, / The ocean's burden and the kingdom's both."[22] The pseudo-Virgilian periphrases, characteristic of Waller's heroic style, become a vehicle for satire: the navy is a literal burden (on the taxpayer), not simply a metaphorical one. In describing the Duchess of York's descent on Harwich, the author of the "Second Advice" uses similes to deflate and not to amplify. When he compares navies to "fopperies," "a small sea-masque" (65–66) set up for purposes of courtship, and likens

---

22. "Second Advice to a Painter," 113–14, in Lord, *Poems on Affairs of State, 1.* In lines 65 and 185–86, below, I have emended the *POAS* text in favor of readings from the 1689 edition (*Third Collection of the Newest and Most Ingenious Poems, Satyrs, Songs, &c. against Popery and Tyranny, Relating to the Times*). There are two good discussions of the "Second Advice" and "Third Advice" as anti-heroic satire: Lord's introduction, *POAS, 1,* xliv–xlvii; and Nevo, *The Dial of Virtue,* pp. 164–72.

the Duchess and her train to the "land crabs" which "at
Nature's kindly call / Down to engender at the sea do crawl"
(57–58), his choice of diction and imagery is as consistent
as Waller's and as well suited to his purpose. The satirist
uses the devices of balance and antithesis as he uses heroic
conventions, reductively. Here is his version of the "glorious
death" of the royal favorite Falmouth:

> Such was his rise, such was his fall, unprais'd:
> A chance shot sooner took him than chance rais'd.
> His shatter'd head the fearless Duke distains,
> And gave the last-first proof that he had brains.
>
> (185–88)

Throughout, he takes the standard topoi of epic panegyric
and turns them to satiric effect: the sound and fury of battle
description, the interested gods, the inevitable comparison
of the King to the sun. Like the panegyrist, he can create
an impressive passage by developing an image at length,
giving a convention new and surprising life. Thus, toward
the end of the poem, he addresses these lines to the King:

> What boots it that thy light does gild our days
> And we lie basking in thy milder rays,
> While swarms of insects, from thy warmth begun,
> Our land devour and intercept our sun? (347–50)

The effectiveness of the lines comes from their combination
of the expected and the unexpected: the familiar associations of the sun as royalist emblem, reinforced in the first
two lines, make the swarming insects an even stronger violation of the decorum of a well-ordered state.

The "Second Advice" and the "Third Advice to a
Painter," probably by the same author, are essentially attempts to give the lie to the heroic interpretation of the
events and personages of the Second Dutch War. "Victory,"
the author of the "Third Advice" says, "does always hate a

rant"; the satirist's duty is to expose the empty boasts of the eulogists, to reveal things as they really are:

> Death picks the valiant out, the cow'rds survive.
> What the brave merit th'impudent do vaunt,
> And none's rewarded but the sycophant.[23]

Marvell's "Last Instructions to a Painter" takes a somewhat different approach. "Last Instructions," unlike its predecessors, does not parody Waller directly, and it relies less on the purely reductive use of heroic devices. Instead, it uses the conventions and imagery of Walleresque panegyric to create a genuine heroic satire—to impale its figures on a pin or blow them up to grotesque, absurd proportions in a style that can be savage or dignified at will.

The satires attributed to Marvell in the 1660s and 1670s fall generally into two groups. The largest number are straightforward personal attacks, normally written in jigging anapests, often witty in a rough-and-tumble way, and always concerned to diminish and deflate ("The Statue in Stocks-Market," "The Kings Vowes," "Upon his Majesties being made free of the Citty"). A smaller group, of more dubious authenticity and markedly inferior quality, consists of poems written in an inflated style, either pseudo-Juvenalian railing or epic pomp ("Britannia and Rawleigh," "Hodge's Vision from the Monument"). Most of the poems in the recent Yale edition of Restoration satirical verse, *Poems on Affairs of State,* fall into one category or the other, a clearly defined "low" or "high" road. Among the poems known to be Marvell's, only in the "Last Instruc-

---

23. "Second Advice," 220–22; "Third Advice," 71, in Lord, *POAS, 1.* George deF. Lord, "Two New Poems by Marvell?" *Bulletin of the New York Public Library, 62* (1958), 551–70, has argued that the "Second" and "Third Advice," because of similarities to the "Last Instructions" in style, emphasis, and political outlook, should be attributed to Marvell. But Ephim G. Fogel, "Salmons in Both, or Some Caveats for Canonical Scholars," *BNYPL, 63* (1959), 223–36, 292–308, has argued against the attribution, and the objections he raises are cogent enough to put the issue once more in doubt.

tions" does he combine the witty particularity and colloquial vigor of his lampoons with the elaboration and
elevation of the second group.[24] It is this quality of styliza-
tion, this union of colloquial force and aesthetic distance,
that makes Marvell in the "Last Instructions" a significant
forerunner of Dryden and Pope.

What distinguishes the use of heroic devices in "Last Instructions" from that in the "Advices" or from such experiments in epic satire as John Oldham's *Satyrs upon the
Jesuits* is not so much its consistency or extent as its skill,
imagination, and flexibility. The style of satire, Dryden
argued in his "Discourse concerning Satire," will at best
combine the dignity and force of Juvenal with the wit and
urbanity of Horace. Modern critics have pointed out that
Dryden's own poetry is based on the "imaginative unity" of
opposite styles, allowing the poet to "modulate between the
poles of high seriousness and mockery."[25] Much the same
ideal animates Marvell in "Last Instructions." His poem,
rather than being a prisoner of the circumstances that produced it, concerned only to stir up the passions of the
moment, is capable of convincing the uncommitted, the
"Moderate sort." The heroic perspective aids persuasion
by adumbrating powerful standards of judgment.

In some ways, the heroic perspective is the only thing that
holds the poem together. "Last Instructions," in company
with such other major Restoration satires as *The Rehearsal
Transpros'd* and *Hudibras,* suffers from structural weaknesses; it is a detailed running commentary on events, extending to nearly a thousand lines. Nevertheless, the
network of epic allusions is the imaginative heart of the
poem and makes the poet's criticism seem more than merely

24. The canon of Marvell's verse has always been uncertain. Of the poems
mentioned above, "Hodge's Vision" has been shown by Margoliouth not to
be Marvell's, and Lord has given good reasons for excluding "Britannia
and Rawleigh" and "The Kings Vowes" from the canon.

25. Ker, *Essays of Dryden,* 2, 92–93, 107–08; Nevo, *The Dial of Virtue,* p. 9;
Brower, *Alexander Pope,* pp. 3–11.

personal. The evocation of a world more golden than brass, where values are not topsy-turvy, underlines the deficiencies of a world where "female *Stewart . . . Rules the four Seas,*" where an admiral, commanding a fort, "with panting Heart, lay like a fish on Land," where "feather'd *Gallants*" run away at the first signs of battle.[26]

Satire is most clearly accommodated to a heroic norm in the poem's several extended episodes. Approximately two hundred lines are devoted to a parliamentary debate over a proposed general excise, described in mock-heroic terms as a battle. The excise itself is portrayed in mock-fearsome fashion as a monster compounded of Spenser's Error and Milton's Sin and Death. The terms of the description, characteristically, do double duty, describing a beast of properly monstrous proportions and at the same time listing the effects of the proposed tax: "A thousand Hands she has and thousand Eyes, / Breaks into Shops, and into Cellars prys" (133–34). In the catalog of troops that follows, the heroic trappings again and again point up the shoddiness of the world described. The forces of the court parade before us: "early Wittals," "For Diligence renown'd, and Discipline," in their "Loyal haste" leaving "young Wives in Bed" (151–53), followed by "Expectants pale, with hopes of spoil allur'd" (159), Procurers, Papists, Drinkers, and Lord's Sons, marching forth in disorderly profusion. These are opposed by a small band of heroes—e.g. "Daring *Seymour,* that with Spear and Shield, / Had stretcht the monster *Patent* on the Field" (257–58). The ensuing battle (in which the forces of good triumph against great odds) is described in a similar manner; the heroic terms, wittily applied, provide amplification, aesthetic distance, and satiric point. The episode

26. "Last Instructions," 562, 597, 762, in Margoliouth, *Poems and Letters of Andrew Marvell.* The first passage quoted refers to the employment of Frances Stewart, whom the King sought unsuccessfully for his mistress, as model for Britannia on coins and medals.

contains an abundance of names, most of them now unfamiliar, and much direct personal satire. Yet, through his
use of a heroic fiction, Marvell is able to preserve these flies
in amber.

A second lengthy and more or less self-contained section
of the poem is devoted to the humiliation England suffered
when the Dutch sailed up the Thames in 1667, burning and
capturing several English ships virtually without opposition.
In this passage, Marvell, working within the framework of
the elevated heroic style, creates a verse susceptible of a
great range of effects. With deceptive gentleness he describes
the "sporting Navy" of the Dutch (535), aided by Neptune,
Aeolus, and the Tritons, sailing gaily up the Thames, as
though they had come to woo, not to destroy. The insinuating prettiness of the verse, so pointedly at variance with
its content, accentuates the ignominious helplessness of the
English as the Dutch admiral, surrounded by "streaming
Silks" which seem to "Court the Air," with "wanton Boys"
clinging on every rope and shroud, makes his leisurely way
through the rivers of England (537–42). Marvell does not
allow us to forget that the Dutch invasion is a rape, a violation of England's "Crystal Streams, and Banks so green, /
And Beauties e're this never naked seen" (525–26).

Here Marvell works largely by indirection. But elsewhere
he is more direct in painting the extent of England's shame.
"Such the fear'd *Hebrew*, captive, blinded, shorn, / Was led
about in sport, the publick scorn" (735–36). The biblical
analogy, like the echoes of the epic tradition quoted earlier,
applies precisely to the situation. England's natural greatness has been allowed to melt away; the ships that panegyrists like Waller had celebrated as the rulers of the sea
have fallen into decay. Private interests, pride, and sloth
hold unchecked sway, as the natural principles of order that
normally govern the universe and the state of man lie in
abeyance. In powerful lines, Marvell brings into juxtaposition the ideal of a strong and healthy commonwealth (the

seat of whose power is the British navy) and its sad corruption:

There our sick Ships unrigg'd in Summer lay,
Like molting Fowl, a weak and easie Prey,
For whose strong bulk Earth scarce could Timber find,
The Ocean Water, or the Heavens Wind.   (573–76)

In lines such as these, Marvell has succeeded in giving his material a chiseled form and in powerfully evoking an ideal against which human folly can be measured. Though "Last Instructions" does not realize the full possibilities of epic satire, the poem nevertheless succeeds remarkably at its best moments in using heroic conventions and a proliferating wit to bring forth a central unity of theme: a rigorous diagnosis of the illness of the body politic.[27]

It remained for Dryden and others to add to the virtues of "Last Instructions" concentration and a clear sense of form. Where in "Last Instructions" the overriding heroic metaphor applies in succession to a series of details, so that we have in effect a string of conceits, witty footnotes to historical events, *MacFlecknoe, Absalom and Achitophel,* and Rochester's "The Maim'd Debauchee" all embody a central heroic metaphor in a central action. The witty application of heroic imagery in local details is subordinate to and dependent upon the plot of the poem; parts illuminate the whole, and the whole controls the parts. Even more clearly than in the other poems we have been discussing, standards for judgment are implicit in the heroic framework of the satire and are made explicit in the author's manipulations of levels of style.

27. Most earlier commentators do not share my high opinion of "Last Instructions." D. W. Jefferson's characterization of the poem as "littleness and confusion . . . obscure references to insignificant people and their forgotten deeds" ("Aspects of Dryden's Imagery," *Essays in Criticism, 4* [1954], 37), is typical; see also Brower, *Alexander Pope,* p. 11. More recently, Lord and Nevo have spoken of the poem's ambitious scope and its epic qualities, though Nevo ultimately judges the poem to be an interesting failure; see *The Dial of Virtue,* pp. 173–79; and Lord, *POAS, 1,* 97–99.

"The Maim'd Debauchee"[28] gains dramatic focus by its use of a persona—a superannuated rake who, in recalling past glories, reveals to the reader a life utterly empty both in the present and in the past. Much of the poem's effectiveness lies in the ironic contrast between the heroic terminology with which the persona describes himself—battles, fleets, the memories of an old warrior—and the actual content of the life described. The extended simile that opens the poem reads like an excerpt from Dryden's *Annus Mirabilis:*

> As some, brave *Admiral,* in former War
> > Depriv'd of Force, but prest with Courage still,
> Two Rival Fleets appearing from afar,
> > Crawls to the top of an adjacent Hill.　　　(1–4)

For twelve lines, the simile proceeds on its leisurely, expansive course, and it is not until the fourth and fifth stanzas that we begin to see what the persona's heroic life consists of:

> My Pains at last some respite shall afford,
> > While I behold the Battels you maintain:
> When Fleets of Glasses sail around the Board,
> > From whose Broad-Sides Volleys of Wit shall rain.
> > > > (17–20)

The mock-heroic decorum, with its pretense of panegyric, is maintained here. "Fleets of Glasses" and "Volleys of Wit," by the standards of the age, are perhaps less noble than battles with real guns, but wit and companionship are still positive terms. "The pleasing Billows of Debauch" and "Love and Wines unlucky chance" (14–15) refer to drunkenness, impotence, and syphilis, yet they manage to do so in a flattering, gallant-sounding way.

As the poem goes on, the veneer of euphemistic metaphor

---

28. In Pinto, *Poems by Rochester.*

begins to wear thin, and the ugly reality shows through more plainly:

> I'le tell of Whores attacqu'd their Lords at home,
>   Bawds Quarters beaten up, and Fortress won:
> Windows demolish'd, Watches overcome,
>   And handsom Ills by my contrivance done.

(33–36)

The gap between rationalization and actuality is so wide that both "high" terms (the military terms "Fortress," "Quarters," "attacqu'd," and the generally honorific "handsom" and "Lords") and "low" terms ("Bawds" and "Whores," "Windows" and "Watches") serve the end of exposure. The heroic language here parodies Waller's *Panegyric to my Lord Protector*, but the parody is in the manner of Dryden and Pope rather than the "painter" satires: Waller's poem serves not as an object of satire, but as a representative of the genuine epic tradition against which the drunken violence of the rake's life can be measured.[29] In the closing lines, attitudes which have been implicit throughout the poem are brought to the surface:

> Thus Statesman-like I'le saucily impose,
>   And, safe from Danger, valiantly advise;
> Shelter'd in impotence urge you to blows,
>   And, being good for nothing else, be wise.

(41–44)

The irony, interestingly enough, works two ways: If the heroic fiction has served to expose the empty and self-destructive life of the rake, the last lines suggest that the superannuated statesman, retired warrior, and elderly rake are all on a level and that none is worthy of any respect.

In Dryden's two best-known satires, the choice of central fiction similarly directs the reader's response. It is difficult, for instance, to see Shadwell any way other than the way

---

29. Cf. *Panegyric*, 177–78: "Tell of towns stormed, of armies overrun, / And mighty kingdoms by your conduct won."

Dryden wishes; indeed, Dryden's Shadwell has entirely supplanted the historical Shadwell for most readers. The mock-
heroic manner, with its ironic pretense of panegyric, allows
the author to strip Shadwell of all his pretensions without
raising his voice in anger or violating the decorum of his
style. The artistic skill with which it is done, the apparent
impersonality, the aesthetic distance, make the demolition
job in *MacFlecknoe* all the more effective.

> Sh- - alone my perfect image bears,
> Mature in dullness from his tender years.
> Sh- - alone, of all my Sons, is he
> Who stands confirm'd in full stupidity.   (15–18)

The lines parody the language of the proud royal father:
"my perfect image," "his tender years," "he / Who stands
confirm'd," all are dignified, sonorous phrases, clichés of
panegyric or pseudo-Virgilian sentiment. The last line, with
its multiple alliteration and careful balance, is the most
sonorous of all; "stupidity," if you ignore its meaning, is a
fine, round, Latinate word. The contrast between apparent
statement and implicit meaning, the author is suggesting,
is akin to the contrast between the figure Shadwell tries to
present to the world and the "real" Shadwell revealed in
the poem.

The heroic framework and the heroic style are used to
somewhat different effect in *Absalom and Achitophel*. Here
Dryden is not setting out simply to demolish, but like Waller
in *A Panegyric to my Lord Protector*, he is seeking to persuade an audience within a particular political context,
seeking to illuminate contemporary history by interpreting
it in heroic-poetic terms. The personages of *Absalom and
Achitophel* are fully rounded characters, unlike the butt
Shadwell. The two title characters (and among the minor
characters, Zimri) are presented as examples of talents mis-
applied or perverted. Achitophel, like Satan (or like Cromwell, as Royalist writers regularly presented him), is the
great bad man, whose gifts make him all the more danger-

ous.[30] Absalom, partly for prudential reasons (since when the poem was written the possibility remained open that Charles would forgive Monmouth), is seen as gallant and attractive but too easily swayed, subject to the appeals of ambition and self-love. His good qualities make him all the more corruptible.

> Th' ambitious Youth, too Covetous of Fame,
> Too full of Angells Metal in his Frame;
> Unwarily was led from Vertues ways,
> Made Drunk with Honour, and Debauch'd
> with Praise.   (309–12)

The judgment is conveyed by the verse itself, as phrase after phrase balances positive against negative: *Covetous* of *Fame, too full* of *Angells Metal, was led from Vertues ways,* all lead up to the final decisive pairs of terms. Up to the last line, the negative terms are mild, almost apologetic or palliative. But the powerful lowering effect of *Drunk* and *Debauch'd* suggests that the conflict is irreconcilable and that whatever resistance Absalom has heretofore put up will now disintegrate. The lines provide both an explanation of his conduct and standards for condemning that conduct.

Dryden's satires are based on the assumption that artistic skill and persuasive effectiveness are inseparable. The heroic fiction is persuasive in purpose, and the author uses his control over the nuances of style to present powerful implicit arguments in support of his position. The poet's art is directed at having the reader take his positives and negatives as absolute, objective, indisputable, rather than simply partisan. An example is this passage from *Absalom and*

---

30. See, for example, Clarendon's well-known character sketch of Cromwell: "He could never have done half that mischieve without great parts of courage and industry and judgement. . . . Wickedness as great as his could never have accomplished these trophies without the assistance of a great spirit, an admirable circumspection and sagacity, and a most magnanimous resolution" (Clarendon, *History of the Rebellion, 6,* 91–97).

Achitophel dealing with Shimei (Slingsby Bethel, sheriff of London):

> Chast were his Cellars, and his Shrieval Board
> The Grossness of a City Feast abhor'd:
> His Cooks, with long disuse, their Trade forgot;
> Cool was his Kitchen, tho his Brains were hot.
>
> (618–21)

Shimei is measured and found wanting by a number of inter-locking standards—most notably, heroic poetry, Christian-ity, and reason. The first two lines, dignified in their ap-pearance, masquerade as praise, but such two-edged terms as "Chast," "Grossness," and "abhor'd" suggest that some-thing somewhere is askew. Chastity is an admirable thing, but not in cellars and kitchens—which, Dryden suggests with a bit of snobbery, are Bethel's proper sphere and the legitimate concerns of a city official. The memories of epic feasts invoked by the second line help indicate that Shimei's religiosity is excessive and hypocritical, a rationalization for uglier motives. Lines 620–21 are blunter in their language, eschewing irony for direct statement, but the precise, bal-anced phrasing gives the lines the appearance of dispassion-ate analysis rather than snarling invective. The unemployed cooks are a violation both of common sense and of the Puritans' own doctrine that " 'Tis Sin to misimploy an hour" (613). The final line suggests that Bethel's brains and kitchen are inverted, a symptom of the radical disorder from which he and his party suffer. Nature and Homer (or the Bible) are the same: the violation of literary standards sug-gested in the ironic literary references is symptomatic of violations of moral standards and, finally, of reason.

Dryden's heroic satire, like Waller's heroic panegyric, seeks to reconcile apparent opposites: partisanship with impersonality, a commitment to persuasion with a commit-ment to art, contemporaneity with universality, witty allu-siveness with serious intent. Both poets, choosing to work in genres traditionally considered dubious in their origins and associations, sought to extend to occasional forms the prestige of epic poetry—not only "the greatest work which the soul of man is capable to perform," but the best of all teachers.[31] Both use their work to urge and exemplify standards of human behavior, measuring the actual by the ideal. Yet both satire and panegyric, to be convincing, need to reflect the world of the actual with seeming accuracy and vividness. In order to succeed, the work must give the accidental circumstances of history the autonomy of myth, a probable and necessary form, while retaining all their pointed specificity. It is extremely difficult for a writer to do justice to the particular and the general, the real and the ideal, and it is equally difficult to achieve both elegance and force in the heroic style. The experiments in heroic and mock-heroic satire in the Restoration period are, except for the poems of Dryden, rarely more than partial successes. Only the very best of Waller's panegyrics manage entirely to transcend the occasions which called them forth, and neither of his attempts at heroic satire succeeds in doing so. Nevertheless, the problem these poets stated and tried with only limited success to solve is one whose solution occupied Dryden and Pope throughout their careers and is perhaps the central concern of neoclassicism: the attempt to put the product of the moment beyond the reaches of time.

31. Ker, *Essays of Dryden*, 2, 154.

5 "Parent of English Verse"

Dryden thought of Waller as the first Augustan, the first man to attempt to refine upon the powerful but inartistic works of the "former age." In the translation of Boileau's *L'art poétique* which he did in collaboration with Sir William Soame, Dryden singles Waller out for a position equivalent to that of Malherbe in France:

> *Waller* came last, but was the first whose Art
> Just Weight and Measure did to Verse impart;
> That of a well-plac'd Word could teach the force,
> And show'd for Poetry a nobler Course:
> His happy Genius did our Tongue Refine,
> And easie Words wth pleasing Numbers joyn:
> His Verses to good method did apply,
> And chang'd harsh Discord to Soft Harmony,
> All own'd his Laws; which, long approv'd and try'd,
> To present Authors now may be a *Guide*.[1]

In his essays, Dryden praises Waller repeatedly for the sweetness of his verse. He associates Waller's harmony with that of Virgil, writing of Spenser's *Faerie Queene* that its "verses are so numerous, so various, and so harmonious, that only Virgil . . . has surpassed him among the Romans; and only Mr. Waller among the English."[2]

---

1. *The Art of Poetry*, I.131–40, in Kinsley, *Poems of Dryden*. The conventional neoclassical view of Waller's place in literary history is discussed in René Wellek, *The Rise of English Literary History* (Chapel Hill, 1941), pp. 35–36, 40.
2. Ker, *Essays of Dryden*, 2, 28–29.

Dryden and Thomas Rymer treat Waller as an exemplar to their own generation (the words "teach," "taught," "showed" recur in Dryden's references to the older poet), isolating certain qualities of his verse which fit in with their view of what poetry should be. To Rymer and to Francis Atterbury, author of the critical preface to an edition of Waller's poems published in 1690, Waller represents the apogee of poetic achievement.

> He was, indeed, the parent of English verse, and the first that showed us our tongue had beauty and numbers in it. Our language owes more to him than the French does to Cardinal Richelieu, and the whole Academy. . . . The tongue came into his hands like a rough diamond: he polished it first, and to that degree, that all artists since him have admired the workmanship, without pretending to mend it. . . . He undoubtedly stands first in the list of refiners, and, for aught I know, last too; for I question whether in Charles II's reign English did not come to its full perfection; and whether it has not had its Augustan age as well as the Latin.[3]

After the neoclassical mode had been firmly established, critics tended to treat Waller not as an assured master, but as a somewhat uncertain harbinger of the age to come. Thus Johnson writes:

> But of the praise of Waller, though much may be taken away, much will remain, for it cannot be denied that he added something to our elegance of diction, and something to our propriety of thought; and to him may be applied what Tasso said, with equal spirit and justice, of himself and Guarini, when, having perused the

3. Preface to *The Second Part of Mr. Waller's Poems* (1690), in Thorn-Drury, *1*, xviii–xix. So Rymer writes, summarizing the contents of the sixth chapter of *A Short View of Tragedy:* "Chaucer refin'd our English. Which in perfection by Waller" *(Critical Works of Thomas Rymer,* p. 123).

Pastor Fido, he cried out, "If he had not read *Aminta,* he had not excelled it."[4]

It is uncertain to what extent Waller's reforms were conscious, to what extent he began writing in the late 1620s and 1630s with a definite program. Aubrey's remarks on Waller would seem to indicate a clearly defined purpose from the outset: "When he was a brisque young sparke, and first studyed Poetry, me thought, sayd he, I never sawe a good copy of English verses; they want smoothness; then I began to essay."[5] But the words and tone here clearly are Aubrey's, not Waller's. At most Aubrey is recording the poet's recollection thirty or forty years later, or perhaps simply extrapolating from his practice. The poet's few recorded critical comments largely date from the years after the Restoration, when statements of the necessity of "correctness" had become conventional. Still, his critical dicta are generally consistent. Like Dryden, he speaks of Britain's native genius as "bold and sublime, but negligently dressed." English poets are too "indulgent" to their "faults," do not have sufficient "patience" to "cultivate [their] thoughts." It is necessary, he says, to bridle Pegasus, "favour his flight, and moderate his force."

> Though poets may of inspiration boast,
> Their rage, ill-governed, in the clouds is lost.[6]

Waller shared the neoclassical interest in the "fixing" of the English language. He was a member of a Royal Society committee "for improving the English tongue," and par-

4. Johnson, *Lives of the Poets, 1,* 296. Cf. Goldsmith's comment on Waller's funeral poem on Cromwell: "Our poetry was not quite harmonized in Waller's time; so that this, which would be now looked upon as a slovenly sort of versification, was, with respect to the times in which it was written, almost a prodigy of harmony" (*The Beauties of English Poesy,* in Arthur Friedman, ed., *Collected Works of Oliver Goldsmith* [5 vols. Oxford, 1966]), *5,* 327–28.

5. Aubrey, *Brief Lives,* p. 310.

6. "Upon the Earl of Roscommon's Translation of Horace," 7–14, 39–40; cf. "Prologue to the Maid's Tragedy," 17–18.

ticipated, along with Cowley, Dryden, Thomas Sprat, the Duke of Buckingham, and others, in a short-lived attempt to set up an English Academy after the French model.[7] Comments on Waller's verse usually associate him with the movement toward purifying the language. "Mr. Waller's diction," Fenton writes, "hath been generally reputed the standard of purity." According to Atterbury, "he sought out, in this flowing tongue of ours, what parts would last, and be of standing use and ornament; and this he did so success-fully, that his language is now as fresh as it was at first set-ting out."[8] In "Of English Verse," Waller uses the fact of linguistic change to argue that English verse cannot last, that the idea of poetic immortality is mere self-delusion.

> When architects have done their part,
> The matter may betray their art;
> Time, if we use ill-chosen stone,
> Soon brings a well-built palace down.
>
> Poets that lasting marble seek,
> Must carve in Latin, or in Greek;
> We write in sand, our language grows,
> And, like the tide, our work o'erflows.   (9–16)

Yet an answer to the poem's pessimism is implicit in the highly polished lines. If the fault of English is that it is not

7. Sprat had urged the formation of an English Academy in his *History of the Royal Society;* Dryden, Evelyn, Swift, and Defoe were among the many other authors in the late seventeenth and early eighteenth centuries to advocate the idea. See Spingarn, *Critical Essays of the Seventeenth Century,* 2, 112–15, 310–13, 327–29, 337.

8. Fenton, p. viii; Thorn-Drury, *1*, xx. Cf. the poems by Thomas Rymer and Sir Thomas Higgons on Waller's death, in *Poems to the Memory of Edmond Waller,* pp. 3, 7. Rymer writes: "This Northern Speech refin'd to that degree, / Soft *France* we scorn, nor envy *Italy:* / But for a fit Comparison must seek / In *Virgil's* Latin, or in *Homer's* Greek." Higgons comments more fully on Waller's linguistic reform: "The *English* he hath to Perfection brought; / And we to speak are by his Measures taught. / Those very *Words,* which are in Fashion now, / He brought in Credit half an Age ago. / Thus *Petrarch* mended the *Italian* Tongue; / And now they speak the Language which he sung."

Latin, the obvious remedy is to try to make it a fixed language, like Latin. Waller normally holds that carefully wrought verse will endure.

> Our lines reformed, and not composed in haste,
> Polished like marble, would like marble last.[9]

Waller's diction and syntax are markedly Latinate,[10] though not in the radical manner of Milton. He does not wrench normal English patterns and pull words into new meanings; his Latinisms do not stand out as Milton's do. The frequency of Latin-derived verbs and polysyllabic nouns, used in lieu of more colloquial equivalents, helps give Waller's lines their characteristic formality. Yet this is not its only effect. The Latinate words help make his language not only more grand, but more precise.

Waller will often take a word that has been naturalized into English and use it in its original Latin sense, sometimes punning on the two meanings. The device is, of course, common in Milton; in both poets, it is in part at least an attempt to enrich the language, what Dryden speaks of as the "heightening" of a word's signification.[11] Waller's use of the device is characteristically witty. A convenient poem to examine is "Of her Passing Through a Crowd of People," a Sacharissa poem in heroic couplets with a heavy concentra-

---

9. "Prologue to the Maid's Tragedy," 11–12. Waller uses the couplet a second time, with minor variations, in "To the Duchess [of York], when he presented this Book to Her Royal Highness," 11–12. For another reference to the ability of "polished lines" to last, see "To the Servant of a Fair Lady," 27–28.

10. My remarks on Waller's diction are in part indebted to the careful and detailed analyses of Allison, *Toward an Augustan Poetic*, pp. 24–46. Other useful studies include H. C. Beeching, "A Note on Waller's Distich," *An English Miscellany Presented to Dr. F. J. Furnivall* (Oxford, 1901), pp. 4–9; Josephine Miles, *The Primary Language of Poetry in the 1640's;* Geoffrey Tillotson, "Eighteenth Century Poetic Diction," *Essays in Criticism and Research* (Cambridge, Cambridge University Press, 1942), pp. 53–85; and the same author's *On the Poetry of Pope* (Oxford, Clarendon Press, 1938).

11. Ker, *Essays of Dryden, I,* 171.

tion of Latinate terms. The poem plays with ideas of order and chaos, of love and propriety, in presenting Sacharissa's discomfort in a crowd, "oppressed by those who strove to be her guard." "This disorder" brings "a greater favour" to her servants than they "durst entertain,"

> when thus compelled they pressed
> The yielding marble of her snowy breast.
> While love insults, disguised in the cloud,
> And welcome force, of that unruly crowd.[12]

Many of the key terms bear double meaning. "Oppressed" (overpowered, burdened, pressed against), "compelled," (forced against one's will, pushed), "insults" (exults, causes an affront to Sacharissa's dignity) are all Latin puns. Similarly, "disorder" means tumult in a general sense and, literally, a state in which order is violated. Other terms used in an unusual sense ("confused," "obsequious") similarly turn on the idea of universal order and its violation.

The Latinate terms produce the effect of compression. Words like "oppressed," "obsequious," and "disorder" express a fairly complicated concept in a small space and are more suggestive as well as more concise than possible phrasal equivalents. Moreover, they are more malleable: the poet can stress key terms by their position in the line or couplet. Waller's variations from habitual English syntax normally have a similar effect. Perhaps the most striking instances of Latin syntax in his poems are his frequent ablative absolutes, or participial clauses:

> *Troy walled so high,*
> The Atrides might as well have forced the sky.

> Of those rude tempests which, *for rapine sent,*
> Too oft, alas! involved the innocent.

---

12. "Of her Passing Through a Crowd of People," 6, 9–14. I am indebted to Allison's comments on the language of this poem, though my conclusions differ somewhat from his; see *Toward an Augustan Poetic,* p. 27.

But living virtue, *all achievements past,*
Meets envy still, to grapple with at last,

That sun once set, a thousand meaner stars
Gave a dim light to violence, and wars.[13]

In each of these passages, the italicized phrase has a neat
concision and makes up a metrical and rhetorical unit; the
syntax works hand in hand with the rhetorical patterning.
On the whole, Waller stays closer to ordinary English usage
than Milton does. But his word order, with its frequent inversions, is removed from that of colloquial speech. His aim
is less remoteness from prose than effectiveness as verse: a
verb at the end of the line often provides balance and emphasis; manipulation of word order can produce phrasal
units that can be played off against one another ("Homage
to thee, and peace to all she brings").[14]

The influence upon Waller of Virgil, the patron saint of
neoclassicism, shows itself in many ways—most clearly, perhaps, in the profusion of epithets in his verse. In his reliance
on adjectives and nouns rather than verbs, he resembles
Spenser, Milton, and his favorite, Fairfax, differing from
such poets as Jonson and Donne; his affinities are with the
poets of epic sweep, grandeur, and circumstance, rather than
the poets of colloquial force. As Josephine Miles says, "cere-
mony" and mellifluousness are characteristic of his language.[15] A poem like the georgic *On St. James's Park* is a

13. "Upon His Majesty's Repairing of Paul's," 59–60; "To the King, on
his Navy," 11–12; *A Panegyric to my Lord Protector,* 147–48, 153–54. This
characteristic of Waller's style is pointed out in Allison, *Toward an Augustan
Poetic,* p. 36.

14. Cf. Atterbury's comment: "Since the stress of our verse lies commonly
upon the last syllable, you will hardly ever find him using a word of no
force there. I would say, if I were not afraid the reader would think me too
nice, that he commonly closes with verbs, in which we know the life of
language consists" (Thorn-Drury, *1,* xxi–xxii).

15. *The Primary Language of Poetry in the 1640's,* pp. 30, 82. See also
Allison, *Toward an Augustan Poetic,* pp. 27–29.

storehouse of poetic diction and elegant periphrases—
"feathered cloud," "silver fishes," "gilded barges," "crystal
lake," "swelling tide," "loaded branches," "lofty mound,"
"the harvest of cold months" (for ice). At times the impression of ornamented triviality is overwhelming; less skillful
courtiers have been better poets. Yet in his use of poetic diction and epithets as elsewhere, his guiding principle is
multum in parvo, witty economy; his characteristic elegance
comes from his tight control over language and effect, which
is in part the result of limiting his aims. And his importance
as an exemplar to the Augustans comes in part from his
concentration on technique as an end in itself.

Atterbury's preface comments in detail on "the new turn
of verse which [Waller] brought in, and the improvement
he made in our numbers." Dryden had presented Waller
as having taught his fellow writers verse ordonnance: "the
excellence and dignity of [rhyme] were never fully known
till Mr. Waller taught it: he first made writing easily an art;
first showed us to conclude the sense most commonly in dis-
tichs, which, in the verse of these before him, runs on for so
many lines together, that the reader is out of breath to
overtake it."[16] Like Dryden, Atterbury reflects unfavorably
upon the verse of Donne and his contemporaries as "harsh,
untuneable," containing "no distinction of parts, no regular
stops, nothing for the ear to rest upon."

> Mr. Waller removed all these faults, brought in more
> polysyllables, and smoother measures, bound up his
> thoughts better, and in a cadence more agreeable to the
> nature of the verse he wrote in; so that wherever the
> natural stops of that were, he contrived the little break-
> ings of his sense so as to fall in with them.[17]

As George Williamson and Ruth Wallerstein point out,
Waller did not invent the heroic couplet; he is rather "a
consolidator of poetic developments and . . . the acknowl-

16. Ker, *Essays of Dryden*, *1*, 7; Thorn-Drury, *1*, xx.
17. Thorn-Drury, *1*, xxi.

edged leader of a restrictive movement."[18] But as one of the first writers habitually to employ the form, he helped develop its characteristic techniques. The term "heroic couplet" normally implies metrical closure (after the couplet and in most cases after the line), but that is not its sole characteristic. Miss Wallerstein writes: "In defining the classical couplet we imply by the term not merely that there shall be a distinct pause, but that the two lines shall form an organic and distinct unit of thought."[19] Marlowe in *Hero and Leander,* Drayton in *England's Heroical Epistles,* Spenser in *Mother Hubbard's Tale* all write largely in closed couplets, but they do not (to use Dryden's term) "conclude the sense" within these couplets. Their verse is essentially continuous, interested in getting on with the story. They use devices of balance and antithesis sparingly and casually, and only half of their lines employ the caesura (as compared with roughly two-thirds for Waller and Dryden, four-fifths for Pope).[20]

The distinguishing mark of the heroic couplet, as practiced by Waller, Dryden, and Pope, is its elaborate patterns of parallel and contrasting elements. Parallel and antithetical figures are common in the prose and poetry of most languages; we find them in the great Greek and Roman orators and in most of the writers of the Elizabethan period

18. Williamson, "The Rhetorical Pattern of Neo-Classical Wit," in *Seventeenth Century Contexts,* p. 261. See also Ruth Wallerstein, "The Development of the Rhetoric and Metre of the Heroic Couplet," *PMLA, 50* (1935), 166–209. Earlier studies which consider Waller's place in the development of the couplet include Henry Wood, "Beginnings of the 'Classical' Heroic Couplet in England," *American Journal of Philology, 11* (1890), 55–79; and A. Hamilton Thompson, "Writers of the Couplet," *Cambridge History of English Literature* (Cambridge and New York, 1907–17), 7, 55–96, esp. 61–67. See also Allison, *Toward an Augustan Poetic,* pp. 62–87.

19. "Development of the Heroic Couplet," p. 168.

20. I am using the figures of Felix N. Schelling in "Ben Jonson and the Classical School," *PMLA, 13* (1898), 221–49, based in each case on 100-line samples. There is a good discussion of the difference between Waller's verse and that of the Elizabethan couplet writers in Wallerstein, "Development of the Heroic Couplet," pp. 169ff.

and the seventeenth century, Lyly and Bacon, Spenser and
Donne. But in the heroic couplet these elements are primary
and are built into the structure of the verse. In the couplet
of Waller, Dryden, and Pope, key words are emphasized by
their placement in the line, and the line, markedly sym-
metrical, is frequently balanced around a single pivot.

Within the basic pattern of balance and antithesis, a great
deal of variation is possible. Line can be contrasted with
line, half-line with half-line. Recent studies have pointed
out the great variety of effects Pope can achieve with his
couplet.[21] Waller rarely achieves this range, but he shows
great skill in his more limited repertoire. I quote the following lines from *To the King, upon His Majesty's Happy Return,* as fairly typical:

> While *to yourself severe, to others kind,*
> With *power unbounded,* and *a will confined,*
> Of this vast empire *you* possess the *care,*
> *The softer part* falls to *the people's* share.
> *Safety,* and *equal government,* are things
> Which *subjects* make as happy as their *kings.*

$$(103-08)$$

The words in italics are parallel and antithetical terms. In
lines 103–04, each element in the first half of the line cor-
responds to and contrasts with an element in the second half.
The second of these lines, with its unstressed "and" in central position, represents a common pattern in Waller, the
line which breaks into two halves, with four strong stresses.
In the second couplet, line is set against line, with the parallel elements inverted chiastically in the second line. Line
107 presents an unequal balance, with two pauses. In line
108, the antithetical terms occur at the beginning and
the end of the line; the pattern is not unusual for Waller,

---

21. See W. K. Wimsatt, Jr., "One Relation of Rhyme to Reason," and
"Rhetoric and Poems: Alexander Pope," in *The Verbal Icon* (Lexington,
University of Kentucky Press, 1954), pp. 153–66, 169–85; and Tillotson, *On
the Poetry of Pope,* pp. 124–40.

though he does not customarily invert verb and object ("sub-jects make") when the verb is not an emphatic word. Waller is careful to vary the placement of the caesura; Pope, in a letter discussing versification, comments on Waller's skill in arranging his pauses.[22] Here as elsewhere Waller compli-cates the movement of the couplet by interweaving cross-patterns of alliteration and assonance (as in the second couplet above: em*p*ire, *p*ossess, *p*art, *p*eople's).

The couplet form of necessity makes rhyme an important structural element in the verse. Waller's rhymes are gener-ally emphatic and effective. He rarely uses feminine rhymes and almost never rhymes a word on a secondary accent; most of his rhyme words, like Pope's, are monosyllabic. Normally, his rhymes involve key words. In the first thirty-six lines of *To the King, upon His Majesty's Happy Return,* only two couplets rhyme words that do not carry heavy rhetorical stress ("though / do," "all / shall"), while in the two early poems "Of the Misreport of her being Painted" and "Of her Passing through a Crowd of People" (totalling forty-four lines), again only two rhymes involve unemphatic words ("below / so," "so / bow"). The point of many of the couplets is summed up in the rhymes, as, for instance, in the clearly contrasted terms in the opening lines of the poem "Of the Misreport of her being Painted":

> As when a sort of wolves infest the *night,*
> With their wild howlings at fair Cynthia's *light.*

Such terms are frequently parallel or antithetical ("joy / destroy," "oppose / foes," "press / cease"). Most of the rhyme words are nouns or verbs—seventeen nouns, twelve verbs, three adjectives, four adverbs, one conjunction in *To the King;* twenty-four nouns, eleven verbs, five adjec-tives, four adverbs in the two shorter poems. More often than not the rhymes are between different parts of speech: twelve against six in *To the King,* eleven against eleven in

22. Letter to Henry Cromwell, Nov. 25, 1710, in George Sherburn, ed., *Correspondence of Alexander Pope* (5 vols. Oxford, 1956), *1,* 107.

the other two. The most frequent combination is noun against verb (occurring thirteen times in the three poems). Here the contrast in structure normally accompanies a contrast in sense; again the rhyme words carry much of the weight of the couplet, as subject and verb, verb and object express the lines' central relationship.

> As ships, though never so obsequious, fall
> Foul in a tempest on their admiral.

> The revolted sea
> Trembles to think she did your foes obey.[23]

The poet Shenstone suggests a further neoclassical nicety in rhyme: "Rhymes, in elegant poetry, should consist of syllables that are long in pronunciation; such as 'are, ear, ire, ore, your;' in which a nice ear will find more agreeableness than in these 'gnat, net, knit, knot, nut.' "[24] *To the King, upon His Majesty's Happy Return* contains only five rhymes on short vowels in its first eighteen couplets. Here too Waller uses his variations from the norm to good advantage; such words often supply force in lieu of agreeableness ("live / forgive," "think / sink," "filled / killed").

A characteristic of Waller's verse frequently remarked on by Augustan critics is his use of the "turn." Dryden praises the "beautiful turns of words and thoughts," "those beauties which gave the last perfection" to the works of Waller and Denham.[25] The turn is a musical figure involving repetition; in figures of this kind, according to Puttenham, "the care is no lesse ravished with their currant tune, than the mind is with their sententiousnes."[26] A clear and full defi-

23. "On her Passing through a Crowd of People," 7–8; *To the King, upon His Majesty's Happy Return*, 17–18. For a good discussion of the uses of rhyme, especially in the poetry of Pope, see Wimsatt, "One Relation of Rhyme to Reason."

24. William Shenstone, "On Writing and Books," *40*, in *Works in Verse and Prose* (2 vols. London, 1768), 2, 161; quoted in Tillotson, *On the Poetry of Pope*, pp. 123–24.

25. Ker, *Essays of Dryden*, 2, 108.

26. Puttenham, *The Arte of English Poesie*, pp. 206–07.

nition of the turn is given by Anthony Blackwall in his *Introduction to the Classics* (1718):

> The most charming *Repetitions* are those, whereby the principal Words in a Sentence, either the same in Sound, or Signification, are repeated with such Advantage and Improvement, as raises a new Thought, or gives a musical Cadence and Harmony to the Period. Those in *English* are call'd fine *Turns;* and are either upon the Words only, or the Thought, or both.[27]

A turn on the thought alone would presumably involve playing with synonyms—as in, for example, the closing lines of Waller's "On the Discovery of a Lady's Painting":

> The sign of beauty *feeds* my *fire.*
> No mortal *flame* was e'er so cruel
> As this, which thus survives the *fuel!*

But normally the turn requires repetition of a word or root. In its simplest form it is mere iteration, and even here Puttenham recognizes many variants: *"Anaphora* or the Figure of Report" ("In vayne . . . / In vayne . . ."), *"Antistrophe* or the Counter turne," and among others, the "Redouble," the "Eccho sound" ("Much must he be beloved, that loveth much"), and the "Coocko-spel" ("is gon, is gon away"). Even at its simplest, the device often entails some variation of meaning, form, or emphasis. In the fully developed turn, which Puttenham calls *"Traductio,* or the tranlacer," "Ye turne and tranlace a word into many sundry shapes as the Tailor doth his garment, and after that sort do play with him in your dittie."[28]

In Milton, the turn is a central element in the structure and progression of the blank verse line and is capable of wide variations in tone. The lyric simplicity of the first example

---

27. Quoted in Williamson, *The Proper Wit of Poetry*, p. 117. I have not been able to consult the original.
28. Puttenham, pp. 208–13.

and the power and subtlety of the second are appropriate
to the two speakers, Eve and Satan.

> Sweet is the breath of morn, her rising sweet,
> With charm of earliest Birds; pleasant the Sun
>
> .   .   .
>
> And sweet the coming on
> Of grateful Ev'ning mild, then silent Night
>
> .   .   .
>
> But neither breath of Morn when she ascends
> With charm of earliest Birds, nor rising Sun
>
> .   .   .
>
> Nor grateful Ev'ning mild, nor silent Night
>
> .   .   .
>
> Or glittering Star-light without thee is sweet.
>
> Know ye not mee? ye know me once no mate
> For you, there sitting where he durst not soar;
> Not to know mee argues yourself unknown.[29]

Pope's turns are sharper, wittier, leaning toward the aphoristic and antithetical; frequently the turn provides the structural sinews of the couplet, and the repetition of the word
opens out its meaning. In each example below, the repetition involves a shift in meaning, forcing us to face up to the
implicit ambiguity (moral as well as verbal) in the central
terms:

> And without sneering, teach the rest to sneer.
>
> With too much Thinking to have common Thought.
>
> Might hide her Faults, if *Belles* had Faults to hide.[30]

---

29. *Paradise Lost*, IV.641–56, 828–30.

30. *Epistle to Dr. Arbuthnot*, 202; *Epistle II: of the Characters of Women*,
98; *Rape of the Lock*, II.16, in Butt, *Poems of Alexander Pope*. The last
example and the second Milton passage are cited in Wimsatt, *Verbal Icon*,
pp. 179, 211; I am generally indebted to Wimsatt's remarks on the turn.

Waller's turns, particularly in his panegyrics, tend to be simpler than those of Milton or Pope.

> Mirror of poets! mirror of our age!

> The Queen of Britain, and the Queen of Love!

> Our nation's glory, and our nation's crime.

In each of these examples, the two meanings are complementary rather than sharply antithetical. Ben Jonson, addressed in the first passage, is a pattern (mirror) to all other poets, and in his plays the age is reflected (with its "spots . . . or graces") as in a mirror. St. Paul's Cathedral is the glory of the nation, and its neglect is the shame of the nation; "nation's" in one case reflects possession, in the other responsibility. The simplicity and directness of the parallels, with their lack of metrical variety, weaken their effectiveness somewhat; Waller's turns sometimes give the impression of redundancy rather than concision. In a line like "At once they promise what at once they give" or "Resolved to conquer, or resolved to die," we appear at first glance to have no contrast but a simple emphatic repetition. Yet even here there is a double meaning: "At once" means at one time and immediately, "resolved" means first determined, then resigned.[31]

In Waller's poems in heroic couplets, the turns work hand in hand with patterns of balance and antithesis. The turns in the lyrics are delicate rather than emphatic. They do not always rise above the trivially decorative: in the opening lines of "To Mr. Henry Lawes," for example, though the "tranlacing" of the two terms, with the chiastic inversion in line two, is metrically skillful, the lines are quite bathetic:

> *Verse* makes heroic virtue *live;*
> But you can *life* to *verses* give.

31. "Upon Ben Jonson," 1; "To the Queen, occasioned upon Sight of Her Majesty's Picture," 12; "Upon His Majesty's Repairing of Paul's," 4; "Battle of the Summer Islands," I.43; *Instructions to a Painter*, 18.

The turn on "body" and "unbodied" in "Of the Last Verses in the Book" has more substance, as does the turn on "chance" in "The Fall":

> Here Venus smiled to see blind chance
> Itself before her son advance
>
> . . .
>
> 'Twas such a chance as this, made all
> The world into this order fall.   (9–14)

Waller's lyrics are often constructed around a single idea,[32] developed at length through synonyms and analogies, though not always with actual repetition of key terms. Several of them do weave a single word or group of words through the verse with great skill. The words "soft," "sleep," and "eyes" run through "Of the Lady who can Sleep when she Pleases." In "Of the Discovery of a Lady's Painting," which deals with the lover's disillusionment when he learns that the "beauty" he "worshipped as divine" is "no beauty," but a product of artful deception, the central argument is summed up by the two recurrent words, "no" (and other variants on the negative) and "beauty." Similarly, in "The Story of Phoebus and Daphne, Applied," the controlling analogy between lover and god of poetry is expressed through turns on key words. Thyrsis, the hero of the poem, resembles Apollo in his "love," in his "song," and, as the two ideas coalesce, in the bays he gains at the end. Another poem, "Of the Misreport of her being Painted," seeks to refute a slanderous accusation against Sacharissa by turning the accuser's own terms against him. The poem turns upon the different meanings of the word "paint," as the poet shows triumphantly that the painter is nature and not art:

> Paints her, 'tis true, and does her cheek adorn
> With the same art wherewith she paints the morn;

32. Cf. Ker, *Essays of Dryden*, 2, 109: "All the sonnets in [the Italian] language are on the turn of the first thought."

With the same art wherewith she gildeth so
Those painted clouds which form Thaumantias' bow.
(19–22)

Waller's "smoothness" is partly an evenness of tone: his effects are all muted, small-scale. Metrically, his verse is regular and harmonious. "Well-placing of words, for the sweetness of pronunciation," Dryden writes, "was not known till Mr. Waller introduced it."[33] He avoids harsh sounds, frequent elisions, and extra-metrical syllables, seldom departing even slightly from the iambic pattern. In spite of the Latinity of his diction, he rarely uses long words; when he does use them, a trisyllable will be coupled with a monosyllable, making up a compact metrical unit ("prevailing foes," "fierce contention," "all achievements past"). Nothing disturbs the smooth sustained flow of the couplet.[34]

We have Waller's own indirect testimony that he formed his characteristic style upon the model of Edward Fairfax's translation of Tasso. He chose, in other words, to reject the example of the generation immediately before him, such Jacobean poets as Jonson and Donne, and turned instead to the heroic poetry of the Elizabethan age. Dryden's remarks on the relationship between Waller and Fairfax are predicated upon the assumption that the poets of the "former age" or "the former part of this concluding century," whatever their virtues, ignored "the beauties of our numbers":

> For Spenser and Fairfax both flourished in the reign of Queen Elizabeth; great masters in our language, and who saw much farther into the beauties of our numbers than those who immediately followed them. Milton was the poetical son of Spenser, and Mr. Waller of Fairfax. . . . Many besides myself have heard our

33. Ibid., *1*, 169.
34. The qualities of evenness, harmony, and "smooth-flowing conversational ease" are emphasized in the accounts of Waller's style in Wallerstein, "Development of the Heroic Couplet," pp. 200–01, and Miles, *Primary Language of Poetry in the 1640's*, p. 81.

> famous Waller own, that he derived the harmony of
> his numbers from *Godfrey of Bulloign,* which was
> turned into English by Mr. Fairfax.[35]

Waller's own epic ambitions, his conception of panegyric
as heroic, made the example of Fairfax particularly attractive to him. He found in *Godfrey of Bulloigne,* as in *The
Faerie Queene,* didactic purpose clothed in "well-sounding
numbers," confirming his own view of the "use of poetry":
"By the loud trumpet, that our courage aids, / We learn
that sound, as well as sense, persuades."[36] There are of
course marked differences in approach, emphasis, and style
between an epic poet writing a long narrative poem in
stanzas and an occasional poet writing fairly short complimentary poems in couplets. Nevertheless, Waller's stylistic
debt to the earlier authors, especially Fairfax, is a real one,
and recent critics, taking Dryden's hint, have defined the
resemblance in some detail. Miss Wallerstein has pointed
out several qualities in Fairfax's ottava rima that anticipate
Waller's couplets: a "sententious and generalized tone," a
consistent, unemphatic smoothness, and a heavy reliance
upon end-stopped two-line units within the stanza.[37] Verbal
schemes are plainly marked, but neat balance is far more
common than sharp antithesis; the poem moves along at a
rapid clip, and the reader is never tempted to linger over
details. I quote a typical passage:

> Among this squadron rode a gentle page,
> The Soldans minion, darling and delite,
> On whose faire chin the spring-time of his age
> Yet blossom'd out her flowres, small or lite;
> The sweat (spread on his cheekes with heat and rage)

35. Ker, *Essays of Dryden,* 2, 247. Fairfax's translation of *Gerusalemme
Liberata* was published in 1600.

36. "Upon the Earl of Roscommon's Translation of Horace," 23–28.

37. "Development of the Heroic Couplet," pp. 177–81; see also Allison,
Toward an Augustan Poetic, pp. 76–77; and Miles, *Primary Language of
Poetry in the 1640's,* p. 82.

Seem'd pearls or morning dewes, on lillies white,
The dust therein uprold, adorn'd his haire,
His face seem'd fierce and sweet, wrathfull and faire.[38]

The music of Fairfax's verse is a good deal simpler and
neater than the varied, suspended movement of the Spen-
serian stanza; Milton, with his "sense variously drawn out
from one Verse into another," is the poetical son of Spenser
in more ways than one.[39] Aside from the verbal schemes,
the most striking quality of the lines quoted is their air of
graceful unreality. Even dust and sweat are turned to ornament. As with Waller, the sweetness is partly a matter of
vocabulary, of what he chooses to emphasize and chooses to
ignore, and partly a matter of metrical regularity, smoothness of flow. The paradoxical, hyperbolic quality in the
lines is muted, tamed by the graceful flow of the language
and meter.

In the eighteenth century, Waller's "sweetness" and
"smoothness" were conventionally bracketed with the
"strength" of Sir John Denham. "Strength" means forceful,
aphoristic concision of expression—saying a great deal in
a small space. The "strong" poet is able to turn a memorable
phrase wittily and concisely, throw out a striking metaphor
or series of metaphors, illuminate his material in successive
flashes; his aim is to be masculine, forceful, expressive.
Thomas Carew, in his "Elegie upon the Death of Dr.
Donne" (1633), contrasts Donne's "masculine expression,"
"rich and pregnant phansie" to those less original poets
whose "tuned chime" simply "charms the outward sense":

To the awe of thy imperious wit
Our stubborne language bends, made only fit
With her tough-thick-rib'd hoopes to gird about
Thy Giant phansie, which had prov'd too stout
For their soft melting Phrases.

38. *Godfrey of Bulloigne,* IX.81.
39. Preface ("The Verse") to *Paradise Lost,* in Darbishire, *Poetical Works
of Milton,* p. 180.

Jonson is similarly praised in the memorial volume *Jonsonus Virbius* (1638) for his "tough sinewy" verse, his "strenuous lines"; as with Carew's lines on Donne, "strength" implies strength of character:

> Who
> Gave Lawes, by which hereafter all must goe,
> But solid JOHNSON? from whose full strong *quill,*
> Each line did like a Diamond drop distill,
> Though hard, yet cleare.[40]

The possible concomitant defects of strong writing are obscurity and crabbedness. Implicit in such statements as Carew's is the assumption that strong lines preclude smoothness and that it is not the poet's responsibility to pare his "Giant phansie" down to suit his audience. When, in the course of the seventeenth century, harmony and perspicuity came to be looked upon as major stylistic virtues, the developing classicism and rationalism of the age saw strong lines as an aberration. Thus Francis Osborn in 1656 instructs his son to "spend no time in reading, much less writing *Stronglines:* which like tough meat, aske more paines and time in chewing, then can be recompensed by all the nourishment they bring." Hobbes in similar fashion comments scornfully on "the ambitious obscurity of expressing more then is perfectly conceived, or perfect conception in fewer words then it requires. Which Expressions, though they have had the honor to be called strong lines, are indeed no better then

40. "An Elegie upon the death of the Deane of Pauls, Dr. John Donne," 49–53, in *Poems of Thomas Carew;* Herford and Simpson, *Ben Jonson, 11,* 448, 461. The strong-lined style is closely equivalent to the Senecan style in prose, similarly cultivated during the age of Jonson and Donne in reaction against earlier modes. See Morris W. Croll, "The Baroque Style in Prose," in *Studies in English Philology in Honor of Frederick Klaeber,* ed. Kemp Malone and Martin Ruud (Minneapolis, 1929), pp. 427–56; and George Williamson, "Strong Lines," in *Seventeenth Century Contexts,* pp. 120–31.

Riddles, and, not onely to the Reader but also after a little
time to the Writer himself, dark and troublesome."[41]
    Denham, the poet whose name is inevitably associated
with Waller's, served as the neoclassical exemplar of
strength because his verse did not violate the canons of the
new age. He was strong without being too strong, succinct
without harshness or obscurity. His own ideal for his verse,
after all, was to be "deep, yet clear . . . without ore-flowing
full."[42] Miss Wallerstein, commenting on the "strong"
tradition, speaks of its characteristic "terse energy," its
"tough, condensed, penetrating wit."[43] The description is
accurate for Jonson and Donne as well as Denham. But the
key difference is that Denham is working within the developing rhetoric of the neoclassical couplet. His best-known
passages are constructed around sharp antitheses. As Donald
Davie has remarked, he achieves concentration by manipu-
lating syntax. His effects are for the most part bold and
simple, and the few metaphors he uses are wittily precise,
make a point explicitly and economically. His poetry has
the virtues of prose, including the virtue of clarity.[44] I quote
from his poem, "On the Earl of Strafford's Tryal and Death"
(my italics):

> His Wisdom such, at once it did appear
> *Three Kingdoms wonder,* and *three Kingdoms fear*
>
> . . .
>
> Such was his force of Eloquence, to make
> *The Hearers* more concern'd than *he that spake;*

41. *Advice to a Son* (6th ed. Oxford, 1658), p. 15; *Answer to Davenant*
(1650), in Spingarn, *Critical Essays of the Seventeenth Century, 2,* 63. The
two passages are cited in Williamson, "Strong Lines," pp. 121, 124–25.

42. *Cooper's Hill,* 191–92, in *The Poetical Works of Sir John Denham,*
ed. T. H. Banks (New Haven, 1928).

43. "Development of the Heroic Couplet," p. 194.

44. See Donald Davie, *Purity of Diction in English Verse* (New York,
Oxford University Press, 1953), pp. 62–69, 206.

> Each seem'd *to act* that part, he came *to see,*
> And *none* was more a looker on than *he*
>
> .   .   .
>
> Now *private pity* strove with *publick hate,*
> *Reason* with *Rage,* and *Eloquence* with *Fate:*
> Now *they could him,* if *he could them* forgive;
> He's not *too guilty,* but *too wise* to live.
>
> (7–8, 11–14, 17–20)

Yet there are a good many things beyond Denham's powers, as beyond Waller's. The best verse, in Pope's celebrated formulation, combines strength and sweetness. Each is a virtue, but neither in isolation is adequate to the greatest poetry. Dryden remarks that his fellow poets, even if they succeeded in making "well-running verses," yet "want genius to give them strength as well as sweetness." Dryden's great achievement, in Pope's view, was that he was able to reconcile the two qualities, synthesize a new style:

> The *Easie Vigor* of a Line,
> Where *Denham's* Strength, and *Waller's* Sweetness join
> Waller was smooth; but Dryden taught to join
> The varying verse, the full-resounding line,
> The long majestic March, and energy divine.[45]

The Augustan compromise sought to unite energy and order, wit and judgment—in the terms of the *Essay of Dramatic Poesy,* justness and liveliness.[46] Dryden and Pope aimed at verse which was forceful and concise, yet clear and harmonious, joining vigor and ease. Waller was the chief exemplar for them of the second set of qualities; to paraphrase Johnson's remarks quoted in the beginning of this chapter, if they had not read Waller, they could not have excelled him.

---

45. Ker, *Essays of Dryden,* 2, 218; *Essay on Criticism,* 360–61; and *The First Epistle of the Second Book of Horace: To Augustus,* 267–69.

46. Ker, *Essays of Dryden, 1,* 36.

Dryden and those who followed him believed in history as linear progress, and Waller's reforms seemed to them both inevitable and right. The grace and elegance of his well-turned couplets seemed to them the formal embodiment of the values of an age in which verse was an instrument of rational discourse among educated men. Waller conceived of poetry as a means to civilized persuasion. Convinced both that poetry was an art and that it should serve a purpose, Waller wrote a verse of wit tempered by judgment, governed by a constant awareness of purpose, audience, and occasion. His art is a cautious art of limitation, but within these limitations he was able to do a few things very well. In his technical innovations, as in the major thematic concerns of his work, he expressed the ideals of order, sanity, and reasonableness which dominated the century to come.

Index

Adams, Robert M., 74–75
Addison, Joseph, 55–56, 57, 59, 72, 92–93, 115
Aiken, Pauline, 91 n.
Allison, Alexander Ward, 4, 112 and n., 172, 207 n., 208 n., 209 n., 211 n., 220 n.
Anacreon, 94, 100, 101 n.
Andrews, Charles M., 18 n.
Antiphilus, 100
Ariosto, Ludovico, 183–84, 184 n.
Aristotle, 98, 116, 117 n., 127–28, 130, 136 n., 139 n.
Art, autonomy of: in Cavalier poetry, 61, 64; in Waller, 64–67, 84–86
Atterbury, Francis, 1, 204, 206, 209 n., 210
Aubrey, John, 10 n., 34 n., 50, 120 n., 174, 205
Audra, E., 173 n.
Auerbach, Erich, 126 n.
Augustus, 117, 127, 166–67
Ausonius, 104
Ayres, Philip, 85

Bacon, Francis, 78, 212
Barlowe, Arthur, 179 n.
Bateson, F. W., 86 and n., 110, 153 n.
Bedford, Lucy, Countess of, 122
Beeching, H. C., 207 n.
Bennett, A. L., 119 n.
Bennett, Josephine Waters, 152 n.
Bethel, Slingsby, 201
Bethell, S. L., 73 n., 74 n., 76 n., 98 n.

Biographia Britannica, 1
Blackwall, Anthony, 214–15
Boileau, Nicolas, 72 n., 176, 203
Born, Lester K., 134
Boyle, Robert, 68 n.
Bridgeman, Orlando, 29
Broadbent, J. B., 111
Brower, Reuben A., 175 n., 193, 196 n.
Browning, Andrew, 36 n.
Browning, Elizabeth Barrett, 2
Buckingham, George Villiers, 1st Duke of, 128, 136–42, 144
Buckingham, George Villiers, 2d Duke of, 35, 206
Burgess, Theodore, 117 n., 119 n.
Burnet, Gilbert, 30, 36
Burton, Robert, 94
Bush, Douglas, 1, 3, 85 n.
Bussby, F., 8 n.
Butler, Samuel: on Waller, 58 and n., 59; as a satirist, 186–87, 193

Carew, Thomas, 61–62, 69, 82 n., 94, 221–22
Carlisle, Lucy Percy, Countess of, 54
Catullus, 91, 94, 95–96
Cavalier poetry, 4, 52, 56–57, 60–64, 76, 111, 113, 120
Cawley, Robert R., 179 n.
Chaloner, Richard, 31, 33 n.
Charles I, 31, 126, 128, 135; policies of, and Waller, 21–30, 41, 137–43, 144–45, 145 n., 150 n., 152

227

INDEX

Monmouth, James, Duke of, 126, 174, 200

Morley, George, 8 and n.

Mornay, Mlle. de, 69 n.

Moulton, Charles W., 3

Mulgrave, John Sheffield, Earl of, 72 n.

Neoclassicism: Waller's role in the development of, 3–6, 110–14, 172–202 passim, 203–05, 205–25 passim; lyric poetry, criticism of, 70–73; "fixing" of the language, 205–07 CRITICAL CANONS: wit and judgment, 57–59, 59 n., 77–80, 147–48; order and energy, 70–71, 224

Nevo, Ruth, 4, 116 n., 134 n., 142 n., 153 n., 175 n., 190 n., 193 n., 196 n.

Newcastle, Margaret, Duchess of, 68

Nicholas, Sir Edward, 27

Nichols, John, 134

Northumberland, Algernon Percy, 10th Earl of, 34, 145 n.

Ogg, David, 37 n.

Oldham, John, 111, 186–87, 193

Oldmixon, John, 93 n.

Osborn, Francis, 222

Ovid, 86, 118, 141, 159 n., 178 n.; and Waller, 59 n., 65 and n., 91, 92, 94, 172; as occasional poet and panegyrist, 92, 117

Palmer, Geoffrey, 29

Panegyric: Waller as a writer of, 39–40, 52, 115–16, 123–71 passim; history of, 116–23; and satire, 124, 129–30, 133, 172–202 passim; and epic poetry, 126–27, 133–34, 134 n., 135, 139–40, 147, 157–58, 175, 183–84, 188–90, 202, 220; relativity of truth in, 127–30, 163 n., 176, 188–90; parodies of, 129–30, 130 n., 188–92, 198; as prescriptive, 132–34,

134 n., 153–58, 159–68 passim; "outdoing" comparisons in, 139–43, 163 and n., 188–90

XII Panegyrici Latini, 117 and n.

Parliament: Long, 20–21, 23–30, 31, 33; Short, 20–23

Peltz, Catherine W., 72 n.

Pembroke, William, Earl of, 122

Persius, 175

Philips, Ambrose, 71–73

Philips, Katherine, 68 n., 173

Pindar, 117

Pinkerton, John, 2

Pliny the Younger, 117

Pomponne, Arnauld de, 18 n.

Pope, Alexander, 19 n., 73, 94, 124, 144 n., 151 n., 193, 198; influence of Waller on, 5–6, 19 n., 92, 173 and n., 183 n., 184 n., 202; versification, 169, 211–12, 212 n., 213, 214 n., 216–17, 224 WORKS: *Epistle II: Of the Characters of Women,* 216; *Epistle to Augustus,* 176, 224; *Epistle to Dr. Arbuthnot,* 216; "Epistle to Miss Blount, on her leaving the Town, after the Coronation," 173; "Epistle to Miss Blount, with the Works of Voiture," 173; *An Essay on Criticism,* 224; *An Essay on Man,* 71; *Messiah,* 162 n.; *Pastorals,* 92, 173 and n.; *Rape of the Lock,* 173, 184, 216; *Windsor-Forest,* 19 n., 150, 151 n., 162 n.

Portland, Jerome Weston, 2d Earl of, 34 and n.

Portsmouth, Louise de Kéroualle, Duchess of, 184

Prior, Matthew, 101–02

Propertius, 65 n., 91–92, 96 n.

Puttenham, George, 116–17, 117 n., 214–15

Pym, John, 27, 28, 29, 32–33, 33 n., 39 n., 42 n.

232